GCSE

BUSINESS

STUDIES

R E V I S E

G U I D E S

Stephen Ison
Keith Pye

Longman

LONGMAN GCSE REVISE GUIDES

SERIES EDITORS:
Geoff Black and Stuart Wall

TITLES AVAILABLE:
Art and Design
Biology*
Business Studies*
Chemistry*
Computer Studies
Economics*
English*
English Literature*
French
Geography
German
Home Economics
Information Systems*
Mathematics*
Mathematics: Higher Level and Extension*
Music
Physics*
Psychology
Religious Studies*
Science*
Sociology
Spanish
Technology*
World History

* new editions for Key Stage 4

Longman Group UK Limited,
Longman House, Burnt Mill, Harlow,
Essex CM20 2JE, England
and Associated Companies throughout the World.

© Longman Group Limited 1996

First Published 1988
2nd Edition 1996

ISBN 0582 27686 1

British Library Cataloguing-in-Publication Data
A catalogue record for this book is available from the British Library

Set by 27QQ in 10/12 Century Old Style
Produced by Short Run Press Ltd
Printed in Exeter, Great Britain

CONTENTS

EDITORS' PREFACE

Longman Revise Guides are written by experienced examiners and teachers, and aim to give you the best possible foundation for success in examinations and other modes of assessment. Much has been said in recent years about declining standards and disappointing examination results. While this may be somewhat exaggerated, examiners are well aware that the performance of many candidates falls well short of their potential. The books encourage thorough study and a full understanding of the concepts involved, and should be seen as course companions and study guides to be used throughout the year. Examiners are in no doubt that a structured approach in preparing for examinations and in presenting coursework can, together with hard work and diligent application, substantially improve performance.

The largely self-contained nature of each chapter gives the book a useful degree of flexibility. After starting with Chapters 1 and 2, all other chapters can be read selectively, in any order appropriate to the stage you have reached in your course. We believe that this book, and the series as a whole, will help you to establish a solid platform of basic knowledge and examination technique on which to build.

Geoff Black and Stuart Wall

ACKNOWLEDGEMENTS

We are indebted to the following examination groups for permission to reproduce their questions. The answers given are entirely the responsibility of the authors.

Midland Examining Group (MEG)
Northern Ireland Council for the Curriculum, Examinations and Assessment (NICCEA)
Northern Examinations and Assessment Board (NEAB)
Southern Examining Group (SEG)
University of London Examinations and Assessment Council (ULEAC)
Welsh Joint Education Committee (WJEC)

We are also indebted to Warrington & Runcorn Development Corporation for the use of the advertisement in figure 6.9 and to Sarah Chappell, Joanna Foxcroft and Ursula Jacobs for providing student answers.

Our thanks also go to Geoff Black and Stuart Wall for their advice and comments.

Stephen Ison and Keith Pye

GCSE IN BUSINESS STUDIES

CHAPTER 1

THE EXAMINATIONS & ASSESSED COURSEWORK

Business Studies must conform to the Key Stage 4 requirements which have been established for that subject. Each examination Board has a number of aims which have been set for Business Studies. As such you will find it useful to familiarise yourself with the aims which are relevant to the Business Studies syllabus you are studying. For example, the syllabus of the University of London Examinations and Assessment Council states that candidates should develop:

1. an ability to make effective use of terminology, concepts and methods relevant to business studies and to recognise the strengths and limitations of the ideas used;
2. an ability to apply their knowledge and understanding in a wide range of contexts, distinguishing between facts and opinions, and evaluating data in order to make informed judgements;
3. knowledge and understanding of the features and dynamics of business activity from a range of perspectives. The perspectives concerned are theoretical (e.g. economics, sociology and psychology) and rôle-specific (e.g. the consumer, the shareholder, the employee and the manager).

It goes on to state the following:

1. Candidates are required to demonstrate specified knowledge and understanding of:
   (a) the relationship between business activity and the environment within which it takes place; and
   (b) the structure, organisation and control of the main forms of business.

2. Candidates are required to demonstrate specified knowledge and critical understanding of business by applying the specified content to the following:
   (a) the aims and objectives of business, and the criteria for judging success, e.g. wealth creation, market share, profitability;
   (b) roles, relationships and management in business, e.g. recruitment, motivation, training, communication;
   (c) the sources, uses and management of finance, e.g. capitalisation, balance sheet analysis, cash flow forecasting;
   (d) production and marketing objectives and related strategies, e.g. cost/output relationships, pricing, product promotion.

SHORT ANSWER QUESTIONS

DATA RESPONSE QUESTIONS

CASE STUDIES

CONTENT

If you study the syllabuses of the six Examination Groups you will find that they cover the following main areas:

1. Business environment
2. Business structure and organisation
3. Business objectives
4. People in business
5. Business finance
6. Production
7. Marketing

This book aims to deal with these areas in a number of chapters. Table 1.1 illustrates a table of contents and helps you to see which chapters and topic areas are relevant to your particular syllabus.

CHAPTER AND TOPIC	SEG	MEG	NEAB	NICCEA	ULEAC	WJEC
3. The background to business	●	●	●	●	●	●
4. Types of business	●	●	●	●	●	●
5. Management	●	●	●	●	●	●
6. Location, size and growth	●	●	●	●	●	●
7. Finance for business	●	●	●	●	●	●
8. Purchasing and production	●	●	●	●	●	●
9. Marketing	●	●	●	●	●	●
10. International trade	●	●	●	●	●	●
11. Business accounts	●	●	●	●	●	●
12. Business documents					●	●
13. Population	●	●	●	●	●	●
14. Recruitment, selection and training	●	●	●	●	●	●
15. Motivation	●	●	●	●	●	●
16. Communication	●	●	●	●	●	●
17. Industrial relations	●	●	●	●	●	●
18. Aiding and controlling business	●	●	●	●	●	●
19. Business in a changing world	●	●	●	●	●	●

Table 1.1

THE EXAMINATIONS

Table 1.2 will give you an idea of the different examination papers you can expect from the six Examination Groups.

EXAMINATION GROUP	PAPER	TIME (Hours)	MARKS* %	CANDIDATES	QUESTIONS
MEG Syllabus code 1351	1 AND 2 OR	2 1	50 25	This is the 'Basic' tier and is aimed at those students expected to obtain grades D-G. In exceptional circumstances a student may be eligible for an award of grade C.	Each paper will contain a number of compulsory questions.
	3 AND 4 OR	2 1	50 25	This is the 'Standard' tier and is aimed at those students expected to obtain grades B-F. If attainment falls below the standard required for grade F, then grade G may be awarded. If attainment is above that required for grade B, then, in exceptional circumstances, a grade A may be awarded.	Each paper will contain a number of compulsory questions.
	5 AND 6	2 1	50 25	This is the 'Higher' tier and is aimed at those students expected to obtain grades A-C. In exceptional circumstances a grade A* or D may be awarded.	Each paper will contain a number of compulsory questions.
	Candidates will be entered for *one* tier (Basic, Standard or Higher) with papers 1, 3 and 5 comprising the common core. In addition, candidates will undertake papers 2, 4 or 6. The paper will consist of four optional sections: accounting, business and change, commerce and technology and change. The candidate will be entered for one optional section.				
NEAB Syllabus code 1411	The information for the NEAB examinations is presented in the following Table:				

Tier	The tier is aimed at grades:	The candidate will be assessed by the following papers. The time allowed for each examination and the make-up of each paper is also given:		
		Paper 1 (37.5%)	Paper 2 (37.5%)	Paper 3 (only option B (25%))
P	D-G	1 hour	1 hour	1 hour
Q	B-F	$1\frac{1}{2}$ hours	$1\frac{1}{2}$ hours	1 hour
R	A*-D	$1\frac{1}{2}$ hours	$1\frac{1}{2}$ hours	1 hour
Candidates could be awarded one grade above and one grade below that given in tiers P, Q and R if there is evidence to support that award.		Case study of a simulated business situation. Short answer and structured questions.	Short answer and structured data response questions.	Problem-solving exercise based on given data.

Instead of undertaking Paper 3 (option B) candidates may choose coursework (option A). The coursework has a weighting of 25%.

EXAMINATION GROUP	PAPER	TIME (Hours)	MARKS* %	CANDIDATES	QUESTIONS
NICCEA	1	1½	30	There are two tiers of entry for the examination, S and T. Candidates will be entered for one tier.	Case study: given to the candidates approximately 8 weeks before the examination. The examination will be based on the case study and will comprise a number of unseen questions. All questions will be compulsory.
	2	2	50		Four compulsory multipart questions.
SEG	1	2	75	There are three tiers: 'Foundation' which is targeted at grades D-G, although an award of C may be made. 'Intermediate' which is targeted at grades B-F, although an award of A or G may be made. 'Higher' which is targeted at grades A*-D, although Grade E may be awarded.	Different papers are set for each tier and comprise questions based on a case study given to the candidates about 8 weeks before the examination. All questions will be compulsory.
ULEAC Syllabus code 1501	1	2	75	This is the 'Foundation' paper and thus allows students to be awarded a grade D-G.	Short answer/multiple-choice questions.
	OR				
	2	2	75	This is the 'Intermediate' paper and this allows students to be awarded a grade B-F.	Short answer/structured questions.
	OR				
	3	2	75	This is the 'Higher' paper and this allows students to be awarded a grade A*-D.	Structured/open-ended questions.
WJEC	1	2	75	Aimed at grades D-G, although an award of grade C may be made.	The three papers consist of a number of short answer questions and longer stimulus response questions.
	OR				
	2	2	75	Aimed at grades B-F, although an award of grades A or G may be made.	
	OR				
	3	2	75	Aimed at grades A*-D, although an award of grade E may be made.	

NOTE* % marks do not total 100 as the remaining marks are for assessed coursework.

Table 1.2 GCSE Business Studies – Examination papers

As you will see there are three main types of examination questions, although not every examination group uses all three.

1 > SHORT ANSWER QUESTIONS

These test specific areas of the Business Studies syllabus. If your Examination Group uses this technique, then you could be asked questions such as: 'In what ways do producer and consumer goods differ?' You will then be given one or two lines in which to answer the question.

2 > DATA RESPONSE QUESTIONS

These present a short passage, table, graph or some other form of data, and use it to develop a number of questions. In answering the questions, you will find some of the relevant information in the data. Data response questions aim to test whether you can relate what you know to particular situations or pieces of information. Some of the Examination Groups will use the term **structured questions** for what are essentially data response questions.

3 > CASE STUDIES

Case studies are used as part of the assessment process. The case studies form one whole paper and are based on a particular theme. That theme might be the experience of a particular company over a number of years. Questions might concern, for example, the company's financial problems, its methods of recruitment, its management structure, and locational decisions. Also, you might be called upon to give your own advice. The SEG and the NICCEA allow the case study to be given to the candidates approximately eight weeks before the date of the examination, although obviously not the questions.

It is important to note that a number of the Examination Groups incorporate **compulsory questions** as part of their examination papers. This means that you have no choice and so have to do all the questions set.

COURSEWORK

As part of the assessment process, you will be required to undertake compulsory coursework. Table 1.3 gives a summary of what is expected and the percentage of marks available from the six Examination Groups. The coursework is not meant to be simply a desk exercise. Instead, you will be expected to relate your 'classroom' Business Studies to the local environment. It is suggested that you should be actively involved in collecting and assembling the information to be used in the assignments. More detail on the preparation and presentation of coursework can be found in Chapter 2.

EXAMINATION GROUP	MARKS %	COURSEWORK
MEG	25	One assignment of no more than 2,500 words, representing about ten hours work.
NEAB	25	Option A only – you will be required to submit one assignment of approximately 3,000 words. A list of titles will be provided by NEAB.
NICCEA	20	Candidates must undertake one coursework assignment. The coursework should not exceed 2,500 words.
SEG	25	Candidates should base the coursework on *one* of the options which is part of the Business Studies syllabus, covering at least two sections of that option. The options are: 1. Business and change 2. Information technology 3. Commerce 4. Finance and accounting 5. Enterprise The coursework is undertaken as a 'file of work' and there is no specified length.
ULEAC	25	The examining group will set six assignments from which you will have to select two. Each assignment is worth 12.5% and should not exceed 1,000 words.
WJEC	25	Candidates must undertake two assignments each worth 12.5%.

Table 1.3 GCSE Business Studies – assessed coursework

GETTING STARTED

Everyone has their own method of preparing for examinations and your teachers may give you lots of helpful advice on the best methods to adopt. There is no one best approach; each of us is different and what works for one person may not work for you. However, this chapter suggests a number of useful techniques you might consider when planning your revision and taking your examinations. It also considers how to present coursework, which we have seen is an important part of the GCSE in Business Studies.

EXAMINATION PREPARATION

1 ⟩ REVISION

The first, and perhaps most obvious, point to make is that there is no substitute for hard work. Having worked steadily throughout the course, you must carefully organise your time in the last three or four months before the examination, so that you gain your proper reward for that work. Do not, therefore, leave your revision until the last minute.

Instead, work out a revision timetable well before the examination. On a blank piece of paper, construct a chart, as in Fig. 2.1.

Day	am 9	10	11	noon 12	1	2	3	4	pm 5	6	7	8	9
Monday													
Tuesday													
Wednesday													
Thursday													
Friday													
Saturday													
Sunday													

Figure 2.1 Revision Chart

You will not be able to work every single hour, so block out the times when you usually have meals, go to school or college and enjoy leisure time. Over the period of your revision for the examinations you might, of course, reduce your usual amount of leisure time. Going out with friends should fit around your revision, rather than your revision fit around going out with your friends! Once you have done this, you can then allocate the time you have left to revise.

In doing this, you will have to take into account the number of subjects you have to revise. Try to give roughly the same time each week to each of your subjects. Making a timetable should indicate why it is a good idea to start revising early, although it is never too late to do something. Once you have a study timetable it is important to stick to it.

In Business Studies, you should try to cover the whole syllabus as there are **integrated questions** (see Ch. 20) and **compulsory questions** which test your knowledge over a range of topics.

Before revising, you need to decide where will be the best **place** to revise. It may be your bedroom, the school library or even the local town library. Wherever you choose, it will need to be fairly quiet, have sufficient lighting and be comfortable. You may even find sitting on your bed is the best place provided you do not fall asleep! Above all you need to be organised.

Once you have prepared a revision timetable or organised a programme which suits you, then you have to settle down and actually revise the various areas or topics within the subject.

An aim of this book is to aid you in that revision. When revising, bear in mind the format of the examination papers of the examining body for which you are entered. We have seen that the six Examining Groups mentioned in Chapter 1 use a mixture of **question types**: compulsory structured questions, integrated case studies, short questions and task-related questions, such as designing a job application form. Try to be familiar with each type of question used by your Examining Body. Practise answering such questions in this book. With questions being compulsory and integrated, this again makes it important that you revise the whole syllabus.

For a number of Examining Groups, the examination paper acts as an **answer book** with blank lines left for you to answer the questions. Each Examination Group will produce papers which are slightly different in format, so it is important that you obtain copies of past papers or specimen papers. At the end of each chapter, you will find examination questions from the various examination groups, together with tutor's outline answers. Although you should not view these answers as being anything other than suggestions, they should help you to gain some idea of what the examiner expects of you. Chapter 20 also gives a number of integrated questions, i.e. questions which cover more than one area of the syllabus. You may find it useful to use this chapter after you have finished the course. Each chapter concentrates on a particular topic and has subheadings which help to highlight the main elements within that topic. If this is your own book and not a school/college book, then you may like to use the margins to add your own notes and comments as you revise. One good way to revise is to read your class notes on a topic, then to read the relevant chapter in this book and attempt the questions at the end of the chapter.

You may like to enlist the help of others in your revision, for example by asking a member of your family to test you. It is not worthwhile doing this, however, until you have revised the topic by yourself.

We suggest that you read over the work written in class or for homework. Carefully note any comments made by the teacher or lecturer as this will reduce the possibility of you making the same mistakes in the examination. The work you have undertaken for assignments should also prove useful revision material. You are likely to be at some disadvantage if your written English is not very good, so you may have to spend some time trying to improve this area. At the very least, learn to spell the more important terms used in Business Studies; words such as 'interest' and even 'business' are often incorrectly spelt.

In fact **spelling**, **punctuation** and **grammar** are assessed both in the final examination and the coursework. At the time of writing, there are four categories for assessing candidates for spelling, punctuation and grammar. They are:

▶ **Below threshold performance**
▶ **Threshold performance**: Candidates spell, punctuate and use the rules of grammar with reasonable accuracy.
▶ **Intermediate performance**: Candidates spell, punctuate and use the rules of grammar with considerable accuracy; they use words and phrases – including specialist terms – with some facility.
▶ **High performance**: Candidates spell, punctuate and use the rules of grammar with almost faultless accuracy, displaying a range of grammatical constructions; they use a wide range of specialist terms adeptly and with precision.

For each of the Examination Groups, 3–5 % of the total marks will be awarded for spelling, punctuation and grammar.

TAKING THE EXAMINATION

You need to go to bed early on the night before the examination. Late-night revision is often counter-productive, especially if it makes you tired during the examination itself. Make sure you have set the alarm clock, particularly if the examination is in the morning. Teachers find every year that some students enter the exam room late. You will not normally be allowed any extra time. Make sure you have checked and double checked where the examination is, as well as the time it starts. You might even visit the place where the examinations will be held before the day they start, so that you can experience the atmosphere. Also make sure you have the necessary equipment: two pens (black or blue), a ruler, two pencils (HB), a rubber, pencil sharpener and a watch.

You may not have a choice of desk in the exam room. However, if you can choose, sit away from the windows, particularly if it is a hot day. Also, avoid desks near the doors as these could be noisy due to candidates arriving late and leaving early.

Spend some time **reading through the instructions** on the examination paper. Make sure you notice which questions, if any, are compulsory and then think about the questions, perhaps jotting down some ideas in rough. You will gain no marks for irrelevant information. The examination is not about writing down everything you know, so avoid writing waffle.

Write as **neatly** and as **clearly** as you can. Try not to use slang language such as: 'High interest rates will make firms go bust.' Avoid giving opinions, such as: 'I think that ...' Try to justify your points; for instance, you might write: 'There are three reasons why it could be argued that ...'

Use all the time you have available rather than leaving the examination room early. You will not be able to change anything you have written once you have left the room. In **checking** over your work, you could spot mistakes or think of other points to add. You should always aim to leave time at the end of the examination to read through your answers.

Each examination paper will allocate marks to each question. These can be found on the right-hand side of each question. They should allow you to calculate the **marks per minute** and so the amount of time you should spend on each question. If, for example, the examination paper is to take one and a half hours and there are 30 marks to be awarded on the paper, then roughly three minutes should be spent on each mark. Use this as only a rough guide, and remember to set a little time aside for reading through the question paper carefully and checking your work at the end. However, working out the marks per question should help you to avoid spending 10 minutes on a question worth only 2 marks while spending only 2 minutes on a question worth 10 marks.

There is always the temptation after the exam to chat with others who have taken the same paper. This kind of 'post mortem' should be avoided if possible. What is done is done! Those you talk to may only depress you by convincing you that you could have written more, answered different questions or even answered the same questions in a better way. It is far better to forget the examination paper you have finished and start thinking about the next one.

COURSEWORK

As you will have noted from Table 1.3 in ch. 1, the six Examination Groups have a **compulsory coursework element** which accounts for 20–25% of the overall assessment. This section gives you some guidance on how to prepare and present coursework assignments.

The starting point is to find out exactly what the Examining Groups' *requirements for coursework* are; Table 1.3 will give you a general outline. For instance how many assignments do you have to undertake? Are there any guidelines on length? What is the marking criteria?

Your teacher/lecturer will help you in your choice of assignment and may even suggest a title. You should pay close attention to the advice he or she gives. Teachers have considerable experience in assessing whether the topic area chosen is suitable for an assignment. ULEAC and NEAB *prescribe* what coursework is to be undertaken and students are given a choice of two out of six titles set by ULEAC.

66 Is it possible to obtain information on your chosen coursework? 99

However, if you *can* choose, you may pick an area of study which interests you. You could start by looking through the Business Studies syllabus and making your choice that way. Remember the topic must be part of the Business Studies syllabus of your Examining Group. Make sure that you are able to *obtain information* on the topic you may have chosen. With this in mind, it may be a good idea to base your assignment on the local community. For example, an area of study could be an industrial dispute at a local factory, where you look at the reasons for the dispute and what was done to try to resolve it. If the dispute is still taking place, of course, the management may be unwilling to talk to you. So do take your teacher's advice on the suitability of a topic as they will be able to tell you how accessible the relevant information is.

Certain topics will lend themselves more easily to an investigation than others. Try to avoid those that will naturally lead you to use a textbook. A badly chosen topic can lead to poor marks and may turn into an exercise of re-hashing your textbook.

You may like to choose a topic which you have *already studied* in class, although this may not always be possible. The choice of assignment should flow out of what you have been doing in class. It should therefore be seen as an important part of the course rather than something 'stuck on' as an extra. In fact, the work for your project may help you in your written examination papers.

If you have some idea of what you would like to do after leaving school, then you could also take this into account when choosing your assignment. For example, if you are interested in banking as a career, then an assignment on the services a bank provides for business will prove very useful. It will give you some idea of what a bank does and may also give you the opportunity to talk to a bank manager. The assignment may even be something you could present to a bank manager if, at some stage in the future, you are interested for a bank post.

Once you *have* chosen a topic area, you will probably need to narrow it down. For example, you could choose the *location of industry*, which is part of the syllabus area referred to as 'business environment'. But it would not be possible for you to deal with *all* the firms in your area. You will therefore need to narrow it down to *one* firm, perhaps one which has moved into your area recently. Remember, a good piece of coursework will contain relevant theoretical material which you have learned in class as well as the practical aspects which result from your study of this particular organisation or firm.

We have already suggested that your title might pose a question. The advantage of setting yourself coursework based on a question is that it will involve you in *analysis*. This means examining all the evidence and then coming to a conclusion. If you do this, it will show the examiner that you have been involved in *making judgements* based on your Business Studies rather than simply gathering as much information as possible and *describing* the situation. For instance, the title 'Why did Nestlé locate in York?' is more likely to involve analysis and judgement than the title 'The location of Nestlé in York'. In the latter title you would probably only *describe* the location. In the former title you could outline the reasons for *any* firm's location in theory and then relate this theory to the specific case of Nestlé locating in York. This would inevitably involve you in judging which of the textbook reasons did, or did not, apply. Coursework which is made up mainly of scrap-book type material, such as photographs, newspaper cuttings or articles from magazines, will be given few marks. So be careful to choose a title which will involve analysis as well as description.

However, when setting a question as part of your title, make sure it is an answerable one. So, 'What would be the effect on South Wales businesses of a new Japanese motor manufacturing plant opening in Cardiff?' would be virtually impossible for you to answer, even if you devoted all of your free time to Business Studies and forgot your other subjects. On the other hand, the question 'What would be the possible impact on Jones (Newsagents) Ltd of a new Japanese motor manufacturing plant opening in Cardiff?' though still difficult, would give you a better chance of coming up with an answer. This is because you would be concentrating on a *limited aspect*. You could perhaps 'quantify' (i.e. measure) the present situation of Jones (Newsagents) Ltd. You could then carry out some research on present levels of employment, pay, etc. and analyse the data collected. Your analysis might include an *estimate* of the changes which the opening of the new plant might bring. You could then come to some sensible business conclusions.

Remember too, that the question set should not simply require an answer of 'yes' or 'no'. For example, a title such as 'Did firm B locate in Cambridge because of the M11 motorway?' may lead to a very restricted conclusion. So, although you should concentrate on a specific issue, choose a title which leaves some scope for a discussion of the points for or against an issue.

The following are titles which you might consider for your GCSE coursework. You may not like the exact titles, but at least they may give you some idea of areas of study. Clearly you would substitute the name of your specific firm for firm X or firm Y in the list below. Remember, though, that some firms are worried about confidentiality. So you may still prefer to use firm X or some other name you can think of.

Is the topic area you have chosen too broad?

Setting yourself a question in your title can be useful.

A specific question or issue is easier to analyse.

Some possible coursework titles for you to consider

1. How does firm X, which is a sole trader, differ from firm Y, which is a partnership?
2. What are the functions of the management of firm X?
3. Does the management structure of firm X conform to the textbook explanation?
4. How different are the *departmental* management functions of firm X from those found in the textbook?
5. What leadership types are used in firm X? What are their advantages? What are their disadvantages?
6. Why is firm X located in town T?
7. What factors influence consumers who use out-of-town shopping areas?
8. How has firm X been able to take advantage of economies of scale?
9. What are the *external* economies and diseconomies of scale for firm X located in town T?
10. What benefits has firm X obtained from vertical integration?
11. Why has firm X been able to survive as a small firm?
12. How does the current Health and Safety legislation affect firm X?
13. Why did firm X merge with firm Y?
14. What is the environmental impact of firm X?
15. What sources of finance did firm X use in setting itself up?
16. Why does firm X use *batch production* to make its products, while firm Y uses a *flow line* method?
17. How has the automation of firm X's production affected its operation?
18. How important is the product life cycle to firm X?
19. What relevance has the product life cycle for firm X?
20. What benefits are there in a supermarket having loss leaders?
21. What factors influence the way firm X advertises?
22. Why does firm X undertake market research?
23. What problems has firm X faced in marketing product P?
24. Why did firm X switch its distribution of goods from road to rail transport?
25. What export procedures does firm X follow?
26. What are the benefits of tourism to town T?
27. How did firm X develop a job description and advertise for a junior clerk/receptionist?
28. How does firm X advertise a job vacancy?
29. What factors does firm X need to take into account when advertising a job vacancy?
30. How does firm X undertake its job interviews?
31. How are the production staff of firm X motivated?
32. Does the satisfaction obtained from job J conform to the textbook explanation?
33. Why are some workers in firm X paid on piece rates, and others on standard rates?
34. Is it true that *written* communications are more efficient within firm X than *verbal* communications?
35. What factors influence the workers in firm X to join a trade union?
36. What types of trade union exist within firm X?
37. What is the role of the shop steward within trade union Z?
38. How are industrial relations within firm X managed – from the company's, the union's and the worker's points of view?
39. What assistance has central government given to firm X?
40. Which services of bank C can firm X make use of?

In considering these titles, you may notice a number of things:

> ▶ The titles are written as *questions* because, as we have said, those assignments which are purely descriptive will not be awarded high marks. Asking, then answering, a question is more likely to lead to *analysis* and it is analysis that gains most marks.

❝❝ Coursework is not a textbook exercise. ❞❞

> ▶ The majority of titles require you to undertake **primary research**. This means you will need to make first-hand investigations outside the classroom. You will have to contact businesses or organisations such as trade unions to obtain information or to find out their views on certain issues. You will not be able to undertake your assignment by desk research alone. Some titles, such as number

3 above, will of course involve some desk research from one of the textbooks you use. As a Business Studies student you should be interested in how business is organised outside the classroom, i.e. in the 'real world'. GCSE coursework will give you the opportunity to investigate just that.

▶ Although primary research has much to commend it, you may obtain some information from **secondary research**. This is research which has been undertaken by somebody else. For example, in number 26 above, the town council for town T may have undertaken some work on the effect of tourism on their town and you may be able to make use of it.

▶ The majority of titles involve **local study**. Undertaking an assignment does not mean you have to go to another part of the country. Instead you can visit a local business, interview a local bank manager, go to an out-of-town superstore to undertake a questionnaire, observe how a local newspaper deals with an industrial dispute or advertises certain job vacancies, and so on. In fact, a number of the Examination Groups stress the need for assignments to have a local flavour.

A good piece of coursework will strike a balance between the various points made above. It will contain some secondary as well as primary material. It will be essentially practical, but will also relate to theory. It will probably be a local study, but it might also be set in a national context or situation. Remember to keep your Examination Group's 'assessment criteria' in your mind throughout. These criteria are, if you like, the rules of this particular 'sport'. Like a skater, you will be judged on 'technical merit' as defined by these criteria. So do your best to follow them at all times.

At the end of each chapter of this book you will find a section entitled 'Coursework'. This gives you one or two assignments which you may find useful for that topic area. You might want to adapt them to suit your own interests or situation. In any event, they could be used as a guideline.

4 ▷ WHERE DO WE GO FROM HERE?

Once you have decided on your title or topic area, then you will need to formulate a 'plan of attack'.

A TIMETABLE

The first stage is to draw up a timetable.

Those students who do well at coursework undertake their assignments in good time, and avoid a blind panic a few days before they have to hand in their work. You may find that you need more time than you think; you may need more material or the information you thought would be useful may turn out to be inadequate. You also need to remember that it takes time to present your assignment logically and neatly. For these reasons, you need a coursework timetable. You might, in fact, put your timetable in the front of the folder in which you keep all the information for that assignment. The MEG gives, as a general guide, ten hours per assignment in terms of student-centred activity. You might like to use this as a rough guide in planning your coursework.

You will also have coursework from other subjects, so careful planning is essential to make sure you do not overload yourself. Figure 2.2 gives a breakdown of tasks which might help you to plan each assignment.

 Plan your coursework time carefully.

Dates	Stages	Tick when completed
	1 Decide on the assignment title. 2 Decide what information is required. 3 Make contact with the relevant individuals/firms. 4 Collect the information. 5 Analyse the information, draw diagrams and plan out the assignment. 6 Work out the conclusions. 7 Write it up. 8 HAND IT IN (on time).	

Figure 2.2 A timetable

We have deliberately avoided putting dates on the various stages, though these will obviously be very important. You will need to discuss the timetable you have drawn up with your teacher/lecturer. Figure 2.2 may help you to decide whether you have included all the necessary stages in your plan. Try to give yourself enough time for each stage so that you can complete all the stages by the hand-in date.

Coursework will teach you a great deal about *organisation*, not only of your time, but in arranging interviews with people, in clarifying your thoughts and in presenting material. You will need to store information carefully, and to make sure the various parts of the project do not go astray. Imagine how disastrous it would be if you lost an assignment which was almost finished one week before it had to be handed in!

OBTAINING THE INFORMATION

Your teacher/lecturer will be able to offer some guidance as to *where* information can be obtained and the form your coursework assignment should take. You must be careful that the assignment is *your own work*. In fact, candidates may be required to sign a declaration to certify that the work undertaken *is* their own. Certain Examination Groups also require the teacher/lecturer to sign a declaration stating that, to the best of their knowledge, all the work that has been submitted is that of the candidates. Therefore, if you produce an assignment copied directly from books or other sources, you will earn no marks. However, you will obviously need to *use other sources* at times. But when you do, you should draw up a 'bibliography', i.e. a list of the materials you have used.

BUSINESSES

As far as possible, your assignment should be based on the local community. Local firms and businesses are a good source of information. Companies provide a whole range of literature, such as company reports and details of their product ranges in catalogues, etc. You could write to a company asking for this information, perhaps enclosing a stamped-addressed envelope. Try to be selective in using this information. In other words, only present information that is relevant to the points you are making in your project.

Local banks and building societies are often only too willing to provide information on their activities. One of their staff may allow you to interview him or her. The *Yellow Pages* will have a section on banks and building societies, and will provide useful local addresses.

Yellow Pages may also provide other useful telephone numbers, such as the Consumer Protection Adviser; the Inland Revenue; and the Office of Fair Trading. One of the best ways to obtain information from businesses is by the use of an *interview*, perhaps accompanied by a *questionnaire*. We now look at these two items in rather more detail.

> Have you considered all the possible sources of information?

INTERVIEWS

The data/information you require could be obtained from an interview with a relevant party. Figure 2.3 gives an outline of possible contacts within a business or organisation who could possibly provide information for certain assignment areas.

Assignment area	Possible contact within a business
Management functions	Personnel department
Location of business	No one person
Local corner-shop/supermarkets	The owner/manager
Sources of finance	Finance department
Share issue	Finance department
Production techniques	Production department
Automation	Production department
Product life-cycle	Marketing department
Advertising	Marketing department
Road/rail transport	Distribution department
Tourism in the local economy	Local authority
Job vacancies	Personnel department
Application forms	Personnel department
Payment systems	Personnel department
Trade unions	Local trade union representative/shop steward
Bank services	Bank manager

Figure 2.3 Possible contacts for arranging interviews

Certain businesses may be too small to have the various departments listed. Here it may be the *owner* of the business who will be able to provide you with the information you require. In undertaking an interview it will be useful for you to decide which questions you are going to ask beforehand. To obtain an interview, either telephone the company or write a letter to the appropriate person or department.

Figure 2.4 gives a brief check-list that you could use to make an effective telephone call.

How to make an effective telephone call

---

1. Before dialling

▶ Decide whom you need to speak to or at least which department. This will help the switchboard to put you through quickly.
▶ Have some general idea of what information you require.
▶ Have ready a list of dates and times that you are able to attend for an interview.
▶ Have a pen and paper handy to take down any points which are important.
▶ Make a note of the telephone number you are dialling. You may need to telephone again if the person you want to speak to is not available.

---

2. During the call

▶ When the person you want to speak to answers then state your name clearly and the school/college you attend. For example: This is Helen Farnhill, of Parkside Comprehensive School.
▶ Speak clearly, stating the reason for your call.
▶ Write on the paper you have ready, the date and time the person is able to see you. Make sure you take this down correctly. You could read the time back to be absolutely sure.
▶ Find out where you need to report to for the interview.

---

3. After the call

▶ Note down the extension number you used in case you need to telephone again.
▶ Enter the date and time in your diary, on a calendar or even on the front of your assignment folder so you do not forget, for if you fail to attend it may be difficult to obtain another interview.

Figure 2.5 Points to remember in making effective telephone calls

Instead of telephoning you may prefer to write a letter. This will certainly be cheaper. As well as being cheaper, you may be able to state what you require more precisely than you could through a telephone call. You will also be able to keep a copy so that you have a record of what information you have asked for. You should state clearly what information you require so that less time will be wasted when you have the interview. Figure 2.5 provides a general letter which you could adapt to meet your needs.

Make your requirements clear.

---

19 Highton Road,
Nelson,
Lancs
M51 1PT

20th February 1995

Dear Sir

My name is HELEN FARNHILL, and I am a student at Parkside Comprehensive School, undertaking GCSE Business Studies. As part of the course, I am undertaking an assignment on the problems of designing an application form.

I would very much appreciate an interview to talk about problems you face. I am able to attend each Monday and Friday after 4pm.

I look forward to hearing from you.

Yours faithfully

H. Farnhill

Figure 2.5

If you know the name of the person you are writing to, then end the letter *Yours sincerely*. However, if you are on first-name terms, which is unlikely, then use *Sincerely* or *Kind regards*. See Figure 2.6 if you want to check how to end your letter.

Figure 2.6 Different ways of starting and finishing a letter

Dear Sir....	Yours faithfully
Dear Mrs Hird....	Yours sincerely
Dear Peter....	Sincerely *or* Kind regards

If possible, type the letter. If not, then make sure that you write clearly. The particular letter in Figure 2.5 should be addressed to the Personnel Officer, The Personnel Department.

Remember to keep copies of all the correspondence because you may include them in the appendix at the end of your assignment. If you do obtain an interview, there are a number of points of which you need to take account:

Points to remember when conducting an interview.

▶ Be prepared.
▶ Make sure you have your questions ready.
▶ Be on time.
▶ Take a pen and paper.
▶ Dress reasonably smartly.
▶ Ask for any literature which the company publishes which may be useful.
▶ Tell the person you meet that you will send them a copy of the assignment when it is completed.
▶ Once you have obtained the information you require, *thank them* for their help. Other students may require information from that company in the future, so you have a responsibility to them.

QUESTIONNAIRES

Questionnaires are an efficient way of obtaining information from a number of people, although you could produce a questionnaire for just one interview. They are used extensively in market research and normally involve an interviewer taking individuals through the questions and watching them fill in the answers. If the title of your assignment is something like 'What factors influence consumers who use out-of-town shopping areas?' or 'What factors influence workers to join a trade union?' then a questionnaire would prove most useful.

The questions should be aimed at a selected group. In the above examples, these would be supermarket consumers and trade-union members. When producing and using a questionnaire there are certain points to remember:

Plan your questionnaire carefully.

1. You may wish to **pilot** the questionnaire first, to make sure that it produces the right kind of responses. You could show your draft questions to your teacher/lecturer, try them out on your family and friends or on a small sample of the people you want to survey. It is better to solve any problems early on, before using the questionnaire in the final survey. Make sure the questions are relevant. Students tend to include too many unrelated questions in their questionnaires.
2. Be careful to avoid asking questions which could prove embarrassing. For example, asking the age of consumers using an out-of-town shopping area would be inappropriate, as would asking trade-union members their wage rate.
3. You will have to decide whether you are going to conduct the questionnaire yourself or whether you are going to circulate the questionnaire and ask the respondents to return the completed form. The latter method is costly and may also result in a poorer response.
4. Arrange the questions in a logical order.
5. Try not to ask 'loaded' questions, such as 'Would you say that the service given by this supermarket is poor?'
   Yes ☐
   No ☐
   Don't know ☐
   It would be far better to ask: 'How would you view the service given by this supermarket?'
   Good ☐
   Average ☐
   Poor ☐

6. Above all, if you are going to undertake a questionnaire outside a business premises, e.g. in a supermarket, make sure you obtain the manager's permission first – especially if you are going to ask questions about the quality of service.

In designing the questionnaire you may devise four main types of questions:

1. Yes/no questions
   These are questions such as:
   Have you done any shopping in this supermarket in the last month?
   Yes ☐   No ☐
2. Multiple-choice questions
   These require a tick in the correct box/boxes. You could use these if asking questions like:
   Why do you do your shopping in this supermarket?
   Location ☐   Competitive prices ☐   Greater variety ☐
   Longer opening hours ☐
   With this sort of question you may need to leave a space for 'other responses'.
3. Good/average/poor questions
   You could ask a question like:
   How would you view the range of products on sale?
   Good ☐   Average ☐   Poor ☐
4. Open-ended questions
   You could use questions which require *comments* from those interviewed, such as:
   Why do you shop at this supermarket?

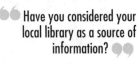
Questions with definite answers are easier to analyse.

Some of these questions will lead you to quantifiable (i.e. measurable) conclusions, and some will not. The quantifiable ones are usually better because you can analyse them more easily, and draw diagrams such as pie charts based on them. Open-ended questions tend to give you as many different answers as the number of people questioned. Therefore you should probably avoid them.

NEWSPAPER ARTICLES AND MAGAZINES

Both national and local newspapers are a useful source of information. Local newspapers may be more relevant as they mainly deal in local issues. The following information may be available from your local press:

▶ local job advertisements
▶ advertisements promoting a firm's products
▶ information on company mergers
▶ local authority initiatives
▶ proposed new business parks
▶ industrial relations issues.

Magazines such as *Marketing Weekly* and *Personnel Management* could also prove useful. Obtaining information from these may involve a visit to your local public library. So, make sure you know when it is open, and where the relevant materials are kept.

THE LOCAL PUBLIC LIBRARY

Your local library may be organised into *sections*:

Have you considered your local library as a source of information?

▶ **Borrowing section:** you will be able to take books out for a limited period of time. Books in the category 650 will be of particular interest since they include those related to Business Studies.
▶ **Reference section:** although you are not allowed to take books out of this section, it may prove the most useful as it includes newspapers, magazines and government publications.

Some government publications may be helpful:

▶ *The Annual Abstract of Statistics* presents the major statistics of the central government departments.

▶ *Regional Trends* presents information on a wide range of economic and social data on a regional basis.

▶ *Social Trends* presents information on patterns of household wealth, income and expenditure.

The reference section is likely to offer photocopying facilities, so you should be able to reproduce the information you require. Remember too, that the library staff are there to help you. However, you do need to have some specific idea of the information you require. Try to become familiar with the way the library operates, including the card indexes, and possibly the computer listings. But do not be frightened – if in doubt, ask at the desk for help in finding your way about.

BOOKS

There are certain books which you may find useful purely for reference purposes. They will provide you with the theoretical background to any practical investigation. You could, for example, take an assignment which compares the *textbook idea* of things with a particular *practical situation* in your local area. Titles for projects such as 'Does the satisfaction obtained from job X conform to the textbook explanation?' clearly involve comparisons of this type. Remember, the examiner will be looking for evidence of your technical knowledge of the subject as well as at the way in which you relate this knowledge to a local situation.

TELEVISION AND RADIO

There may be a programme on the television, or on the radio, which you can use as part of your assignment. These can be recorded and the information extracted for use in the coursework assignment. As we have already said, you must make a note of any programmes you use for reference in your bibliography.

6 ▷ PRESENTING AN ASSIGNMENT

❝❝ Take time over your presentation. ❞❞

Remember that coursework will make up 20–25% of your final marks in GCSE Business Studies, depending on which Examination Group you are entered for. It is important therefore that you treat all aspects of it seriously, including its presentation.

Certain Examination Groups give guidance on the presentation of assignments, and the view is that any format is acceptable as long as it is logical and systematic. An assignment could be logically presented using the following headings:

▶ title and objectives
▶ research
▶ analysis
▶ conclusion
▶ bibliography
▶ acknowledgments.

The completed assignment could be word processed for neatness and appearance. This may be especially advisable if your writing is difficult to read.

The six headings listed above can be expanded upon as follows:

THE TITLE AND OBJECTIVES

❝❝ Give your coursework a clear structure ❞❞

For example: 'What are the reasons for the location of firm X in Town T?' This should be followed by a brief introduction explaining what you are aiming to do.

THE RESEARCH

This section gives a description of what information is required and how it is to be collected – perhaps, for example, by arranging an interview with individuals in firm X, possibly using a questionnaire. If so, include a copy of the questionnaire actually used. Explain how you selected people for interview, and why those particular persons were chosen. Perhaps describe how you conducted the interviews, with reasons for any procedures you adopted. In other words, use this section to account for the *methods* used in your investigation.

THE ANALYSIS

You may find this the hardest part of your assignment. Analysing the data means studying what information you have obtained and deciding which aspects you feel are relevant and important in answering the question you have set yourself. Suppose your assignment deals with 'Why did firm X merge with firm Y?' Then, from the information you have gathered, you will need to *use* the data to suggest why the merger did in fact occur. In analysing any information you have obtained, the following points may prove useful:

▶ Keep referring back to the question you have set yourself in the assignment. This will help to make sure you are answering it. Only *relevant data* should be presented and discussed in the analysis.

▶ Check that you are using appropriate methods to present your information. In other words, which types of table or diagram will best display your information? What type of arithmetical or statistical technique will help make sense of the 'raw data' you have collected?

▶ Check that you have obtained enough information. You may find, when you come to your analysis, that you do *not* in fact have sufficient information to answer the question. This is one good reason to complete your assignment in good time, so that if you meet such problems you still have enough time to deal with them.

▶ Remember that your teacher/lecturer is there to help you if you need help. He or she could give you valuable advice on how to proceed and which techniques to consider, or to avoid!

THE CONCLUSION

Here you can relate your findings to your project title, especially a title which is based on a question. For example, your conclusion might be that firm X located in town T partly because of the motorway network close by, and partly to be close to its supply of raw materials. In the conclusion, you are drawing together your findings and commenting upon them in the light of the task you originally set yourself.

You might wish to discuss some of the implications of your findings for the future. For instance, if you have identified a particular problem facing a firm you might be able to suggest how it could overcome that problem. Such 'recommendations' can be usefully placed in the 'conclusion' section of your project.

What you need to avoid, and what is unlikely to gain you many marks, are statements like: 'The coursework was very enjoyable to do and I learned something.'

On the whole, remember that the conclusion is an account of your findings related to the original task you set yourself.

BIBLIOGRAPHY

A dictionary definition of bibliography is a 'list of books, etc., of any author'. In undertaking your assignment you may have used a number of textbooks, a newspaper article and an advertisement from a magazine. You could include details of these in your bibliography. You should notice that the parts of a reference to a book are usually written in the following order:

1. author's name or names
2. title of the book
3. publisher
4. date of publication

Your bibliography should be in alphabetical order, according to the name of the author or periodical. It is also a good idea to make a note of the page numbers you use, just in case you need to refer back to the book or article at a later date. These are good practices which will help to make your coursework appear more professional.

ACKNOWLEDGMENTS

You may also include an acknowledgments section, thanking those individuals or institutions which have helped you in producing the assignment. For example: 'I would like to thank Mr B. Evers of Wilson Construction PLC for his help and the information he gave me in this assignment.'

In presenting your assignment you should use graphs, tables, diagrams and photographs as well as written information. Make sure you draw these clearly and label them carefully. This type of illustrative material must, at all times, be relevant to the assignment, illustrating points that are being raised. It should not be tacked on at the end or included just because it 'looks nice'.

Check your Examination Group's requirements for presentation.

You also need to be aware of how many words the assignment should be. Table 1.3 gives a guidance on the length of assignments as laid down by the various Examination Groups.

It may be preferable to present your assignment in a *folder*. This means that all the work is kept together, and this can help to give a better impression.

Of course, an assignment can take an *oral* or *visual* form. If you do submit an audio or video tape as part of your assignment, it is still likely that you will need to present a brief *written* outline of the assignment, together with information on the various interviews and events which have taken place.

CHAPTER 3

THE BACKGROUND TO BUSINESS

SCARCITY AND CHOICE

OPPORTUNITY COST

RESOURCES

MEETING OUR NEEDS

TYPES OF ECONOMIC SYSTEM

THE MARKET ECONOMY

THE PLANNED ECONOMY

THE MIXED ECONOMY

BUSINESS OBJECTIVES

THE BUSINESS PLAN

GETTING STARTED

If you look around your home you can hardly fail to notice the influence which business has on your life. The goods you possess, whether for immediate consumption such as food, or to give you satisfaction over a longer time period such as a television, will have been produced by a **business**. If you watch independent television you will not be able to escape advertisements making you aware of the goods and services which businesses provide. If your household purchases a national daily newspaper you will also notice that this includes advertisements of goods and services on offer. Your local newspaper will also include advertisements for employment vacancies, which may be of importance to you if you are considering leaving school in the near future or if you are looking for part-time work. One of the aims of a course in Business Studies is to develop your knowledge and understanding of **business and its environment**. This applies at the local, national and international levels of business.

This chapter sets out the background to business. Why do businesses produce goods and services? What resources do they use in the production of these goods and services? What is meant by production? Within what kind of economic system do these businesses operate? Do they all set themselves the same objectives? What is meant by a Business Plan?

ESSENTIAL PRINCIPLES

1 SCARCITY AND CHOICE

Individuals, as **consumers** within an economy, require a large number of goods and services. Businesses aim at producing these with a view to making a profit.

Most individuals are restricted in what they can buy because of the size of their income. Some will, therefore, spend much more of their income on **basic necessities**, such as food, drink and housing. Others will have more income and therefore be able to buy **luxuries**, such as microwave ovens, CD players and video recorders. If you think about your own situation as a student, then there will be many goods and services you would like to buy. Goods, such as one of the latest top-twenty CDs, a book or a new pair of shoes; or services, such as a haircut, an evening out at the cinema or a football match. You will not be able to buy all the goods and services you would like to because of the limited amount of **resources** you have. These limited resources will, in your case, be the money you obtain each week either as pocket money or for doing particular jobs. This being so you will have to make **choices**. Some of the goods and services you want you will be able to buy but others you will not. This need to choose follows from the fact that although you have **unlimited wants**, you have **limited resources**, in other words your resources are **scarce**.

In the same way, businesses will have to choose how they use their limited resources. Do they use their limited funds to extend their factory or buy a new machine? Do they spend money on developing a new product or do they spend more on advertising the products they are already producing? A business must continually make these and many more decisions.

Governments also have to make choices as to how to spend the money they obtain from taxpayers. If more is spent on providing educational services, this might be at the expense of the National Health Service.

2 OPPORTUNITY COST

Make sure you state that opportunity cost is the next best alternative foregone, not just any alternative!

As mentioned above, as a student you may have unlimited wants but limited resources, so that you will have to make choices. These choices will involve **opportunity cost**. If, for example, you use your money to go to a football match, then you will not be able to use that money to go to the cinema. In making your choice you will have a **scale of preferences**; perhaps football is first, the cinema second and swimming third. The cinema would then be the *next best* alternative you have had to do without, as a result of spending your money on a football match. The next best alternative you have foregone is called the opportunity cost. The opportunity cost of your visit to the football match is then the visit to the cinema which you have had to give up. The concept of opportunity cost is just as relevant to business and the Government. A business which chooses to buy, say, a new fleet of lorries, will forego what it sees as the next best alternative. This might have been to build a new warehouse in which to store its finished products. In this case, the opportunity cost of buying the new fleet of lorries is the new warehouse. Governments will also have similar choices to make involving opportunity cost. For example, an extra £1 billion on building schools may mean fewer new hospitals.

3 RESOURCES

The resources of an economy which can be used to produce goods and services can be divided into four categories (called the **factors of production**):

▶ land
▶ labour
▶ capital
▶ enterprise.

A. LAND

Do not forget that land also includes the resources on or below the surface.

You may feel that land is simply the surface of the earth on which factories and offices can be built. It is this, but it is also the material resources, which are on or below the surface. It therefore includes: agricultural products; mineral deposits, such as coal, iron ore, tin and oil; and the resources obtained from the sea, rivers and lakes.

B. LABOUR

If land is classed as a *natural* resource then labour is classed as a **human resource**. Labour is not just the physical or manual work which individuals undertake in providing goods and services. It is also the mental and intellectual skills which individuals use in the course of production.

C. CAPITAL

Unlike land and labour, capital is a **manufactured resource**. It includes factories and a wide variety of machinery and technology, such as computers. Capital can take a number of forms:

Fixed capital

This is made up of such things as factories and machinery. Fixed capital is needed by a firm before it can start producing.

Circulating capital

This is sometimes called **working capital** and includes the stocks of raw materials which the business will need to manufacture its products. It will also include partly finished products which are not yet ready to be sold, and finished goods which are not yet sold.

D. ENTERPRISE

Land, labour and capital are used to produce goods or services but they need to be organised. Enterprise brings the factors of production together. The person who does the organising is called the **entrepreneur** or businessperson.

4 > MEETING OUR NEEDS

A. PRODUCTION

Businesses have to meet the needs of their customers whether they provide goods or services. If they fail to meet those needs they will very quickly go out of business. Businesses must therefore carefully consider what the consumer requires and how the consumer's tastes are changing over time.

When you go into a shop and buy a product such as a loaf of bread then you are completing a whole **chain of production**. This has started with the farmer planting the grain and has ended with you buying the bread from a retailer. You may think that production is just the process of manufacturing the bread. This is not, however, the whole picture because production is also made up of the provision of the raw materials; in the case of the loaf of bread, this would be flour, salt, yeast and water. The chain of production will also include the services which ensure that the finished product finds its way to the consumer. These services include the transport of bread to the shops, the selling (retail) of bread from the shops and the attempt to make you buy that type of bread (advertising).

It is possible to divide production into three broad areas – primary, secondary and tertiary production – as can be seen in Fig. 3.1.

Types of production

Companies in the **primary production** area of production are involved in the extraction of raw materials, whether above or below the earth's surface. This means that primary production covers farming, forestry and fishing, as well as mining, quarrying and drilling for such raw materials as coal, limestone and oil.

Secondary production involves the manufacture of goods, i.e. the process of turning the raw materials into products. You can, perhaps, make a list of such companies in your town or city. These companies may manufacture finished products which are ready for the end-user to buy or semi-finished products which will be used in making other products. If you refer to Fig. 3.1, you will also notice Construction, which involves the building industry, and the Utilities, including the industries of gas, electricity and water.

As seen in Fig. 3.1, the manufacture of goods can be separated into two types: **consumer goods** and **producer goods**. You may be more familiar with *consumer goods* as you will find many examples in your home. The **single-use consumer**

It can be difficult to learn a great deal of information. Sometimes a diagram, such as Fig. 3.1, is useful in giving you the important points.

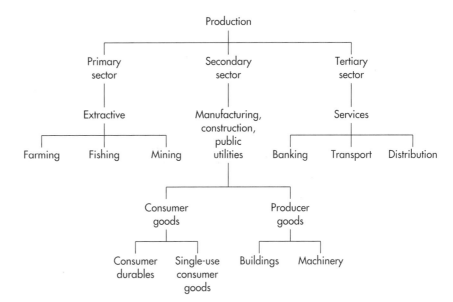

Figure 3.1 Types of production

goods are items which are used only once, such as food and matches. **Consumer durables**, on the other hand, are long-lasting and can be used again and again, such as the washing machine, refrigerator or television. **Producer goods** are used by companies and individuals in the manufacture of other goods (which could in turn be consumer goods). Producer goods include such items as lathes, drills and computers and they can also be called **investment goods** or **capital goods**.

Tertiary production: once the goods have been manufactured, that is by no means the end of the chain. A number of activities will still have to occur before the goods reach the consumer. They will have to be transported, advertised and distributed through wholesale and retail outlets. Banking and financial services will be involved in insuring the finished product and, even before manufacture, in raising the money to begin production (see p. 76). *Tertiary* production, therefore, involves all these service activities such as banking, transport, and distribution. Services are sometimes classed as **intangible goods**, as they meet our needs in much the same way as goods do.

Growth of the tertiary sector

Over the past 30 years, in the UK, there has been a decline in the primary and secondary sectors and a growth in the tertiary sector. This has been the case whether the share of total output or the share of total employment are used as measures. The tertiary sector currently has 68% of the share of total output. This compares with only 4% for the primary sector and 28% for the secondary sector. In terms of the share of total employment, the figures are much the same with the tertiary sector employing 74% of total employment, and the primary and secondary sectors 1% and 25% respectively.

There is no one reason for the changes which have taken place, although the following reasons have been put forward:

The changing pattern of demand: It has been argued that as an economy develops and its population becomes richer, then consumer demand shifts away from goods and towards services. This means increased expenditure on such services as tourism, meals in restaurants, health care and education.

Increased competition from newly industrialised countries: One argument put forward is that countries, such as Taiwan and South Korea, have developed their manufacturing industries and have become major competitors to the secondary sector in the UK. This has particularly been the case since the newly industrialised nations have often had the benefit of relatively low wages.

Lack of competitiveness: Low labour productivity, a slow rate of replacement of capital equipment (relative to our major competitors), and a lack of care and attention given to the design and quality of our manufacturing goods have also been presented as a reason for the decline of the secondary sector in the UK.

B. SPECIALISATION

In early society, individuals would produce for themselves all the products they needed. If they produced a surplus of any product, then they would exchange some of that surplus for the other products in short supply. This is known as a system of **barter**. Perhaps you could think of the problems barter would create (see ch. 7)!

The introduction of money (see also ch. 7) solved one of the problems of barter, in that it allowed individuals to specialise. They were now able to produce the goods, or to provide the services, that they were better at producing. With the money they obtained, they could then buy the goods and services they needed. Specialisation has developed to a point where individuals can now specialise in one small part of a productive process. You should be able to note many examples of specialisation in the area in which you live. Think particularly of the manufacturing business where the process of producing the goods may be divided into a large number of small steps, many undertaken on a production line. This is known as the **division of labour**.

C. THE INTERDEPENDENCE OF BUSINESS

Figure 3.1 gives some idea of the **interdependence** of business. All the members of society involved in **production** are also **consumers**, as are those who are not directly involved in some aspect of production. *Individuals* would find it difficult to exist by their own efforts in modern society as they rely on others to specialise and produce the goods and services they require. In other words, individuals are **interdependent**. So too, are businesses. Take the case of a chocolate manufacturer, which must rely on **primary producers** to supply its raw material, namely cocoa beans. The beans have then to be imported so a chocolate manufacturer must also depend on the **tertiary sector**, i.e. the transport services of road and sea.

The business will also require a skilled workforce capable of producing the chocolate products. In return, the employees will be dependent upon the manufacturer to provide employment and the income which goes with it. With that income, the employees of the chocolate manufacturer can become the consumers of the goods and services of other businesses.

Once the chocolate has been produced, the manufacturer must seek to sell it. This may require the services of an advertising agency to bring the product to the notice of the consumer. Wholesale distributors may purchase the product in bulk from the manufacturer. Retail outlets will then purchase the product for consumers. The manufacturer is, of course, reliant on the consumer whether in the UK or abroad. If the demand is inadequate then the business will not survive.

Other services will also be important for the chocolate manufacturer. Extra finance may be required to expand the factory, to obtain new machinery or to buy a new fleet of lorries. For this reason, the services of the local bank may be needed. Also, the banks will have a whole range of additional facilities to help the manufacturer in importing and exporting the product (see ch. 7). The business will need to insure the products, particularly when they are in transit, as there may be a risk of damage or accident. The manufacturer will also be dependent upon communications of all types – not just the work of the advertising agency but also the provision made by the postal and telecommunications services (see ch. 16).

Finally, there will be an interdependence between the manufacturing company and the Government. The Government will require the company to pay corporation tax on the profits made from the production of goods and services, and the company's employees will also be subject to income tax. In return, there are a number of benefits the Government will provide for the company. The company may be in an area of the UK which receives grants and subsidies as part of the UK and EU Regional Policy. Even if it is not, central and local Government will have helped provide the infrastructure – roads, schools, energy supplies and health care – all of which benefit the company.

5 > **TYPES OF ECONOMIC SYSTEM**

So far we have looked at the major purpose of business activity: to provide the goods and services which meet our needs. This involves the areas of primary, secondary and tertiary production, and varying degrees of specialisation by those in employment. All this productive activity will be undertaken in a particular type of economic system, which is largely determined by political factors. There are three main types of economic system:

 Make sure you can keep the different economic systems separate in your mind!

▶ the market economy
▶ the planned economy
▶ the mixed economy.

6 ▷ THE MARKET ECONOMY

In an extreme ('pure') market economy, there would be no government involvement at all. What is produced would depend solely on what business views as profitable and what the consumer demands. The pure market economy can be seen to have certain features: private enterprise, freedom of choice and competition.

Private enterprise

There is no state ownership of business, hence no nationalisation takes place. All businesses are either owned by an individual (sole trader) or by a group of individuals (partners or shareholders). The resources in the economy are owned by private enterprise and their use depends on the 'signals' provided by the market mechanism (see below).

Freedom of choice

The owners of land and capital are able to use their resources in whatever way they regard as most beneficial to them, e.g. giving the highest profit! Consumers can spend their income as they wish and workers can undertake the type of employment they prefer.

Competition

This is an important feature of a market economy. It is usually argued that a large number of businesses competing with each other will produce a cheaper product of better quality. In other words, competition will promote greater efficiency.

The market economies are sometimes called **free enterprise**, *laissez-faire* or **capitalist** economies. There is perhaps no economy which quite meets the idealised form of a pure market economy, although some countries, like the US, are close.

A. THE MARKET MECHANISM

We have seen that an economy has resources of land, labour, capital and enterprise. Decisions have to be made as to how to use these resources. We see below that, in the planned economy, it is the Government which decides how these resources should be allocated and the prices which should be charged for the goods and services they produce. In the market economy, however, these decisions are left to private businesses and are the result of the market mechanism.

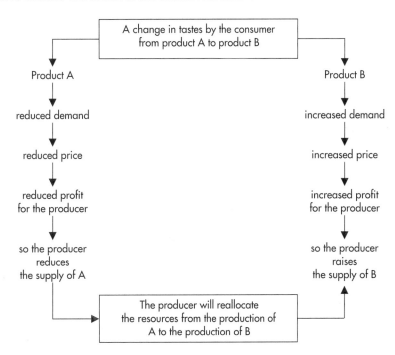

Figure 3.2 The market mechanism

The Figure 3.2 outlines how the market mechanism operates. When you buy goods or services, you are signalling to the producer that you have a preference for their product. The more 'signals' of this type that producers obtain from other consumers, the more they will produce of that product. The reason for this is that, other things being equal, the greater the demand for their product, the higher the price they will be able to charge, and therefore the higher the profit level they will obtain. When you spend your money on a product it is like voting. In this case, you are voting for a particular company's goods or services. The more income you have then the more 'votes' you possess.

A change in the price acts as a signal to the producer to alter supply, as we can see in Fig. 3.2. The producer will move resources away from the production of those products which have a falling demand, to the production of those products which have a rising demand. In the case of Fig. 3.2, the move would be away from product A and towards product B.

B. ADVANTAGES OF THE MARKET ECONOMY

1. The market mechanism allocates resources automatically without any need for government intervention.
2. Businesses compete with each other. This should result in increased efficiency and a better range and quality of product, from all of which the consumer can benefit.
3. All individuals within the economy have freedom of choice.

C. DISADVANTAGES OF THE MARKET ECONOMY

1. Businesses will charge the price that most consumers are willing to pay. This could mean that certain individuals will be unable to obtain the goods and service they require.
2. Competition may not in fact take place. Larger businesses may take over the smaller firms or squeeze them out of existence. What is called a **monopoly** situation may then occur. This may be against the interests of the consumer. The monopoly may charge higher prices, knowing that no alternative sources of supply are available.
3. With no government intervention, businesses will only take account of their own private costs of production: the cost of the raw materials they use, and the wages, rent, rates and interest they pay. They will not take account of the social costs they impose on others as they produce. For instance, the firm may cause pollution, perhaps of the air or rivers, or bring about congestion as its vehicles use local roads. It might increase noise levels by operating its machinery or cause visual intrusion by building a factory which overlooks local houses. These costs to society as a whole, as a result of the firm's production, are called **social costs**, and are likely to go unchecked in the market economy without government intervention.

7 ⟩ THE PLANNED ECONOMY

The planned economy uses its resources in a way decided by the Government or state. A planned economy includes two features: resources are owned by the state, and the production of goods and services is determined by the state.

Resources are owned by the state

In the case of businesses, the profits are used for the benefit of the economy and not for the owners/shareholders as in the market economy, the view being that this creates a more equal society.

The production of goods and services is determined by the state

Resources will be allocated according to the Government or planning authorities' view as to the desires of the consumers and not by the profit motive or self-interest. However, they may wrongly predict those desires. They may find that there is an overproduction of certain goods and services that the consumer does not want and an underproduction of other goods and services which are in high demand.

The planned economy is sometimes called the **command** or **controlled economy**. You may not think of Britain as a planned economy, but during the Second World War the Government did take control of the economic resources of the nation so that they could be used to meet the war effort.

A. ADVANTAGES OF A PLANNED ECONOMY

1. All businesses are state-owned so that it is not possible for a private monopoly to develop.
2. The state decides what is to be produced so that any wasteful competition can be avoided.
3. The state can take account of the social costs and the social benefits in deciding what to produce.

B. DISADVANTAGES OF A PLANNED ECONOMY

1. The Government decides what is to be produced. If it misjudges the requirements of the consumer, then shortages or gluts of certain goods and services can occur. Shortages result in long queues for products; gluts lead to large stockpiles of unwanted products.
2. Since the state owns all the factors of production, this may reduce the incentives to work harder. There is no opportunity for individuals to own their own businesses and to make profits.
3. There will be a lack of competition between businesses and a lack of variety for the consumer. Private monopoly may merely be replaced by public monopoly.
4. In the market economy, resources will be allocated automatically through the market mechanism. In the planned economy, there will be state planning. This may involve a lot of resources and lead to large planning bureaucracies which are slow to take decisions.

8 ▷ THE MIXED ECONOMY

This type of economic system sets out to combine the advantages of both the market economy and the planned economy. In fact, most economies in the world can be viewed as mixed economies although some are closer to the market economy and others to the planned economy. In the mixed economy, resources are owned partly by private individuals and enterprises, and partly by the state; they are allocated partly by the market mechanism and partly by government intervention. In the UK over the last few years, the economy has moved more in the direction of the market economy with certain nationally owned enterprises being privatised, such as British Telecom, British Gas and British Airways (see ch. 4). It has also been the case that since the 1980s, East European economies have abandoned central planning in favour of placing an increased importance on private enterprise.

9 ▷ BUSINESS OBJECTIVES

As a student you may set yourself objectives. At present, your main objective may be to obtain high grades in your GCSE examinations. Businesses will also have objectives and these will normally be formulated by the management of the company, the Board of Directors. By business objectives, we mean the targets that the company is aiming to achieve. Businesses may have more than one objective, but profit is likely to be one of them. A business may set out to maximise its profits, i.e. to make as much profit as possible. This is an objective which the *owners* of the business are likely to prefer, whether sole traders, members of a partnership or shareholders (see ch. 4). In a medium or large company, the shareholders may have less say in the running of the company. Effective control of the company may be in the hands of the top management. Management may have different objectives in mind than shareholders. The managers may seek, as their main objective, to sell as much of the firm's output as possible, i.e. to maximise the volume of sales. The managers' status or promotional prospects may depend more on the sales revenue or size of the company than on the profit performance of the company. Lastly, a business may view the growth of its productive capacity as its main objective. It may set out to achieve this by taking over other businesses.

MANAGEMENT OBJECTIVES

The top managers of a business may set other objectives, which benefit themselves directly rather than the company. One such objective could be an improvement of their own status. This could be achieved by increasing the size of their own department or the number of staff they are in charge of. On the other hand, the objective of management may be a 'quiet life', avoiding unnecessary risks. Some businesses may not set objectives which maximise anything, whether it be profits, sales revenue or growth. They may simply aim to do the best they can in the circumstances. This could be seen as a **satisficing** rather than a maximising objective.

The objectives throughout the business may be different. For example, the overall objective set by a company may be to maximise profits, whereas a particular department's objective may be to maximise its quota of employees or its sales performance. Objectives may also change through time, sometimes as a result of conflict. Suppose a business pursues sales maximisation without too much thought for the profit objective, its shareholders are then likely to be concerned, and at the Annual General Meeting may challenge (and change) the direction of the company.

Certain companies are not profit-making private businesses. Nationalised industries may, for example, have as their main objective the provision of a satisfactory service to the community, i.e. a social objective. They may have added to this a further objective of making a certain level of profit or of at least breaking even.

The objective a business sets for itself will depend on what type it is – sole trader, partnership, limited company, etc. – and its size. The advantage of setting objectives is that it provides a *target* against which it can judge its success over a period of time.

10 ▷ THE BUSINESS PLAN

The **Business Plan** is probably the most important document that any company can have and yet it is also the least well known or used.

All large companies have a Business Plan which is updated each year but very few small companies have one.

The idea behind a Business Plan is like having a map before you set out into relatively unknown territory. You would not be wise to set out into the Highlands of Scotland for a few days camping without making sure that you have a good map. Similarly, it is not at all sensible to try to set up and run a business without some idea of where you are going.

When businesses first begin, they are normally run by one person and that person usually understands what he or she is trying to do. Within a very short space of time, however, the business can grow to a size where one person cannot keep all the possibilities and options in his or her own head and cannot fully understand all the possible ways in which the business needs to be controlled.

Without a Business Plan, it is very difficult to succeed in business. These days it is almost impossible to obtain any form of financial assistance from a bank without a fully worked-out Business Plan.

Let us now look at what any good Business Plan will contain.

A. EXECUTIVE SUMMARY

The **executive summary** gives a brief summary of all of the main points and conclusions of the Business Plan so that a reader might be given the 'gist' of the Business Plan very quickly without having to read everything.

B. THE COMPANY

It is sensible to include a description of your company: how it began, what it is called and what it is in business to do. Many companies find it useful to have a written **'mission statement'** so that everyone – inside and outside the business – knows what it is trying to do. The 'mission statement' may sound very grand but it is intended to be a *realistic* statement and not simply a 'wish'. For example:

By the year 2000, Bloggs & Company will endeavour, through excellence in customer service and consistently high quality research and development, to become the largest manufacturer (by turnover) of high quality plastics in the UK.

This section may also contain descriptions of such things as the company's recruitment policy and its policy with respect to the suppliers of services and components. Many companies, these days, require those companies that supply them with components also to have 'quality systems' and full Business Plans.

It is also wise, here, to look at the 'location' of the company and to explain why it was located in that particular place and whether it has gained any benefits from it. Location is *very* important for most businesses.

C. THE MANAGEMENT

Banks and other lenders will need to understand the quality and experience of the **management** of the company. This section will contain details of the names, ages, experience and qualifications of the management. It is also usual to say *why* the managers want to work in the company and how they see its future.

D. PRODUCT(S) AND PRICING

This section describes the products and/or services which the company offers (or intends to offer). This will normally be very detailed, listing each product or service and saying why the company is producing or offering it, what market it is designed to reach and how successful it has been.

It will also say how those products have been priced and how the company intends to increase or decrease them over the next few years.

E. PLAN OBJECTIVES

A Business Plan is drawn up for a specific period of time:

Bloggs & Company
Business Plan
1996/97 to 1998/99

This would be a 'three-year' plan covering the 'financial years' beginning with 1996/97.

A 'financial year' can start at any time and its beginning is usually chosen by the company when it is set up. Many companies use the calendar year – i.e. January to December – for their financial years whilst others simply start from when they were established – say, August to July.

The 'Tax Year' is set by Parliament and, at the moment, runs from April 6th in any one year to April 5th in the following year. The reasons for such a strange year are historic but many small companies use the 'tax year' as their 'financial year' to make their dealings with the taxman easier.

For whatever period of time the Business Plan is to cover, it will state what the objectives of the company are to be. These will normally be divided into a number of different subheadings which may or may not relate directly to the company's sub-departments.

The subheadings and objectives may, therefore, be:

▶ **Production**
   Year One.

1. Purchase and installation of a new micro-lithographic machine.
2. Rearrangement of the production line.
3. Etc.

   Year Two

1. Replacement of the packing line with more up-to-date equipment.
2. Installation of a new stand-by generator.
3. Etc.

▶ **Marketing**
   Year One

1. Product development on the old HR250 printer.
2. Market research for the proposed high temperature plastics.
3. Begin advertising in May for the high temperature line.
4. Take a stand at the European Plastics Exhibition.
5. Etc.

Year Two

1. Begin the promotion campaign for the high temperature plastics.
2. Decide on whether to narrow down the product range.
3. Investigate the possibility of exporting to the Middle East and Japan.
4. Etc

► **Sales**
Year One

1. Achieve £100,000 sales for the printer product.
2. Introduce new 'regional' sales structure.
3. Etc.

Year Two

1. Set up agents to handle sales of the new high temperature plastics.
2. Investigate new areas for the 'services' that we might offer.
3. Etc.

► **Personnel**
Year One

1. Make sure that all demographic trends are understood for our factory areas.
2. Employ new manager for the high temperature line.
3. Employ two new 'regional' sales managers and sales people for the new regional structure.
4. Arrange and implement training for all staff concerned with the new production line.
5. Etc.

Year Two

1. Find and recruit two new export managers.
2. Arrange and implement training courses in appropriate languages.
3. Etc.

► **Finance**
Year One

1. Install new accounting package on the main computer.
2. Arrange new sources of finance for the required production investment.
3. Etc.

Year Two

1. Make sure that overseas currency is available, if required, for any purchases of companies or the commissioning of agents abroad to support new export drive.
2. Add 'invoicing' facility to the computer accounting system.
3. Etc.

► **etc, etc.**

F. COMPETITION

Competing Companies

This section will describe who are the main competitors to your company and how they might affect the business over the period of the Business Plan. It might be, for example, that one of your main competitors has announced that they will be launching a new product. This will need to be taken into account in your own Business Plans.

Competitive Advantage

You will need to assess very clearly what advantages you might have over the competition – and what advantages *they* have over you. You might have better quality staff or more modern machinery; they might have a better location or better advertising.

G. MARKETING

Regardless of what has been listed under the company's objectives, it is necessary to show those who will read the Business Plan that you have developed a marketing strategy which has identified *what* market or markets you see yourself as being in, and *how* you will develop them.

H. MANUFACTURING

The heart of most businesses is the manufacturing of their products. Such companies will need to state what their plans are for manufacturing – how the capacity will be increased, how machinery will be kept up-to-date, how new technology will be introduced, etc.

I. RESEARCH & DEVELOPMENT (R & D)

Most companies need to develop their products and their services over time if they wish to keep up with the markets and – if possible – move ahead of their competitors.

Whether your company supplies goods or services it will need to research new ideas and then to develop those ideas to the point at which they can be marketed. R&D is expensive, but is absolutely vital. A producer of pushchairs might be tempted to think that 'a pushchair is a pushchair' – once you have designed a seat with a handle and four wheels you just need to produce it and to sit back and rake in the money. In the modern world, this is not so. Consumers require the very best in design, convenience and appearance and any company that does not carry out R&D will very soon find itself out of business. For example, old-fashioned wheel-bearings used to be made out of steel ball-bearings. These are expensive and difficult to maintain. Research has now produced plastic bearings that last longer, are cheaper for the manufacturer to use, and do not squeak.

J. HISTORICAL FINANCIAL DATA

This section will contain figures for your financial performance over the last few years. It is there so that people using the Business Plan can see how the company has developed in the past.

K. FINANCIAL PROJECTIONS

The heart of the business plan is where the calculations of what it will cost are based – in the Financial Projections section.

Here will be found information on what the company thinks it will have to spend and what it believes it can earn on sales over the period of the Business Plan.

It may contain:

▶ a cash flow analysis for each year
▶ an income statement for each year
▶ a projected balance sheet for each year
▶ some key 'ratio' analysis.

L. LOAN/INVESTMENT

If the company sees that it will require overdrafts, loans or investments, it will need to say so in this section and say what it feels will be the effects of the money. Most importantly it will need to say what 'return' it can offer on the investment and how much interest it is estimating it will have to pay for the overdrafts and loans. These will, of course, have been 'built in' to the financial projections in the previous section.

EXAMINATION QUESTIONS

QUESTION 1

'Britain is a good example of a "mixed economy"'

(a) State briefly what is meant by a mixed economy. (2 lines provided)   (2 marks)

(b) Name two other kinds of national economies and give a brief description of each.
(4 lines provided)   (4 marks)
       (NICCEA)

QUESTION 2

An economy's resources are used by businesses in the production of goods and services. The goods produced can be either producer goods or consumer goods. The consumer goods may be either single use or durable and they directly satisfy the wants of the consumer.

(i) What is meant by the term '*resources*' mentioned in the above passage?
(2 lines provided)   (2 marks)

(ii) In what way do producer goods and consumer goods differ?
(4 lines provided)   (4 marks)

(iii) Give 2 examples of both single use consumer goods and consumer durables.
(2 lines provided)   (4 marks)

QUESTION 3

Study the following data and answer the questions printed below.

	1965	1975	1985
% of Employment in:			
Primary	20	?	10
Secondary	50	45	?
Tertiary	30	40	50
Unemployment %	4	6	10
Working Population (000's)	300	320	350

Table 3.1 Distribution of Employment 1965–1985 in the county of Midshire

(a) Give TWO different examples of jobs that might be classified as:
    (i) tertiary activities (one line for each example)   (2 marks)
    (ii) primary activities. (one line for each example)   (2 marks)

(b) What percentages of the workforce were employed in
    (i) primary activities in 1975? (one line)   (2 marks)
    (ii) secondary activities in 1985? (one line)   (2 marks)

(c) How many people worked in tertiary activities in 1985. (Show your working.)
       (3 marks)

(d) Using the figures from the table, state and explain TWO main changes that have taken place in employment over the last 20 years.   (4 marks)
    1. (3 lines provided)
    2. (3 lines provided)

(e) How many people were unemployed in Midshire in 1985? (3 lines provided)
       (2 marks)

(f) State and explain TWO ways in which the State can help people who are unemployed.
    1. (3 lines provided)
    2. (3 lines provided)   (4 marks)
       (MEG)

A TUTOR'S ANSWER TO Q.1

QUESTION 1

(a) A **mixed economy** includes elements of both the free market and the planned economy. This means that resources – i.e. land, labour, capital and enterprise – are allocated partly by the market mechanism and partly by the government (or planning authority). These resources are both privately and publicly owned.

(b) The free market and the planned economy

The *free market economy* relies on the market mechanism (supply and demand) to allocate resources rather than on government intervention. The market determines the price of the products and the price acts as a signal to producers and consumers. For example, a high price will encourage more production and discourage some consumption. The market will eventually settle on a price that brings 'harmony' between producers and consumers. All the resources are privately owned by individuals or businesses. In the *planned economy*, resources are owned by the state and the planning authority within the state decides what is to be produced. Planners may produce more than consumers wish to buy, i.e. there will be overproduction. The extra output will then have to be held in storage. Wrong decisions by planners can therefore cause serious problems.

STUDENT'S ANSWER TO Q.2

> ❝ Enterprise might also have been mentioned. ❞

> ❝ Usually thought of as part of land or raw materials ❞

> ❝ Good points. Resources can be classified as land, labour, capital and enterprise. You have mentioned most of these. ❞

> ❝ Good examples of producer and consumer goods *but* the question asked you how they *differ*. ❞

> ❝ Accurate examples ❞

> ❝ Some slip-up in part (ii) but a reasonable attempt overall. ❞

(i) Resources as mentioned in the above passage are those things such as raw materials used in the making of goods. Land, coal deposits, labour and machinery are resources.

(ii) Producer goods are things like machinery and factories. Consumer goods are things like food and clothes.

(iii) Single-use consumer goods:

i) food

ii) cosmetics.

Consumer durables:

i) TV set

ii) fridge.

A Review Sheet for this chapter can be found on pp. 233–4.

CHAPTER 4

TYPES OF BUSINESS

GETTING STARTED

In your local town or city you will be able to find examples of the different types of business. It is important in any Business Studies course to obtain a clear understanding of the different forms of business organisation which exist. As Fig. 4.1 shows, there are three broad types of business:

► Private sector companies
► Public sector companies
► Co-operatives.

There is a distinction between these businesses in terms of **ownership**:

1. **Private sector companies** are owned and controlled by individuals. They may vary from one person businesses to large companies with many owners (shareholders).
2. **Public sector companies** are said to be owned by the state on behalf of the general public, and include the nationalised industries.
3. **Co-operatives** are either owned by the people who work in them (producers' co-operative) or by the consumers who purchase from them (retail co-operative).

As well as the ownership distinction there is the **legal** distinction. For this you will need to understand a little of:

1. The Companies Acts
2. The Industrial and Provident Societies Acts

and how they affect the business organisation.

SOLE TRADERS

PARTNERSHIPS

UNLIMITED AND LIMITED LIABILITY

PRIVATE LIMITED COMPANIES

PUBLIC LIMITED COMPANIES (PLCs)

BECOMING A LIMITED COMPANY

MEMORANDUM OF ASSOCIATION

ARTICLES OF ASSOCIATION

PUBLIC SECTOR COMPANIES

PRIVATISATION

CO-OPERATIVES

ESSENTIAL PRINCIPLES

1 ⟩ SOLE TRADERS

Consider the following business: SMITH'S PLUMBING ENGINEERS.

Dave Smith started out working for himself as a plumber five years ago. He thought the name Smith's Plumbing Engineers sounded good and, having advertised himself in the *Yellow Pages*, he has never been short of work.

A. OWNERSHIP AND FINANCE

❝❝ Make sure you understand the main differences between the various types of business. This knowledge is the basis for answering many types of question. ❞❞

▶ As the name suggests the sole trader is a **one-person** business where the individual may have been responsible for starting off the business.

▶ It is very easy to set up a business like this. There are **no legal formalities** and, for this reason, they are the most common form of enterprise.

▶ The sole trader will need to provide the **capital** of the business. This could be from personal savings or a loan from a bank. Dave obtained a loan which he used to purchase a van, specialist plumbing tools and to pay for an advertisement in the *Yellow Pages*.

B. ADVANTAGES OF SOLE TRADERS

1. Dave Smith (the owner) is working for himself, so he has an **incentive** to run the business as efficiently as possible.
2. Only a relatively **small amount of capital** is necessary to start up the business.
3. Dave Smith is in sole charge and therefore can **take decisions quickly** because no one has to be consulted.
4. Dave Smith does not have to **share the profits** with anyone.

C. DISADVANTAGES OF SOLE TRADERS

1. If the business loses money then his personal belongings are at risk because he has **unlimited liability** (see page 36).
2. If the owner dies or is ill it is difficult to keep **continuity** within the business.
3. The owner may have difficulty in obtaining **extra capital** for expansion.
4. The business may not do as well as it could because the owner may lack new ideas, as a result of **working in isolation**.

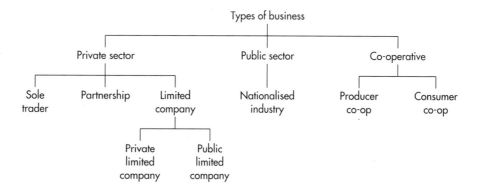

Figure 4.1 Types of business

2 ⟩ PARTNERSHIPS

The sole trader can solve a number of the problems he or she faces by forming a **partnership**. Dave Smith may decide to go into partnership with a friend of his, Jim Collier. Jim has experience in installing central heating systems. He is also willing to put £5,000 into the business. After some discussion, they decide to call the partnership SMITH AND COLLIER PLUMBING AND HEATING ENGINEERS.

A. OWNERSHIP AND FINANCE

▶ They are covered by the **Partnership Act (1890)** which defines a partnership as 'the relation which subsists between persons carrying on a business in common with a view of profit'. Which means a partnership is made up of members who are in business and whose aim is to make profits. So a charity could not be a partnership.

▶ Partnerships are allowed to have 2–20 members – although there are exceptions. This is the case with banks which, if they are a partnership, are not allowed more than 10 partners, and also with firms such as accountants and solicitors who are allowed to have more than 20.

▶ Many partnerships can be set up **without a contract** between the partners. However a written agreement is preferable since it will help to solve any disagreements which may occur. Dave and Jim do not have a written agreement, and this could create problems if they find they cannot work with each other.

▶ All the partners are equally responsible for the debts of the partnership; they have **unlimited liability** (see below).

▶ A partner may simply provide capital for the partnership but take no active part in the day to day running of the business. This partner is known as the **dormant** (or **sleeping) partner**.

B. ADVANTAGES OF PARTNERSHIP

1. **More capital** will be available for the business to expand – in our example, £5,000 more.
2. Partners will bring different **ideas** to the business.
3. **Specialisation** (see page 24) can occur with the individual partners concentrating on those areas of the business at which they are most efficient. Jim is the central heating specialist as well as being able to do the accounts, whereas Dave specialises in the general plumbing but also orders the raw materials required.
4. All partners are entitled, unless they decide otherwise, to an **equal share** of the profits and must contribute equally to the losses.

C. DISADVANTAGES OF PARTNERSHIP

1. Like a sole trader, the partners still have **unlimited liability**.
2. There could be **disagreements** among the partners which, unlike in the case of a limited company which is a separate legal entity from the owners, could lead to the total break-up of the partnership.
3. The actions of one partner are **binding** on the others. So it is important that the partners are chosen with care.
4. There may be problems when one of the partners dies, particularly if that person's capital is taken out of the business by the family of the deceased. In this case, the partnership may have to be dissolved (ended) and a new partnership made up of the remaining partners.

3 ❯ UNLIMITED AND LIMITED LIABILITY

Before dealing with public and private limited companies, it is important to explain what is meant by the terms **unlimited** and **limited liability**.

A. UNLIMITED LIABILITY

Sole traders and partnerships have **unlimited liability**. This means that if the business cannot pay its creditors (the individuals or firms to whom it owes money) then the owners may be declared bankrupt. If this is the case, then the owners' personal possessions, such as home and car, can be taken and used to pay for the debts of the business.

❝❝ Students often mix these two up. So beware! ❞❞

B. LIMITED LIABILITY

With **limited liability**, the owners' (i.e. the shareholders responsibilities for the debts of the company are limited to how many shares they have in the company. For example, a shareholder with £100 of shares will only lose the £100 if the company goes into liquidation, and not all his or her personal possessions. The benefit of this is that potential shareholders will not be put off by the possibility of losing everything they own.

A sole trader or partnership may wish to remove the risk of unlimited liability by forming a **private limited company**. This would mean that the sole trader would need at least one other person, who more than likely would be a member of the sole trader's family. Dave and Jim decide on such a course of action, as outlined later in this chapter. Dave and Jim's company will be called CAMBRIDGE PLUMBING AND HEATING ENGINEERS LIMITED and it will have its own legal personality, being separate from its owners.

A. OWNERSHIP AND FINANCE

▶ A private limited company – identified by writing **Limited** or **Ltd** after the company's name – may have a number of owners from two to no upper limit, called **shareholders**.

▶ The owners obtain shares which entitle them to a share of the profits in proportion to the number and type of shares possessed.

▶ Certain restrictions are placed on private limited companies. The shares cannot be sold on the Stock Exchange and cannot be advertised for sale publicly through newspapers, etc., so they have to be sold privately (thus '*private* limited company') with the agreement of the other shareholders. Shares may first have to be offered to existing shareholders.

▶ Private limited companies are likely to obtain the majority of their finance by issuing shares but money may also be borrowed from a bank.

▶ The shares cannot be sold to the general public and this has the effect of limiting the amount of finance that can be raised.

B. ADVANTAGES OF PRIVATE LIMITED COMPANIES

1. **More capital** is available as there are more owners.
2. The **owners are protected** from losing their personal possessions by limited liability. To those trading with a limited company the word 'limited' serves as a **warning** in that if the company goes into liquidation then the owners are not responsible for any debt beyond their own shareholding in the company.
3. The company will have its own **legal identity** so that, unlike a partnership, it can carry on in business unaffected by a shareholder's death.
4. They have only to publish their accounts in a summarised form. They are able, therefore, to retain some **privacy**. However, the accounts have to be available to the public if the public asks for them.

C. DISADVANTAGES OF PRIVATE LIMITED COMPANIES

1. In becoming a private limited company, the sole trader or partnership will **lose some control** over the running of the business and will be accountable to the shareholders who have voting rights. This can be avoided to some extent by the founder member or members owning the majority of the shares.
2. Although more capital can be raised than by a sole trader or by a partnership there is still the problem that **shares cannot be sold to the general public** on the open market.

PLCs are the largest type of business in the private sector and they are identified by the letters 'plc' written after the name of the company, e.g. Cadbury Schweppes plc.

A. OWNERSHIP AND FINANCE

▶ The number of **shareholders** can range from two upwards.

▶ The **shares can be sold to members of the general public** initially, through advertising in the national newspapers. The shareholders then become part-owners of the company and have certain rights:

1. to receive the company's annual reports/accounts
2. to attend, vote and speak at the company's Annual General Meeting (AGM)
3. to elect the Board of Directors and the Chairman of the Board.

▶ As many PLCs have their shares traded on the Stock Exchange, the shareholder can sell the shares (now 'second-hand') to anyone who is willing to buy them (see ch. 7).

❝❝ You may need to *name* a large company in manufacturing or construction which is in the private sector. This will normally be a PLC such as ICI plc. ❞❞

B. ADVANTAGES OF PLCs

1. As with a private limited company, the shareholders have **limited liability**.
2. **More capital** can be raised than by a private limited company because shares can be sold to the general public.
3. The growth of a PLC allows it to take advantage of **internal economies of scale** (see ch. 6).

C. DISADVANTAGES OF PLCs

1. As the PLC grows in size, it may experience **diseconomies of scale** (again see ch. 6).
2. There may be **communication problems** between the management and workforce.
3. Shares can be transferred easily by the shareholders of a PLC and they could be bought by a company intent on a **takeover** bid.
4. The company's **full annual accounts have to be published**.

It is unlikely that Cambridge Plumbing and Heating Engineers Limited will ever make moves to become a PLC. Only if the company decides, for example, to manufacture its own central heating systems would it consider 'going public'. In that case, it would sell shares on the open market to obtain the finance to start manufacturing the system.

6 ⟩ BECOMING A LIMITED COMPANY

If the business wants to become a limited or public limited company then it will have to be registered. Figure 4.2 explains the procedure with which Dave and Jim will have to comply if they want their business to become a private limited company. Figure 4.2 also outlines the procedure for becoming a PLC.

The founders of the company have to file the relevant documents with the Registrar of Companies.

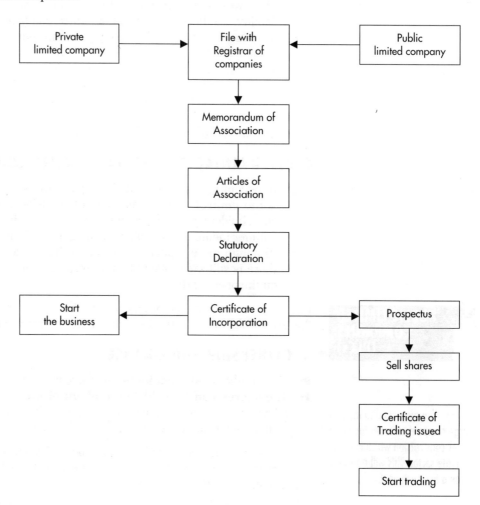

Figure 4.2 The procedure for becoming a limited company

7 > MEMORANDUM OF ASSOCIATION

The **Memorandum of Association** deals with the company's relationship with the outside world. The main contents of the memorandum are listed below:

A. THE COMPANY'S NAME

This allows the Registrar to make sure that no two companies are using the same name. A private limited company's name must contain the word 'limited' (or the letters 'Ltd') and a public limited company's name must contain the letters 'plc'. Dave and Jim will not be able to use the name 'Cambridge Plumbing and Heating Engineers Limited' if any other company has already registered the name.

B. THE COMPANY'S ADDRESS

This shows where the company has its registered office. Dave and Jim have premises on a trading estate which includes an office. Their address is: 52 The Estate, Highfield, Cambridge CB3 7EQ.

C. THE OBJECTS OF THE COMPANY

This states the purposes for which the company is formed, such as 'for the manufacture of chocolate' or, as in our example, 'to provide a plumbing and heating service'. Future shareholders, therefore, have some idea of the company in which they are investing their funds. In practice, such 'objects' clauses usually outline many different types of activity in order to cover any future change which the business might wish to pursue.

D. A STATEMENT

A statement is required that the liability of the shareholders is limited.

E. THE AMOUNT OF CAPITAL

This specifies the amount of capital to be raised by issuing shares and the type of shares, e.g. £100,000 divided into £1 shares. A public company must have at least £50,000 of share capital.

F. AN AGREEMENT

This confirms the agreement of those who sign the memorandum that they wish to form a limited company and that they agree to purchase the stated number of shares.

8 > ARTICLES OF ASSOCIATION

This deals with the internal relationship of the company, i.e. the day-to-day running of the company. The **Articles of Association** cover:

1. the procedure for calling a general meeting
2. the methods of electing directors
3. the rights and duties of directors
4. the borrowing power of the company
5. rules about the transfer of shares
6. the division of profits.

As regards point 5, for a private limited company, the Articles of Association will contain a restriction on the right to transfer shares.

Once these two documents have been completed, they are sent to the Registrar of Companies along with the **Statutory Declaration**. This states that the promoters of the company have complied with the requirements of the Companies Acts. The Registrar of Companies will then check the details and make sure everything is in order before issuing a **Certificate of Incorporation**. This sets up the company as a legal entity. It is the 'birth certificate' of the company. The *private* limited company can now commence business.

A *public* limited company also needs a **Certificate of Trading**. This is issued by the Registrar of Companies when he is satisfied the company has raised sufficient finance to cover its proposed plans. The company will have to advertise the sale of its shares, decide on how they are to be issued and then start trading (see ch. 7).

9 > PUBLIC SECTOR COMPANIES

Public sector companies are concerns which are owned by the Government on behalf of the general public and are of two types:

1. **public corporations**, such as the BBC, are a special sort of public enterprise which is set up by a special document called a **Royal Charter**;
2. **nationalised industries**, such as The Post Office Group.

A. OWNERSHIP AND FINANCE

> Make sure you understand the main differences between private and public sector companies.

Post Office
MoD
British Rail (No)

1. Unlike private limited companies and public limited companies which are owned by the shareholders, public corporations and nationalised industries are **owned by the state** and there are **no shareholders**.
2. Each nationalised industry is **set up by an Act of Parliament** and has a separate legal identity from the Government.
3. Nationalised industries are influenced by four groups:
   (a) the Government, which is responsible for the general policy of the nationalised industry;
   (b) a Minister or Secretary of State within the Government who is responsible for the interests of the nationalised industry within Parliament and for ensuring that the industry operates in the interests of the public;
   (c) the Board of Directors which is responsible for the day-to-day running of the industry – the Government appoints the Chairman; and
   (d) consumer consultation councils which monitor the activities of nationalised industry and act as a **'watchdog'**. (See ch. 18 for an explanation of **consumer protection**.)
4. Nationalised industries must aim to 'at least' **break even financially**, although the interest of the public may lead them to make losses.

B. THE REASONS FOR NATIONALISATION

1. Certain industries are **natural monopolies**, which means they can be better organised nationally to take advantage of economies of scale (see ch. 6). The argument here is that anything less than a national monopoly would be 'inefficient'.
2. Certain industries are **costly to set up and run**. Unless the early investment is paid for by the Government, they might not begin operations at all. For example, the Channel Tunnel Group faced large problems in raising finance; if it had been a nationalised concern the State could have provided the initial finance.
3. Certain industries have been brought under Government control for **strategic reasons**. Rolls Royce engines are important to Western defence, which was one of the reasons why the company was nationalised when it faced problems in 1971. (The company was returned to private ownership in 1987.)
4. Certain industries would have faced **bankruptcy** if they had not been nationalised and this would have resulted in high **job losses**, e.g. British Leyland in the early 1970s.
5. Certain industries have been nationalised in the past to **avoid duplication** of services, e.g. British Rail.
6. Certain industries are under national ownership for **safety reasons**, e.g. British Nuclear Fuels.

10 > PRIVATISATION

> Try to be aware of any other companies that are likely to be privatised.

Since the election of the Conservative Government in 1979, a number of nationalised industries have been **privatised** or **denationalised**. This means that they have been transferred from the status of nationalised industries to that of PLCs. Examples include:

- British Aerospace
- National Freight Corporation
- British Airways
- British Telecom
- British Gas
- Water
- Electricity
- British Airports Authority
- Sealink
- Jaguar

At the time of writing, British Rail is in the process of being privatised.

A. THE REASONS FOR PRIVATISATION

The main reasons put forward for privatisation are:

1. Greater **competition** between businesses leading to increased efficiency, better quality, lower prices and greater choice for the consumer. This is because firms will need to improve the goods and services they provide if they are to sell more than their competitors.
2. It **allows the management to manage** the company rather than to face interference from the Government, which may be against the interests of the company.
3. If the company makes a profit, then the benefits will go to improving the company or as dividends to the shareholders. If the company makes losses, then the company will have to carry the consequences. This could lead to the company being **better organised** because the management will not have the Government to fall back on to 'bail them out'.
4. It is hoped that more of the general public will be able to own shares as nationalised industries like British Telecom and British Gas are privatised. In other words, there will be greater **public participation** in the running of British industry.

B. CONTRACTING OUT

One element of privatisation has been the **contracting out** to private contractors of services which were originally supplied by the public sector. This has included:

▶ **local authority services** such as street cleaning, refuse collection, the maintenance of parks and recreation grounds and the provision of school meals;
▶ **NHS provision** such as cleaning, catering, laundry – although it could be expanded to include the ambulance service; and
▶ **Ministry of Defence**, again including catering and cleaning together with vehicle repairs, and the refitting of warships.

Contracting out is undertaken by **competitive tendering**, whereby firms bid for the privilege of running a particular service. The logic behind contracting out and tendering is similar to that of privatisation in that it aims to improve efficiency through providing a better service at a more competitive price. It is also intended to increase competition between rival suppliers leading to new ideas and improved management techniques. Two arguments have been put forward against contracting out:

▶ Private companies who have obtained the tender are deemed to offer an inferior service, both in terms of reliability and quality. This is based in part on the fact that private companies often use low bids in order to obtain contracts.
▶ The working conditions and remuneration of staff of the private companies is often below that of the pre-contracted out service, mainly as a means of achieving cost savings.

11 ▷ CO-OPERATIVES

Co-operatives are a different kind of business organisation and fall into two categories:

1. retail co-operatives
2. producer co-operatives.

A. RETAIL CO-OPERATIVES (CO-OPERATIVE RETAIL SOCIETIES)

The retail co-operative movement was started in 1844 by a number of weavers in Rochdale who became known as the 'Rochdale Pioneers'. You will know the consumer co-operatives as retail shops, 'Co-ops', which can be found in the main shopping areas of most towns.

Ownership and Finance

1. Retail co-operatives are not covered by company law but draw their legal personality from the **Industrial and Provident Societies Acts**.
2. Anyone can buy shares, which cost £1.00 each with an upper limit of £10,000.

❝❞ The differences between retail and producer co-operatives can often create problems. Make sure you know the differences ❝❞

3. The shareholders or members, as they are called, have **one vote** no matter how many shares they have; this is unlike a PLC where the shareholders have votes at the Annual General Meeting in relation to the number of shares owned.
4. Although they possess **limited liability** the shares do not increase in value and **cannot be sold on the Stock Exchange**. If the owner wants to dispose of the shares they have to be sold back to the co-operative society.
5. The **members share the profits**. This could be in the form of:
    (a) a rate of interest paid on the basis of share owned; or
    (b) reduced prices in the shops as a result of the profit being ploughed back into the business.
6. The members elect a **management committee** which is responsible for the day-to-day running of the society.
7. Retail societies are members of the **Co-operative Wholesale Society (CWS)** from which they purchase their stock.

B. PRODUCER CO-OPERATIVES

There is no strict definition of a producer co-operative. Many are small, with as few as ten workers, but they can be much larger.

Ownership and Finance

1. The aim of producer co-operatives is one of **equity, equality** and **mutual self-help**. The idea is that they are run on democratic lines with each member of the co-operative having one vote on decisions that have to be taken, irrespective of the amount of capital they have put into the business or of how hard they work.
2. They register with the **Registrar of Friendly Societies**. This can create a problem in that a minimum of seven members is needed and so a prospective co-operative may take a number of non-working founder members who may have only a limited knowledge of the ideas of the co-operative movement.
3. The **finance is provided by the members of the co-operative**, who have an equal claim to a share of the profits. A certain amount of the profit will be ploughed back into the co-operative.
4. Extra finance can be obtained by expanding the co-operative through accepting more members. **Problems can occur with a larger co-operative** in that it may take longer to arrive at decisions and more disagreements may occur.

EXAMINATION QUESTIONS

QUESTION 1

State two reasons for the Memorandum of Association. (2 lines provided)   (2 marks)

QUESTION 2

Explain what is meant by 'unlimited liability'? (2 lines provided)   (2 marks)

QUESTION 3

'The private sector and the public sector are different ways of achieving the same thing.'

(a) Explain the essential difference between the private sector and the public sector.
    (6 lines provided)   (4 marks)
(b) Give an example in each case of a large organisation engaged in secondary production:
        (i) in the private sector   (2 marks)
        (ii) in the public sector   (2 marks)
(c) What is the 'same thing' that both are supposed to be achieving?
    (2 lines provided)   (3 marks)
                                                            (NICCEA)

QUESTION 4

Jeni Farnhill started to design and make wedding dresses five years ago in her home. The business has expanded and now she has four people working for her in small premises in her local town. At present, she is a sole trader but Jeni is in the process of registering her business as a private limited company with the name Gala Dresses Ltd.

(i) Outline the main features of a private limited company.
(3 lines provided) (3 marks)
(ii) State three reasons why Jeni Farnhill may have decided to become a private limited company. (3 lines provided) (3 marks)
(iii) In becoming a private limited company why are the Memorandum of Association and the Articles of Association important to the shareholders?
(5 lines provided) (4 marks)

TUTOR'S ANSWER TO Q.3

(a) The private sector is made up of businesses which are either owned by an individual or a group of individuals. This sector includes the sole trader, partnerships, private and public limited companies and co-operatives. In the case of private and public limited companies, the owners are the shareholders. The public sector includes businesses which are owned by the Government, whether it be central or local Government.

(b) (i) Here you need to name an example of a large company in manufacturing or construction which is in the private sector. This will normally be a PLC such as ICI plc.
(ii) British Nuclear Fuels. Make sure you read the question carefully because it asks you for examples of *secondary* production, not primary or tertiary.

(c) Both the private and public sector are supposed to be achieving the production of goods and services in order to satisfy human needs. In other words, they are different ways of organising production, i.e. of bringing together the resources of land, labour and capital.

STUDENT'S ANSWER TO Q.4

❝ Registered with the Registrar of Companies using the Memorandum of Association and the Articles of Association **❞**

❝ Before you start an examination question make sure that you read *all* parts of the question. Too much has been written about the Memorandum and Articles of Association in part (i), given that these are in part (iii). This is not wrong, but it does waste time! **❞**

4. (i) A private limited company, otherwise known as Ltd., is one which offers shares, but the shareholding is restricted. Shares tend to belong to members of the family or employees and cannot be sold through the Stock Exchange to the general public. Liability is limited, that is, in case of bankruptcy, the shareholder is only liable to lose what he has put into the company (price of the shares) and not his personnal assets. Ltd. company must be registered in the Memorandum of Association and the Articles of Association. In these, the name and address of the company must be given, its aims and objectives; in the Articles of Association details are given about the general running of the company such as shareholders' meetings.

These are good points.

This is a good answer in terms of the space provided on the examination paper. It is well worth making sure that you understand all there is to know about the Memorandum and Articles of Association, as questions are often set on these.

(ii) Jeni Farnhill may have decided to become a Ltd. because it has limited liability, capital is increased and membership is restricted to private individuals.

(iii) The Memorandum of Association and the Articles of Association are important to the shareholders because they provide information about the company such as its name and address, the capital it intends to raise and a statement that liability of the shareholders is limited; and it gives details of how shareholders meetings are to be conducted and the rights of the members.

COURSEWORK

1. In your *local* area choose a type of business organisation.

    It can be either:
    (a) a sole trader, e.g. a local corner shop
    (b) a partnership, e.g. a local firm of solicitors
    (c) a private limited company (Ltd), e.g. a small family business but make sure it has 'Ltd' after its name, or
    (d) a public limited company (PLC) – your local area should have a PLC, which will normally be a well-known company name.
2. Make arrangements to visit the business of your choice.
    (a) What type of business organisation is it?
    (b) What size is the business (e.g. in terms of the number of people employed)?
    (c) What are the advantages and disadvantages the business faces by being the type of organisation it is?

    For example, if it is a *sole trader*, does it face difficulties raising funds? Would it like to expand? Has the owner ever thought about taking a partner? (If not, why not?)
    If it is a *partnership*, how many partners are there? What are the benefits of having that number of partners?

    (d) Are there any plans for the organisation you have chosen to change its legal form?

    For example, does the sole trader plan in the future to become a private limited company?

    (e) If the company is a PLC then perhaps you could obtain some information on its Memorandum and Articles of Association. You could match up what the text book has to say with the company's Memorandum and Articles.
3. Write up your findings in the way outlined in Chapter 2.

A Review Sheet for this chapter will be found on pp. 235–6.

MANAGEMENT

GETTING STARTED

It is difficult to define the term 'management' for there is no single definition. It is easier to define what management is by explaining what a manager does.

Any business, small or large, will have to be organised. Consider your school: the teachers are usually divided into departments based on subject areas and there are also ancillary or support staff, such as cleaners and cooks. The Headteacher will be involved in managing the school, perhaps helped by a Deputy Headteacher and by the Heads of the various departments. If we take the example of a company called Chocolate Delight plc, a confectionary manufacturer, the staff there specialise in particular types of work and there are managers in charge of making sure that the work is completed. These managers can be seen as leaders who try to make sure that the business is running smoothly. There is a Managing Director responsible for the overall running of the company.

You will need to have an understanding of how management is organised, what management does, and how they distribute work to the staff for whom they are responsible.

The **owners** of limited companies are the shareholders who entrust the **control** of limited companies to the directors they have **elected**. The directors, who are the top management, will **appoint** the middle management of the company who are then **employees** of the company as are the rest of the staff (see Fig. 5.1).

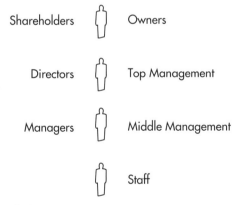

Figure 5.1 The relationship between shareholders, directors and managers

1 > THE FUNCTIONS OF MANAGEMENT

❝ It is easy to confuse the various functions of management, so be careful! ❞

ESSENTIAL PRINCIPLES

A. PLANNING

The managers of Chocolate Delight plc, or in fact any business, will have to make decisions which will affect the running of the company – decisions such as: where to locate the factory, what products should be manufactured, how those products should be made, who should be responsible to whom and how the company's resources are to be used to achieve the best results.

The more skilled the management is in planning, the more successful the company is likely to be.

B. CONTROLLING

Once the plans for the company have been established there must be supervision and checking of those responsible for carrying out the plans.

The management must ensure that their instructions are being carried out and that the company is achieving its objectives.

C. CO-ORDINATING

The management are responsible for the activities of those who work for the company. They must make sure that departments are aware of each other's activities and of the decisions taken, so that there is no duplication, friction or lack of understanding. Co-ordinating really refers to ensuring the smooth operation of the company.

D. MOTIVATING

For any company to be efficient, it must have a staff which is motivated. This can be achieved partly through the wages paid, through fringe benefits and a share of the profits, and also by the ability of the management to promote job satisfaction. The whole area of motivation is dealt with in ch. 15.

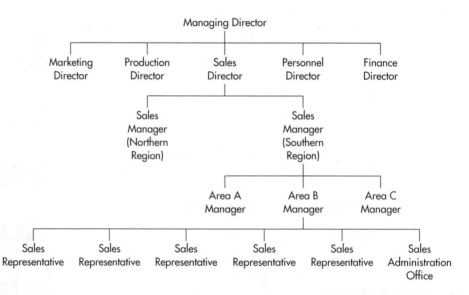

Figure 5.2 Organisation chart for a typical manufacturing company

2 > THE ORGANISATION OF MANAGEMENT

The structure of a business is shown by an **organisation chart**. Figure 5.2 shows such a chart which could refer to Chocolate Delight plc or a typical manufacturing company. If this referred to a wholesaler then there would be no production department but perhaps a buying department.

The chart is like a family tree which shows:

▶ the responsibilities of the management of Chocolate Delight plc
▶ the status of the various levels of management
▶ the lines of communication within the company.

No chart can show all the complex parts of a company's management structure but it does give some idea of how the management of a business is organised.

A. PYRAMIDAL

Chocolate Delight plc might have a Sales Department organised in the traditional pyramidal way as in Fig. 5.3.

Figure 5.3 Hierarchical management structure (Pyramidal chart)

This is sometimes called a **hierarchical structure** and it shows the direct lines of authority in a pyramidal shape. The three Sales Managers are responsible to the Sales Director, and the Sales Representatives are responsible to the Sales Managers. Hierarchical structures are clear and easy to understand for those working in them, but they have the disadvantage that people become 'departmentalised'.

B. HORIZONTAL

Chocolate Delight plc may choose another way of showing structure which tries to avoid the idea of levels of superiority. This is the idea behind the **horizontal** chart which is read from left to right with the most senior management on the left as in Fig. 5.4.

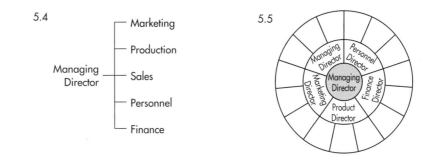

Figure 5.4 (left) Horizontal management chart

Figure 5.5 (right) Concentric management chart

C. CONCENTRIC

This is yet another way of showing the pyramidal structure. This is by using a **concentric** chart which, like the horizontal chart, seeks to avoid emphasising the various levels of authority. The Managing Director will be in the innermost circle and the other management team will be arranged in concentric circles moving out from the centre, as in Fig. 5.5.

D. MATRIX

A business could be organised on a project-based approach as in Fig. 5.6. This type of structure is often referred to as a **matrix**. It is often found in businesses which are developing new products, which in the case of Chocolate Delight plc could be a new chocolate bar. Instead of being accountable to their immediate superior, as is the case in the pyramidal structure, staff are responsible to a project manager who would have to make sure that the current project is completed on time and is up to standard.

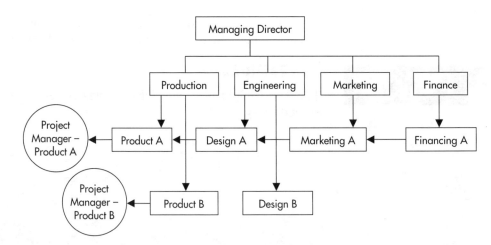

Figure 5.6 Matrix management
chart

In developing a new chocolate bar, production, engineering, marketing and finance staff could be involved along the lines of Fig. 5.6. Together, they could bring their different skills and experience to the particular project, namely the type of chocolate bar the consumer requires, and decide on the machinery needed, how the bars should be made and whether the company has sufficient funds to finance the production of a new product. The benefit of this structure is that the individuals working on the project could operate as a team, and so be easier to organise and motivate. The disadvantage is that the project members may feel insecure because the project will only be for a period of time.

Companies will usually split their management into a number of **departments**. As Fig. 5.2 shows, Chocolate Delight plc has marketing, production, sales, personnel and finance departments. The **advantages** of a departmental organisation are that:

4 ▷ **DEPARTMENTAL FUNCTIONS**

❝ Do not confuse the management functions and the departmental functions with each other. ❞

1. it allows **specialisation** to take place, with individual managers undertaking the duties they are best at;
2. the company can be **better organised** if the various functions of the company are divided into different departments; and
3. each department has its **area of responsibility**, which is clearly set out and is relatively easy to understand.

A. MARKETING

In the case of Chocolate Delight plc, market research assesses the type of chocolate product the consumers desire and how much they are prepared to pay. They must bear in mind the machinery, manpower and raw materials that the company has available. The development of new products or services will also require extra finance and advertising so that production can take place and the consumer can be made aware of the new products or services available. It will be necessary to distribute the products, so different forms of transport will have to be considered, taking into account cost, convenience and reliability. The marketing function will be dealt with in more detail in Chapter 9.

B. PRODUCTION

The production department will be responsible for changing the raw materials or assembling the components into finished products. 'Production' can involve both the manufacture of goods and the provision of services such as banking and insurance although these 'service' companies may not have a production department as such.

The production department of Chocolate Delight plc must take into account the type of factory and machinery they have at their disposal and the level of skilled labour they require. Usually, they are also responsible for ensuring that the finished chocolate bars are properly stored and that the stocks do not become too large.

C. PURCHASING

The purchasing department is responsible for buying the raw materials and anything else the company needs, i.e. everything from office supplies to production machinery.

D. SALES

The sales department is closely linked to the marketing department. Its function is to form a link between the company and the customer, and it is concerned with selling the product or service. The department will employ sales representatives who will build up a network of customers. With Chocolate Delight plc, this will range from large superstores to small corner shops and newspaper kiosks. The representatives may pass on to the marketing department (see ch. 9) vital information about the new products that competitors are introducing and any changes in the tastes of consumers.

E. PERSONNEL

The personnel department is responsible for the human resources of the company. Its aim is to recruit the right people for the firm's departments, to help to organise them and to make sure there is adequate staff development. This covers areas such as staff training, staff appraisal, promotions and routine matters like employees' taxation forms, sickness benefit, holiday pay and pensions. The rates of pay, salary structure and all negotiations with the staff over such matters as working conditions and dismissals will be dealt with by this department (see chs 14 and 15).

F. FINANCE

The finance department deals with all the monetary aspects of the company. This involves monitoring the inflow and outflow of payments, such as the invoices sent for confectionery sold and those received for the costs of raw materials and new machinery, and wages.

There may be other departments, such as research and development (R&D) and design. The activities of all these departments will be overseen by the Managing Director and the Board of Directors.

5 FORMAL AND INFORMAL ORGANISATION

How Chocolate Delight plc organises its staff is very important. If they are badly organised, decision making will be more difficult and the company will not achieve the best results. An organisation chart is shown on page 46 but more generally any organisation really has two separate structures – not only its formal organisation, but also its informal organisation.

A. FORMAL ORGANISATION

The **formal organisation** consists of the channels of communication set up officially within a company. As can be seen from the chain of command in Fig. 5.7, the production worker is responsible to, and takes orders from, the production foreman; the production foreman in turn is responsible to, and takes orders from, the production manager, and so on.

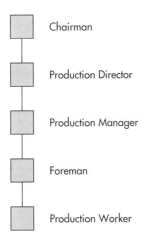

Figure 5.7 The chain of command

Chairman

Production Director

Production Manager

Foreman

Production Worker

B. INFORMAL ORGANISATION

The **informal organisation** cannot be shown in the organisation chart. It operates as workers at various levels throughout the company develop their own ideas and even take their orders from each other or perhaps from their union leader. It is always necessary to consider the informal structure when trying to see how a company really operates. For example, the Managing Director's secretary may be a junior member of the company but might have a great deal of power and influence over what goes on. The formal organisation of the company is established by the management but the informal organisation develops among the whole staff depending on personalities, tradition and many other factors.

The term **leadership** refers to the role taken by an individual or a group in organising other members of staff. There are essentially three types of leadership: autocratic, democratic and *laissez-faire*.

A. THE AUTOCRATIC LEADER

The leaders with an autocratic style decide on all areas within the business, whether it be what is to be produced, how it is to be produced or who should do which job. In Chocolate Delight plc, this style could be adopted at certain times or in certain situations. In a crisis, such as having to produce a particular amount of confectionery to satisfy an urgent export order, the workforce could be told what to do, without any discussion. With an autocratic leadership style, there is little or no communication between the leaders and the staff they are responsible for. The advantage of this style is that decisions can be taken more speedily, but there may then be a need for greater supervision. The staff are also likely to grumble and suffer from a lack of job satisfaction because they are rarely consulted.

B. DEMOCRATIC LEADER

The leadership of Chocolate Delight plc may encourage the workers to participate in the decisions of the company. The democratic leader tries to foster a more friendly, co-operative working environment, where the staff may put forward ideas for new products or new ways of producing existing products. This can promote greater job satisfaction among staff, and bring about new and unexpected improvements as a result of staff involvement. If there is a disadvantage with this style, it could be that it takes longer to arrive at decisions because of the amount of discussion which takes place between the leaders and staff. Output might then be lower than necessary in the period before the decision is actually taken.

C. *LAISSEZ-FAIRE* LEADER

The *laissez-faire* style of leadership is one which leaves the workforce to its own devices, with little control being exercised over it. At certain times, Chocolate Delight plc could use this type of leadership to maximise the flexibility of the organisation and to encourage the workers to make their own decisions.

Figure 5.8 illustrates part of the organisation chart of Chocolate Delight plc. As you will see, the Managing Director is at the head of the whole company but he or she can only directly control the work of the five directors. The Area B sales manager in Fig. 5.2 can be seen to directly control the work of six sales representatives.

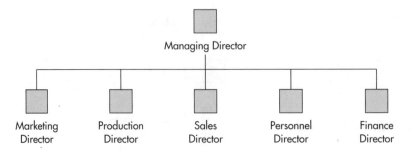

Figure 5.8 The span of control

The span of control is the number of workers a person can control directly and this will vary depending on:

1. the type of work, whether it is repetitive, such as putting chocolates into boxes, or highly skilled, requiring a great deal of supervision; and
2. the ability and the amount of training of those being controlled.

If the span of control is too wide then supervision will be very difficult. If the span of control is too narrow then subordinates may fail to develop their own ideas.

8 CHAIN OF COMMAND

The chain of command within Chocolate Delight plc is from the Managing Director and Board of Directors to the Sales Manager, then on to the Area Manager and finally the Sales Representatives. Decisions will be passed down the chain as shown in Fig. 5.7. A short chain of command may be the most desirable because, the fewer links there are in the chain, the easier it is for the management and workforce to communicate.

9 DELEGATION

The Board of Directors will not be able to do all the work themselves within the company, so they will have to delegate the day-to-day running of the company to others. In Fig. 5.2, the Sales Director will delegate to the two sales managers who cover the northern and southern regions of the UK. They may be given the authority to do the job but the final responsibility will still remain with the Board of Directors. Delegation may take place because the managers may not have time to do the job themselves.

The management of Chocolate Delight plc may, however, be a management who are afraid to delegate, perhaps because:

1. they fear the job will not be done properly, e.g. because they think the workers of the business are not capable;
2. delegation may make the managers' span of control more difficult to monitor.

If authority is not delegated then it is said to be **centralised**. This means that there is a great deal of control from the top (whether it be from the Managing Director or Board of Directors).

Where authority **is** delegated then it is said to be **decentralised**, with decisions being taken at all levels of the company. If there was complete decentralisation then the manager would no longer have a job.

Decentralisation cannot be determined from an organisation chart. The chart does not show the **degree** to which authority and responsibility are delegated, which is the key factor in determining the extent of centralisation; instead, the **decisions taken** have to be looked at. For example, if Sales Manager Southern Region on Chocolate Delight plc's organisation chart frequently took important decisions which the Sales Director deliberately never checked, then this would be decentralisation. Decentralisation would be greater if:

1. many important decisions have to be made at all levels;
2. the company has many divisions which may even run themselves, making their own decisions; and/or
3. there are a large number of good staff at all levels of the company.

E X A M I N A T I O N   Q U E S T I O N S

QUESTION 1

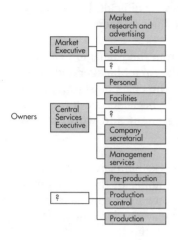

The incomplete chart shown here indicates how various work functions may be performed by specialised departments.

(a) Complete the chart by filling in the blank boxes which have been indicated with a question mark.   (3 marks)

(b) Give two reasons why a firm might organise itself on a departmental basis.
    (3 lines for answer)   (4 marks)

(c) Describe two functions of the marketing department of a firm.
    (4 lines for answer)   (4 marks)

(d) How and why should a sales target set by the Marketing Executive be communicated to a production worker on the shop floor?
    (3 lines for answer).   (4 marks)
                                                                          (NICCEA)

QUESTION 2

The following chart shows the organisation of Green Dragon Toys Ltd.:

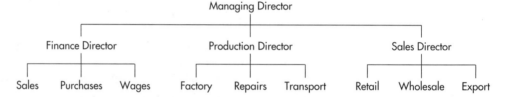

(a) What is the **span of control** in this company? (1 line for answer)   (1 mark)

(b) To whom is the export manager directly responsible?
    (1 line for answer)   (1 mark)

(c) State two advantages to Green Dragon Toys Ltd. of having an organisation chart like this. (4 lines for answer)   (2 marks)
                                                                          (WJEC)

QUESTION 3

A. Griffiths Ltd is involved in the manufacture of sportswear. The company is divided into 5 departments (marketing, production, personnel, finance and sales), and it employs 300 staff. Each of the departments has a director and A. Griffiths is the Managing Director. At a recent Board of Directors meeting it was decided to develop a new range of tracksuits.

(i)   (a) State what is meant by the Board of Directors. (2 lines for answer).   (2 marks)
      (b) How important will the marketing department be in the development of the new range of tracksuits? (3 lines for answer)   (3 marks)

(ii) A. Griffiths has been Managing Director of the business for a number of years and is seen to have an autocratic style of leadership. Is this likely to prove beneficial in the development of the new tracksuits? (4 lines for answer)   (4 marks)

(iii) How important will it be to have an effective chain of command in the development of new products? (2 lines for answer)   (1 mark)

TUTOR'S ANSWER TO Q.3

(i) (a) The Board of Directors is a group of individuals which is elected by the shareholders to whom they are accountable. Their purpose is to run the company. This will involve, above all else, deciding what the company policy is going to be.

(b) The marketing department will have the important task of finding out what type of tracksuit is popular with the customer. This may involve design, colour and range, as well as how much the consumer is prepared to pay. It may use questionnaires or conduct sample surveys in trying to perform this task. The marketing department will therefore be important in the early stages of development of the new range of tracksuits. It may also try to establish how many tracksuits the company can expect to sell and to what groups of consumers.

(ii) You will first need to state briefly what an **autocratic** style of leadership is. This style of leadership is one with little or no communication between the leader(s) and the staff for which they are responsible. This style could prove beneficial in the development of a new range of tracksuits simply because decisions can be more speedily taken, without time-consuming discussions between the management and the rest of the staff. The product could be developed and put on the market far quicker, which may be an advantage if the company has competitors who are also developing new products in the same field.

The disadvantage may be that, because there is limited discussion within the company, the product may not be as good as it might have been if a more democratic approach to leadership had existed.

(iii) An effective chain of command is vital if a new product is being developed. The decision taken at the Board meeting to produce a new range of track suits has to be communicated to the staff within the company. If the chain is faulty then the development could be delayed or the orders misinterpreted by the workforce.

STUDENT'S ANSWER TO Q.1

> A good answer. The student could also have mentioned the benefits of specialisation, with each person doing what they are best at. Using departments also allows individual areas of responsibility to be seen.

> A good point – but if the span of control is to be mentioned, it must be clearly explained.

> A good answer. You could also mention that the marketing department tries to make sure that the firm produces the goods that the consumer wants.

1. (a) Distribution

Production executive.

(b) 1) To help communication. One manager per department so communication flows easily up and down.

2) To prevent having a large span of control. With more departments, there are smaller spans of control.

c) 1) Advertising the product by choosing the best media, and the best presentation of the product to the general public.

2) To carry out the most accurate market research, by collecting relevant information on the product.

> ❝ The Production Executive is likely to ask the Production Manager to pass the information to the production workers. ❞
>
> ❝ This is a good point. Motivation is likely to increase if the workers know what is happening within the firm. ❞

d)   The Marketing Executive should tell the ⟨Production Executive⟩ who should pass the information to the production workers on the shop floor. This is to increase workers' ⟨motivation,⟩ so they understand why they are doing the job and its purpose.

COURSEWORK

ASSIGNMENT THE ORGANISATION OF A LOCAL BUSINESS

1. Choose a business in the area where you live. Size is not important but it should not be too small as you are trying to obtain information on its organisation structure. The choice of business might be made in one of the following ways:
    ▶ A member of your family or a family friend works for the business;
    ▶ A local business interests you – possibly a business you want to work for; or
    ▶ You may have a part time job working for a business, perhaps on a Saturday, and therefore know someone who could help you.
2. Contact the business either by telephone or by post and arrange to meet them. The personnel department is the one which is most likely to help.
3. The first thing to find out is the make-up of their organisation chart. You could present your questions in a questionnaire and cover the following areas:
    ▶ How many departments are there?
    ▶ How has the chart changed as the company has grown?
    ▶ Who is responsible to whom?

    Once this information has been obtained it should be possible to build up an organisation chart.

4. It may be possible to find out other information as well:
    ▶ Is the management leadership autocratic, democratic or *laissez-faire*?
    ▶ Is the span of control too wide or the chain of command too long?
    ▶ Does the management of the business delegate? (If not, why not?)
5. Set out the assignment in the way outlined in Chapter 2.
6. In your conclusion, clearly state whether the business in your opinion is organised in an efficient way. Perhaps you could indicate areas where the business could improve its organisation.

A Review Sheet for this chapter will be found on p. 237.

GETTING STARTED

All businesses will have to make important decisions, many of which will affect how successful they are for many years to come – decisions such as where to locate, what size to operate at and whether or not to take over another firm. There are important benefits to be obtained from choosing correctly. A wrong decision could lead to the business making losses or even going out of business.

CHAPTER 6

LOCATION, SIZE AND GROWTH

LOCATION

INFLUENCES ON LOCATION

NATURAL AND ACQUIRED ADVANTAGES

SIZE

INTERNAL ECONOMIES OF SCALE

EXTERNAL ECONOMIES OF SCALE

DISECONOMIES OF SCALE

OPTIMUM SIZE OF A BUSINESS

GROWTH

VERTICAL INTEGRATION

HORIZONTAL INTEGRATION

CONGLOMERATE INTEGRATION

THE SURVIVAL OF SMALL FIRMS

ESSENTIAL PRINCIPLES

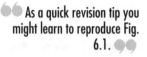

The decision of where to **locate** a business is a very important one. It is perhaps the first decision for the manager or management of a new business to make, whether it is a small one-person business or a large PLC (see ch. 4). If the location chosen is a poor one then the business may be less competitive and therefore less profitable than it could be. For example, a filling station located on a road without much traffic will be less profitable than one located on a main road with heavy through traffic.

Most sites will have advantages and disadvantages, but the best site will normally be the one with the lowest costs for producing the goods and services, and for distributing them to the consumer.

For certain firms, the choice of location is limited. Shipbuilding firms will need to be on the coast and will need to have a deep water estuary. Other firms may be **footloose**, i.e. they may be set up anywhere. But even these firms will benefit by searching for the best possible site.

There are a number of factors which will *influence* a firm's location as shown in Fig. 6.1.

> As a quick revision tip you might learn to reproduce Fig. 6.1.

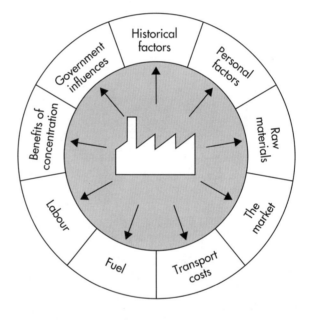

Figure 6.1 The factors influencing the business location

A. HISTORICAL FACTORS

In the Industrial Revolution, many businesses were drawn to the sources of raw materials and power. The pottery industry developed in Stoke-on-Trent because of the proximity of clay, and the brewing of beer in Burton-on-Trent because of the type of water there. Water power was used in driving machinery, so that fast-flowing streams attracted firms such as Richard Arkwright's textile factory at Cromford in Derbyshire. These factors are less important today but do help to explain why certain businesses are in their present location.

B. PERSONAL FACTORS

Certain firms may have located in an area just because the individual who set up the company lived in that area. Henry Rowntree was one such person who founded Rowntrees (now part of Nestlé) in York. Boots the chemists of Nottingham and Morris the car producer at Cowley were also founded in these particular areas because the person who started the company lived there.

C. RAW MATERIAL

Some industries are tied completely to the location of the raw materials themselves, such as the coal- and tin-mining industries. In other industries, the location of the raw materials has an important influence on the place of production. Iron and steel mills initially located near the raw material source because, during the refining of the iron ore, the product lost weight (ore refining is a bulk decreasing industry) and became easier and cheaper to transport. These **bulk decreasing** businesses are likely to locate near their raw material supplies as this will make transport and distribution costs cheaper.

We have seen (above) that a firm may continue to locate itself in an area long after the original reasons for locating there have gone, in the case of our example even after the exhaustion of iron ore. This is called **industrial inertia**.

D. THE MARKET

If the goods being produced are **weight** or **bulk increasing** products then it may be worthwhile locating the firm close to the market, as this may reduce transport costs. The location of the market is one of the most important factors affecting the location of firms which produce goods which are expensive to transport. For example, furniture manufacturers are generally located near to where the furniture is to be sold.

E. TRANSPORT NETWORKS

Historically, being close to an efficient transport network has been very important. Water transport was cheap and reliable, if rather slow. Nevertheless, the canals had an important influence on the location of firms during the eighteenth and nineteenth centuries. The development of railways in the nineteenth century allowed businesses to locate over a wider area with access to a major terminal important for many firms. The railways became less important with the improvements in the road network, particularly after the advent of the motorway system in the 1960s. Extending the motorway system is one of the ways by which the Government hopes to attract industry into areas of high unemployment. Easy access to the motorway system is an important factor in locating factories for many firms.

F. FUEL

Many businesses in the nineteenth century located near to the main source of fuel, usually coal. Much of manufacturing industry was, therefore, set up in the areas of major coalfields. However, with the advent of gas and electricity and with the introduction of a national distribution system, location near to a fuel supply was no longer so important.

G. LABOUR

To produce any goods or services, labour is needed. The problem is that sometimes the right type of labour is very scarce. It can also be difficult to persuade workers to move from one area to another. A firm may be attracted to an area because of the availability of skilled labour and the fact that the area may have a tradition in a particular industry, such as the textile industry in West Yorkshire. On the other hand, a location may be avoided because it has a reputation for strikes and absenteeism.

H. BENEFITS OF CONCENTRATION

As businesses develop in an area, it is likely that they will attract other businesses, leading to a concentration of firms in a particular area. As a result, that area will adapt itself to the needs of those businesses.

Local colleges of education will develop courses relevant to the firms' needs and small specialist firms will set up to provide the main firms with components or to dispose of their waste products. The local banks and insurance companies are also likely to become expert in the needs of their local industry, being able therefore to offer them specialist treatment. All these are known as **economies of concentration**.

I. GOVERNMENT INFLUENCES

Since 1934, the Government has aimed to intervene directly in the location of business, restricting the location of firms in certain areas and encouraging their location in other areas. New towns, such as Welwyn Garden City, Stevenage and Milton Keynes, were established and also 'Assisted Areas'. There are four types of Assisted Areas:

1. Development Areas
2. Intermediate Areas
3. Split Development Areas/Intermediate Areas
4. Split Intermediate Areas/Non-Assisted Areas.

They are areas of high unemployment, and businesses setting up there obtain financial incentives of one form or another. Of the four, there is a greater level of financial assistance available in Development Areas.

The main forms of regional support currently in operation are: Regional Selective Assistance (RSA); Regional Enterprise Grant (REG); Consultancy Initiatives; and the EU Structural Fund.

Regional Selective Assistance (RSA)

RSA is available in Development Areas and Intermediate Areas, collectively known as Assisted Areas. The assistance is primarily available for manufacturing firms although certain service sector projects are eligible. The grants are **discretionary**, being based on whether the project:

(i) is regarded as being viable;
(ii) is unlikely to proceed, or to proceed on a much smaller scale if the grant was not available;
(iii) is seen to benefit the regional and national economy; and
(iv) is likely to create new jobs or protect existing jobs.

RSA cannot be used simply to relocate jobs from one area of the country to another.

Regional Enterprise Grant (REG)

This grant is available only in Development Areas. However, it is also available in South Yorkshire and Derbyshire (both part of the European Regional Development Fund (ERDF) programme for steel areas), and also Fife and Plymouth (both part of the ERDF programme for areas of shipbuilding). The grant is payable to firms with fewer than 25 employees. Like the RSA, the grant is available mainly for manufacturing industry and is for investment projects. The grant is **discretionary** and can allow a firm 15% of the cost of fixed assets with a maximum amount of £15,000. On the other hand, if the project covers the development of new or improved products or processes, then a grant of 50% of the project cost with a maximum amount of £25,000 is possible.

Consultancy Initiatives

In the Assisted Areas and Urban Programme areas, small and medium-sized firms have been able to obtain a subsidy, worth two-thirds of the cost, in order to take advantage of external consultants. The aim is to encourage firms to use outside experts in areas such as marketing, design, business planning and information systems.

EU Structural Fund

The EU Structural Fund is also used to encourage regional development, especially the European Regional Development Fund (ERDF).

The aim of European Regional Policy is to achieve five objectives through the use of the Structural Fund:

1. promoting the economic development of underdeveloped regions – these regions can be seen as 'lagging regions';
2. redevelopment of regions which have suffered from industrial decline – these regions have a rate of unemployment higher than the EU average;
3. assisting areas anywhere in the EU which are experiencing long-term unemployment – this includes workers who have been unemployed for more than 12 months and are over the age of 25;

4. integration of young people into the workforce – this aims to deal with youth unemployment, job seekers below the age of 25, and can cover anywhere in the EU;
5. (a) the reform of the Common Agricultural Policy (CAP) through speeding up the modernisation of agricultural structures; and
   (b) helping those in rural areas, which are defined on the basis of how many individuals work in agriculture, how developed they are as an agricultural region, and also how peripheral they are, within the EU.

Three areas of the UK – Northern Ireland, the Highlands and Islands, and Merseyside – are eligible for assistance as regions whose development is lagging behind.

In 1980 the Government also introduced 'Enterprise Zones'. Here, firms received assistance such as ten years' exemption from rent and rates.

3 > NATURAL AND ACQUIRED ADVANTAGES

The advantages of a particular location can be seen in terms of natural or acquired advantages. **Natural advantages** include the possession of raw materials (e.g. coal, iron ore), the availability of sources of power (e.g. water, coal), nearness to major markets and having an appropriate climate. (In the case of the textile industry, a damp climate meant thread was less likely to break.) All these natural advantages have been of historical importance to location. **Acquired advantages** have more to do with the benefits gained from the **concentration** of firms in the locality, rather than with the characteristics of the locality itself.

Figure 6.2 UK manufacturing – by size 1989

4 > SIZE

A. IMPORTANCE OF SIZE IN THE UK

Once located, a business needs to consider the **size** at which it is going to operate. In all industrialised economies businesses will vary in size. Some will be very small, employing one or two workers, whereas others will be large PLCs (see p. 37), employing thousands of workers. As can be seen from Fig. 6.2, over 90% of UK firms employ less than 99 workers. In other words, most UK firms are small to medium in size. But these firms only account for 24% of the total number of persons employed, and only 17% of gross output. If, however, you look at those firms employing between 5,000 and 14,999 workers, they account for only 1.3% in number of firms, but 15.9% in number of persons employed and 20.8% of gross output. It is the large firms which, though relatively few in number, dominate UK employment and output.

B. MEASURING SIZE

When measuring the size of individual firms we come up against a problem, namely what measure do we use? The *Financial Times FT 500* looks at the largest quoted companies in Europe and the UK using market capitalisation as its main measure; see Fig. 6.3(a). Market capitalisation is measured by 'the number of shares the company has in issue, multiplied by the market price of those shares'. Using this measure J. Sainsbury was seen as the 22nd ranked company in the UK in 1994, with Lloyds Bank 23rd and Imperial Chemical Industries 24th. If however, profit or number of employees were used as a measure then a different picture would be obtained; see Figs 6.3 (b) and (c).

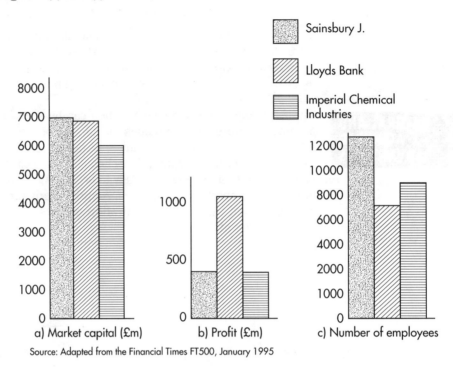

Figure 6.3 Measuring the size of firms

Source: Adapted from the Financial Times FT500, January 1995

C. ECONOMIES OF SCALE

Larger firms are seen as being more efficient in that they can produce their goods more cheaply and sell them at a lower price. These reduced costs are a direct result of the increased size of the firm and are called **economies of scale** (benefits of size).

As you can see from Fig. 6.4, the firm's costs start to fall with increased production and they are at the lowest, in this case, when 3,000 units are produced. This is called the **optimum output** because it is the output with the lowest average cost. After this output the costs start to rise again. These are called **diseconomies of scale**.

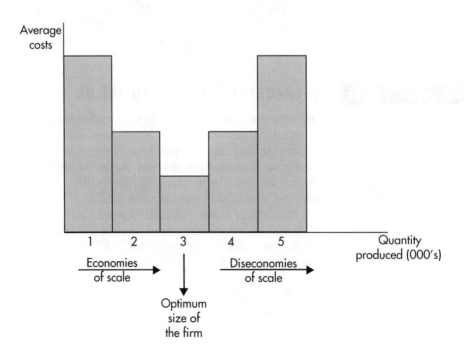

Figure 6.4 The optimum size of the firm

The economies of scale can be either internal or external. **Internal economies of scale** are obtained through the growth of the firm itself. **External economies of scale** are obtained through the growth in the size of the industry as a whole. They are important when the industry is heavily concentrated and are outside the direct control of business itself.

5 ▷ **INTERNAL ECONOMIES OF SCALE**

❝❝ It is very easy to mix up the various internal economies of scale so revise this topic carefully! You can bring this knowledge into your answer to many types of question. ❞❞

As the firm grows in size, there are a number of sources of internal economies:

▶ technical economies
▶ management economies
▶ marketing (trading) economies
▶ financial economies
▶ risk-bearing economies.

A. TECHNICAL ECONOMIES

Large firms are able to make more use of the **division of labour**; with a small output it may not be possible to employ one person wholly on one process or part of a process. However, as output rises a greater degree of specialisation is possible. As workers specialise on particular activities their productivity often increases: 'practice makes perfect'. Adam Smith showed that a pin factory could produce many more pins if each person concentrated on a particular activity (drawing the wire, cutting the wire or sharpening the head) rather than trying to undertake all the various activities. It is this specialisation which is called the division of labour.

The firm can also make more use of **machinery**. For example, a machine may only be used for two hours per day in a small firm, but may be fully used in a large firm. This will save the 'cost' of having expensive machinery lie idle. Larger specialised machinery can be used which produces more output per hour. It may even be possible for the whole process to be undertaken in the form of a production line (mass production). This would not usually be economically possible in a smaller firm.

Benefits can be made from increased **volume**, for example, if a container is doubled in size its surface area increases four times but its volume increases eight times. There are, therefore, savings to be made in using larger containers which will cost relatively less per unit of volume than the smaller ones. Larger lorries (juggernauts), aircraft and blast furnaces are further examples of the benefits that can be obtained from extra size. The 'running costs' of a 4-tonne lorry are less than twice those of a 2-tonne lorry.

Research and development (R & D) is also possible in a larger firm and this could lead to an improvement in the quality of the goods produced and a reduction in costs through better ways of producing the goods.

B. MANAGEMENT ECONOMIES

Larger businesses are able to take on (i.e. appoint) qualified staff who are specialists in a particular area. The small firm is likely, of necessity, to have a work force of 'jack of all trades'.

Management costs will not necessarily increase in proportion to the growth in size of the firm. For instance, you may be able to double the size of the firm without doubling the managerial staff. This will reduce management costs per unit of output.

C. MARKETING (TRADING) ECONOMIES

Marketing economies can be viewed in terms of buying and selling. When a business buys its raw materials, it is likely to obtain preferential treatment, perhaps in the form of a discount, if it is making a **bulk purchase**. A larger business is in a stronger position to **secure good discounts** because it could threaten to go elsewhere if it was not satisfied with the terms, and this threat would be a financially powerful one because of the size of its order. When selling the product, specialist sales personnel can be appointed, who can often obtain larger orders with no extra time and effort than that needed to obtain a smaller order. Administration, transport, advertising and packaging costs can also be spread over large orders. For example, the packaging costs per item are likely to be less for 1,000 items than if 10 items were packed.

D. FINANCIAL ECONOMIES

Most firms need to borrow money to finance their business (see ch. 7). Large firms are able to obtain their finance from banks more easily, borrowing at lower interest rates. A bank will more readily give a loan to a well-known company, than to Joe Smith who is just starting up a window cleaning business. The larger firm is also likely to have more assets to offer to the bank as security for the loan.

E. RISK-BEARING ECONOMIES

Large producers can spread their risk so that they do not have all their 'eggs in one basket'. They can obtain their supply of raw materials from different sources and this will allow them to safeguard against shortages. Larger firms can also produce a wide range of products; for example, Hillsdown Holdings plc owns Smedley's Food Ltd, Chivers Hartley Ltd and Premier Beverages as well as upholstered furniture, house building and office furniture companies. You will probably have a number of its products in your kitchen since its brand names include Typhoo tea, Olde English recipe marmalade and Haywards Pickles. If there is a fall in the demand for one of the products, losses can be offset by profits from sales of the others.

6 ▷ EXTERNAL ECONOMIES OF SCALE

There are economies to the firm which result from the industry as a whole growing in size. Sources include:

▶ economies of disintegration
▶ economies of concentration
▶ economies of information.

A. ECONOMIES OF DISINTEGRATION

As the industry in an area grows, it may mean that certain processes can be done better by a specialist (ancillary) firm. In the West Yorkshire woollen industry, firms specialised in a particular process such as spinning, weaving and dyeing. Other firms specialised in making textile machinery. The same specialisation has occurred in the motor vehicle industry; for example, Lucas has specialised in the production of car lamps and electronics for the major car assemblers in the Midlands. The individual firm can often buy cheaper and better quality components and services from these specialist firms.

B. ECONOMIES OF CONCENTRATION

An industry may develop in a particular area, enabling individual firms to gain advantages:

▶ **Better training**: As local colleges offer courses for the main industry of the area, a pool of skilled labour will eventually develop, to the benefit of individual firms.
▶ **Better transport**: The road and rail networks often improve as an industry develops in an area. These improvements are designed to serve the industries' needs but, of course, benefit each other.
▶ **Better commercial services**, such as banks and insurance companies: These will become expert, having special knowledge of an industry's needs.

All of these will be of mutual advantage to particular firms in the area.

C. ECONOMIES OF INFORMATION

Similar firms in an area will require up-to-date information on such things as raw material supplies and foreign government regulations. There may be a free flow of such information between firms. Firms may also group together to make a joint contribution to R&D, whereas they may not be able to undertake independent research. This will save individual firms both time and money.

7 ▷ DISECONOMIES OF SCALE

We have seen that as a business grows in size, it will obtain certain benefits known as economies of scale. However, a business may grow *too* large. As you can see from Fig. 6.4, its costs will start to rise after a certain level of output. This happens mainly because the larger firm becomes more difficult to manage, to organise and to control.

This is because: decisions take longer, there are no personal links, and there may be no links with the workforce.

A. DECISIONS TAKE LONGER

This happens when a large number of individual views and ideas have to be taken into account. This is often the case where firms have merged and where there are two management teams. There will be an extended chain of command. A sole trader with perhaps two people working for him/her will be able to take decisions on the spot. It may take a large PLC days or even weeks, with many board meetings, to arrive at a decision. That decision will then have to filter down to the workers on the shop floor.

B. NO PERSONAL LINKS

The large firm may become remote, with no personal links with its customers.

C. NO LINKS WITH THE WORKFORCE

As well as being remote from its customers, the management in a large company may become remote from its workforce. This may cause low morale and industrial relations problems (see ch. 17). There is evidence to suggest that as firms increase in size, so do the number of strikes. This may be for a number of reasons:

▶ Workers may feel as though they are not part of the firm and that their views are not taken into account.
▶ The work may be very tedious in large firms where mass production methods are used.
▶ There may be a lack of understanding between the management and the workers; a 'them and us' situation may develop.

Having looked at the economies and diseconomies of scale, it can be seen that there must be some **optimum size**, such that if the firm grows any more the disadvantages will outweigh the advantages. The optimum size is that point where the firm can produce most efficiently. In Fig. 6.4, this is the point of lowest average cost (3,000 units). It may be difficult for a firm to know when it has reached its optimum production level, but it is something of which the firm should always be aware.

9 > GROWTH

Firms will seek to **grow** for a number of reasons:

▶ to reduce their average costs by obtaining economies of scale;
▶ so that they can produce a wider range of products – by diversifying in this way (spreading the risk) the firms will have the other products to fall back on if one of their products fails or goes out of favour
▶ to give the owner or management more power and status. An extreme example of this is provided by the 1980s TV programme *Dallas* in which the characters strive to build an industrial empire and with it to increase their power and status.

HOW DO FIRMS GROW?

Many firms start off as small one-person businesses (see ch. 4) and remain like this for a variety of reasons. Others, however, will grow into large companies employing thousands of workers. How do they grow into these large companies?

New products

Firms are always looking for new products or new ideas which will sell, so allowing the company to grow. Before 1976, Rowntree (now part of Nestlé) did not produce a solid milk chocolate bar. They noted however that all the other solid milk chocolate bars on the market were thin. They therefore decided to produce a thick, chunky bar – and the 'Yorkie' bar was born. You can perhaps think of several new products that have come onto the market recently and are selling well. Many will allow the company to make more profit.

The market

Over time, the demand for certain goods and services will increase, whereas for others it will decrease. Over the last ten years, there has been a growth in the popularity of computers for commercial, industrial and home use. This expansion in the demand has led to a growth in the computer industry. The same could be said of the motor car industry which grew rapidly over the thirty to forty years up to the 1970s. If the demand for goods or services is high and growing, then the firms producing those goods or services are likely to grow.

Integration

It takes time to develop new products and to wait for the demand for the product to grow. As a result, firms have, in recent times, increased their size by merging or by amalgamating with other firms. This is known as **integration** (the joining together of two or more firms). An example is the firm Cadbury Schweppes plc. There are three types of integration:

1. vertical integration
2. horizontal integration
3. conglomerate integration.

A vertical merger takes place between firms which are at different stages of production.

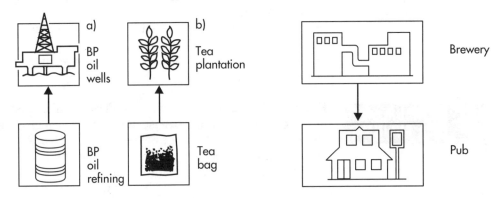

Figure 6.5 Backward vertical integration   Figure 6.6 Forward vertical integration

A. BACKWARD VERTICAL INTEGRATION

> In explaining the different types of integration it is always useful to use real-world examples.

Backward vertical integration is where a firm merges with an organisation supplying its raw material needs (see (a) and (b) in Fig. 6.5). The benefits of this are:

▶ the firm can **control** the quality and quantity of these raw materials instead of relying on other firms;
▶ the firm can cut out the raw material suppliers' profit;
▶ the firm can make sure delivery is on time; and
▶ the firm may be able to obtain certain **economies of scale** (see p. 61–2).

B. FORWARD VERTICAL INTEGRATION

Forward vertical integration is where a firm takes over the retail outlet (see Fig. 6.6). The benefits of this are:

▶ the **standard** of the outlet can be controlled, which is particularly important as the manufacturer may be spending millions of pounds on advertising and will therefore want the product sold in the right conditions at the 'point of sale';
▶ the outlet is **tied** to the manufacturer's product and this may help that product and hinder the product of competitors;
▶ the firm may be able to obtain certain **economies of scale**.

A horizontal merger takes place between firms at the same stage of production. The chocolate manufacturers Rowntree and Mackintosh merged in 1969 (now part of Nestlé) (see Fig. 6.7). There are obvious advantages from this:

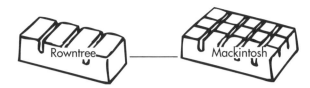

Figure 6.7 Horizontal integration

▶ **economies of scale** can be obtained. These may include technical economies as the enlarged firm increases the size of manufacturing plant, in the course of rationalizing production. More specialisation of labour and machinery can now take place. Also the other internal economies of scale may be available.

▶ the two firms together will now have more influence on the market (**market power**) as the merger reduces the number of competitors.

A conglomerate merger occurs when the firms amalgamate which produce goods or services that are not directly related. The main advantages of this are:

▶ **economies of scale** available to all larger firms

▶ diversified production to **spread risks**; and

▶ to **combat market saturation** – a situation where there is little room for further growth in the firm's output as the demand is already fully satisfied. Therefore, the firm can only grow by joining existing firms rather than by producing and selling extra output.

Purely financial organisations often appear at the head of conglomerates in order to coordinate managerial and financial services. These are sometimes called **holding companies**.

The policy of the Government towards mergers has varied from time to time. If it is thought that a merger could lead to a monopoly developing then it may be referred to the **Monopolies and Mergers Commission**.

If there are so many benefits to be made from firms growing in size, then why are there so many small firms in existence?

A. DEMAND FOR VARIETY

For certain products, demand will fluctuate, with the consumer demanding a wide variety of styles. Firms will then need to change production methods quickly and easily and this can be done more readily if the firm is small. A small firm can produce in 'batches' and move from one type of production to another as demand changes. The mass production technique assumes a constant and high volume of output, in order to set up a full assembly line.

B. INABILITY TO OBTAIN ECONOMIES OF SCALE

For the production of certain goods and services, there will be little scope for obtaining economies of scale and so the firm will remain small.

C. PERSONAL SERVICES

Certain services need personal attention, e.g. hairdressing, plumbing and plastering. Because they concentrate on small-scale work, they tend to remain small businesses. On the whole, those businesses providing personal services tend to be owned by sole proprietors or partnerships where decisions can be made quickly.

D. LUXURY ITEMS

The size of the firm may be limited by the size of the market. Small firms may be able to fill the gaps in the market left by large firms. For instance, the large firm may be less interested in small production runs of high quality items and may, therefore, not compete in providing such products as custom-built cars or made-to-measure suits.

E. AMBITION

The owner of the business may have limited personal ambition. He or she may prefer a small family business so as to retain his or her independence.

F. LACK OF FINANCE

Small firms may be unable to obtain finance in order to expand. A small unknown firm may find difficulty in obtaining a loan as it might be considered a high risk by a bank.

Of course the firm may be small simply because it is a new firm and will need time to develop. So, overall, there are two sets of forces which pull the firm in opposite directions, one suggesting the firm should grow in size, and the other that it should remain small, as seen in Fig. 6.8.

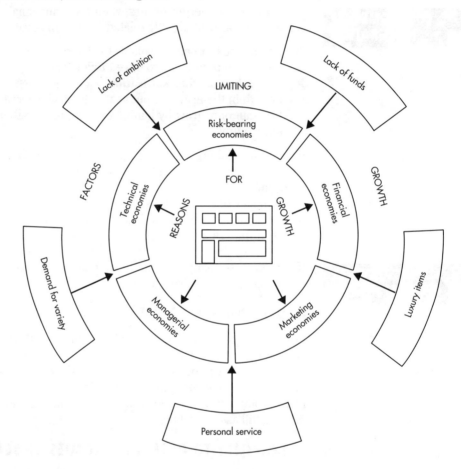

Figure 6.8 Factors for and against the growth of a firm

EXAMINATION QUESTIONS

QUESTION 1

A reduction in a firm's average costs resulting from an increase in the size of the firm is an _____

(ULEAC)

QUESTION 2

Why do a firm's average costs fall as output rises? (3 lines provided)

(ULEAC)

QUESTION 3

A company manufacturing refrigerators has to consider a number of factors in choosing a suitable site in which to locate.

Below is an advertisement which was used by the Warrington-Runcorn Development Corporation in 1986.

1. Of the factors listed what do you view as two important reasons for locating in that area?
    (i) _____ (1 mark)
    (ii) _____ (1 mark)
    What are the reasons for your choice in both cases?
    Reasons: (7 lines provided)   (8 marks)
2. Are there any factors which are not dealt with in the advertisement but which you feel are important in deciding where to locate a business?
    (7 lines provided)   (5 marks)

Figure 6.9

TUTOR'S ANSWER TO Q.3

1. In answering this question you need to consider what type of business is considering moving to Warrington-Runcorn. Refrigerators are likely to be costly to transport, so that one answer could perhaps be:
   (i) The good transport communications network. If the business is relocating from another part of the country, then perhaps the second answer could be:
   (ii) The quality of the housing. You must try to *list* reasons that you could explain further in the next part of the question. The *reasons* for your answer could then be explained in more detail:
       (a) A good transport network is vital for a business in which the transport of the finished product is very costly. The area's closeness to major road, rail, air and sea links with a market of 15 million people close by, is an obvious benefit. The air and sea links will be particularly useful if the business sells the product abroad or uses imported raw materials.
       (b) Your reason for including the quality of housing might be that in moving from another area the company might wish some of its key staff to move. The staff are likely to be more positive about the move if they are told that good quality housing will be available.

2. This is not an easy question because the advertisement has covered most of the important factors. You could, in fact, say that the advertisement has included many of the relevant features for locating in this area. However, perhaps something could have been included on the training establishments available, such as local colleges, which will be important in developing the particular engineering skills required. Or, again, perhaps the advertisement could have been more specific on what firms could qualify for a capital grant.

STUDENT'S ANSWER TO Q.3

⟨⟨ Good ⟩⟩

⟨⟨ You could make the point that the refrigerator manufacturer will be interested in *particular* skills. ⟩⟩

⟨⟨ Very good. All the main points are included. ⟩⟩

⟨⟨ A very good answer, which shows that the student is thinking about the question set. It includes important points in which the refrigerator company might be very interested. ⟩⟩

1. (i)   The skilled workforce available in the area.
   (ii) The communications network and the 15 million consumers in the area.
   Reason for (i): It will not be necessary to attract and move a skilled workforce to the area. Therefore the cost will be less, as people are already housed there, the company will not need to offer housing benefits and removal costs. The company will save time as staff will not need as much training, if they are already skilled.
   Reason for (ii): The company can transport the refrigerators quickly and easily, not just relying on the type of transport. They can quickly obtain raw materials, even if it is necessary to import them, and especially as much of the UK's industry is within an hour's drive. There is the 15 million consumers in the area, which will hopefully be a good market for the refrigerators.

2. Whether there is room for the company to expand if they wish to do so, without having to move plants.
   Which type of manufacturers are already in the area. The refrigerator manufacturing company may not wish to locate there if similar manufacturers are in the area already. It will affect their share of the market.
   The necessary resources available, e.g. dumping facilities for waste, and the power supply. A firm manufacturing can not operate efficiently without these.

C O U R S E W O R K

ASSIGNMENT 1 – LOCATION

1. Choose a local business. The choice can be made either because:
   (a) someone in your family works in the business, or
   (b) it is a business which interests you.
2. Construct a questionnaire. You can either send this to the business or take it with you to use during an interview (if you can arrange one!).

   The areas your questionnaire covers could include:

   (a) What are the reasons which influenced the business in its choice of location?
   (b) Has it been viewed as a good choice? If not, why not?
   (c) Has the business ever moved location? If so, why?
   (d) Are there other similar businesses in the area? If so, do you know why they are here?
3. Once you have collected all this information write it up in the form of a report to be presented to the Board of Directors. State whether you feel the present location is a satisfactory one or whether a better site is available in your area.

ASSIGNMENT 2 – SIZE

1. Choose a small corner shop and a large supermarket in your area. They could be the ones at which your family do their shopping.
2. Large supermarkets are able to take advantage of economies of scale, whereas a small corner shop may not. Compare the two retailers in terms of:
   (a) marketing economies
   (b) financial economies
   (c) technical economies
   (d) management economies
   (e) risk-bearing economies.

   Some of the information can be obtained by simply visiting the two retailers, such as the variations in price. However, you may have to arrange a meeting with the owner or manager for more information.
3. Why does the corner shop remain small? What are the advantages and disadvantages to the customer of each type of retailer?
4. Once you have all this information, a report could be written and presented to the two retailers suggesting an area where you feel they could improve.

ASSIGNMENT 3 – GROWTH

1. Almost everyday in the newspapers there is a report of one company planning a merger with, or takeover of, another company.

   You could monitor one such merger or takeover. Use the newspapers to follow the events, perhaps cutting the relevant bits out of your daily newspaper or taking notes from newspapers in the local library. The financial pages in particular may give details on the companies that are merging and sometimes carry adverts saying why the merger or takeover is a good thing. The information may be a little difficult in parts so you may only be able to note certain aspects of the merger or takeover.
2. With the information you could build up a series of events.
   ▶ Who started the merger/takeover?
   ▶ Which were the companies involved?
   ▶ What was the reason put forward for the merger/takeover?
   ▶ Did the merger/takeover take place?
   ▶ Was the merger/takeover referred to the Monopolies and Mergers Commission?
   ▶ If so, what happened?

   You could also write to the companies involved asking for further information on their activities (e.g. their company reports).

A Review Sheet for this chapter will be found on p. 238.

FINANCE FOR BUSINESS

GETTING STARTED

As you can see from Fig. 7.1 below companies need money for all manner of reasons and they can try to obtain it from a variety of sources. The banks and the Stock Exchange play a major part in this process. We consider the nature of **money** and the role of these institutions later in the chapter.

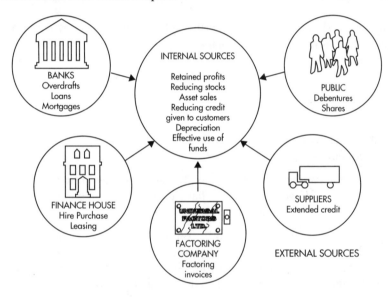

Figure 7.1 Sources of finance for business

ESSENTIAL PRINCIPLES

1 HOW COMPANIES FINANCE THEIR ACTIVITIES

Companies need money to:

▶ buy factories and machines
▶ hire people
▶ pay for other companies which they might want to take over
▶ buy the materials they need to make their products.

Where this money comes from depends on whether the company is just starting out or whether it has been running for a number of years.

A small company just starting out might:

▶ use the savings of its owner
▶ ask the bank for a loan.

A larger, established company would be able to use the retained (or saved) profits of previous years. If it needs even more cash then it will have a number of possible sources of new finance, usually both **internal** and **external**.

2 INTERNAL SOURCES OF FINANCE

Using **internal sources of finance** can be less troublesome, and can save the firm interest charges. Companies can raise finance internally in a number of ways:

▶ retained profits
▶ funds obtained by reducing stocks
▶ funds obtained by selling under-used assets
▶ money made available by reducing the credit available to customers
▶ profits retained for depreciation
▶ money created by making sure that all funds are put to effective use (earning interest).

A. RETAINED PROFITS

This is money which has been earned as a profit in the past and then saved for the future.

B. STOCK REDUCTION

Stocks are the products of the firm that are available for sale in warehouses or stockrooms. Most firms produce more than they need to supply current customers so that they will not be caught out if there is a sudden surge in demand. Stocks are money, however! They are valuable products and if a company builds up too many they can represent wasted money. A firm which reduces its stock levels is, in fact, releasing the equivalent amount of money for its own use.

'Stock' can also mean stocks of components and parts which must be held so that products can be produced. Large stocks of components which have already been paid for are a burden on company finance. Most modern companies are moving towards a system of production in which the parts which make up products are delivered as soon as possible before they are needed – thus reducing the amount of stock which has to be bought and stored. This is called the 'just-in-time' or **JIT system**.

C. ASSET SALES

Although the assets are sold outside the business, the asset itself was held internally by the company *before* its sale. It is, therefore, an *internal* source of finance.

Quite a few companies have buildings or land that they are not using and will not need in the future. If these 'assets' can be identified and sold then they will release large amounts of money for the company to use.

D. LIMITING CREDIT TO CUSTOMERS

Cutting the total of outstanding invoices is a way of releasing cash for the firm's use.

E. DEPRECIATION

If we were sensible and had enough cash – but most of us do not – then we would make sure that, when our car was too old, there would be a fund in the bank ready to replace it. In other words, we would set aside a certain amount every year in order to pay for a new car when it was needed. This may be difficult for individuals but it is absolutely vital for companies which need to replace machines, vehicles and other articles at regular intervals. All companies retain a part of their profits to allow for the depreciation of their assets due to factors such as age and usage. These profits may help the company to fund the future replacement of the assets.

3 > EXTERNAL SOURCES OF FINANCE

A. BANKS

To raise finance **externally**, the company can approach a bank, where they might be offered:

► an overdraft
► a secured loan, or
► a mortgage.

Overdrafts

With an **overdraft facility**, the bank manager agrees to allow a firm to take more money out of its account than is actually in it – up to a certain limit, of course!

Secured loans

The bank may agree to lend a firm an amount of money but might require security. In other words, they want some valuable asset, legally signed over to them, just in case the firm is unable to pay off the debt.

Some secured loans may actually be guaranteed by another organisation. For small businesses, the Government has introduced the 'small firms loan guarantee scheme' which is available through banks.

Mortgages

Mortgages are a special form of secured loan – the bank will lend money in return for the security of property that the firm owns.

B. THE PUBLIC AND FINANCIAL INSTITUTIONS

Finance can also be obtained from the general public or from financial institutions. A small business can often raise money by going to members of the family and asking for help. A larger company can raise money from the general public in one of two ways:

1. by borrowing from the general public or from financial institutions and promising to pay the loan back; or
2. by inviting the general public or financial institutions to become shareholders. In the first case, the company receives the money in return for **debentures**. In the second case, it receives the money in return for **shares**.

Debentures (loan capital)

Debentures are documents which are given to people or institutions who lend money to companies. The document will tell the lender:

► **when** they can expect to be repaid; and
► **how much** in interest they can expect to receive until then.

If the interest is not paid in any one year, then the holders of debentures can actually force the company to close down so that they can be repaid.

Debentures are very special forms of finance for business:

► Holders of debentures **do not own** the company.
► They do not have a vote.
► They have no say in running the business.
► But, their interest *must* be paid every year.

Remember: debenture holders are outsiders who have loaned *the company money; shareholders are the* owners *of the company.*

▶ Also, the interest is paid out *before* anything is paid to the holders of shares.

Shares

A *limited* company – whether private or public – is one in which people can invest money (as owners) by buying **shares**. However, their financial risk is limited to the value of their investment. They cannot be held liable for any of the debts of that company beyond the value of their shareholding (see page 36).

C. OTHER METHODS OF OBTAINING EXTERNAL FINANCE

There are several other ways in which companies might obtain money from outside sources.

Hire instead of buy

Companies might try to hire machines and equipment instead of buying them.

▶ This could be done by **hire purchase** – i.e. paying for the machine in instalments – in the same way that we buy some of our household equipment (TVs, cars, etc). The company would go to a **finance house** for this type of finance.

▶ Alternatively, the company could hire equipment by **leasing**. When a company leases a piece of equipment, it usually has no intention to own it. It pays instalments, just as we do under a hire purchase agreement. However, unlike HP, the machine or the equipment is never actually owned.

Companies have good reasons for leasing machines and equipment rather than buying outright. Repairs and maintenance are often either free or at very good rates and they can keep up with changes in technology much more easily. The most important reason why firms lease however, is money. Leasing involves putting down only a fraction of the cost of the machine and then making monthly payments. This enables firms to use the rest of the cash for other things. For companies, therefore, leasing means that they can:

▶ keep up with new technology
▶ have their equipment and machines maintained by other people
▶ keep most of their money free for other uses.

Extending credit from suppliers

Another way of obtaining money from outside is to raise the finance by extending credit from suppliers. This is not the most pleasant way of raising finance but it is a technique used by many companies. Most firms who supply other firms with equipment, send in their bills (invoices) within a few days of supplying the goods. Most of these invoices allow a month for payment but many companies will take longer to pay.

Factoring

Factoring involves the somewhat strange process of selling the company's bills. For example, a company may have many people who owe money to it. The invoices it has sent out simply have not been paid – usually because the customers are trying to extend their credit times as described above. A company in this position can raise cash by selling the invoices to a special factoring company which will then take on the responsibility of obtaining payment on the invoices. The company will be paid a proportion (say 85%) of the invoices straight away and the factoring company will then keep all the money it collects – eventually – from making the customers pay.

4 ▷TYPES OF SHARE

There are a number of types of share that can be purchased: ordinary shares, preference shares, cumulative preference shares and participating preference shares.

Remember that shares are not loans, they are **investments**! If you lend £1,000 to a company in the form of a debenture and the company runs into trouble and has to be closed down, you will be one of the first to be repaid if there is any money available. This is because you are a creditor of the company – someone who has simply lent it money. If, on the other hand, you had invested £1,000 in shares in the same company then you would be the very last to be given any money back.

▶ Shares, therefore, tend to be risky but rewarding.
▶ Debentures tend to pay less, but be very safe.

A. ORDINARY SHARES

Virtually all companies issue a number of ordinary shares (**equities**). Buying one of these shares makes you a part owner of the company with a right to a say in how it is run. This right is exercised at shareholders' meetings held at least annually. Ordinary shareholders also have the opportunity to share in any profits that are made. If any profit is left over after tax and interest has been paid, then the shareholders will, if the directors agree, receive a share of this profit. It will be paid in the form of a **dividend**. However, the first claim on the profit will go to the preference shareholders (see below). Only after they have been paid their dividend will any remaining amount be available for distribution to ordinary shareholders.

B. PREFERENCE SHARES

These are shares which carry a **fixed rate** of dividend – expressed as a percentage – which is paid out before the dividends to the ordinary shareholders. Preference shareholders do not have the right to a vote.

C. CUMULATIVE PREFERENCE SHARES

A firm may not earn enough profit in one year to be able to pay a fixed rate of dividend on its preference shares. With a cumulative preference share any shortfall is carried forward to the next year.

D. PARTICIPATING PREFERENCE SHARES

These shares receive the usual fixed dividend but may also **participate** in further dividends if any money is left over after all dividends due on other shares have been paid.

5 ▷ ISSUING SHARES

Only public limited companies (PLCs) may issue shares to the general public (see ch. 4) but they may do so in a variety of ways: public issue, offer for sale, placing and/or rights issue.

A. PUBLIC ISSUE

Shares can be advertised (bearing in mind certain rules and regulations) in the press and can be sold directly. This is usually done on the advice of a specialist company called an **issuing house**. The issue is usually **underwritten**. **Underwriters** are people or companies who agree to buy any shares from an issue which are not sold to the public or to institutions. In return, they receive a fee whether they have to take any of the offer or not.

B. OFFER FOR SALE

The shares are sold to the issuing house which then sells them on to the general public, institutions or stockbrokers. Again, the offer would usually be underwritten.

C. PLACING

With this method, the shares are sold in blocks of quite large numbers to institutions. This guarantees that all the shares will be sold but can usually only be done with relatively small numbers of shares.

D. RIGHTS ISSUE

If a company is successful enough it can often return to its own shareholders to sell them even more shares. To make sure that they buy the shares the company will usually offer the new shares at a cheaper price than the current market values. The issue gives each present shareholder the **right to buy**, say, one new share for every three that they currently hold. In financial jargon, this is called a **one for three rights issue**.

6 MONEY AND BANKING – NATURE OF MONEY

What is money? It may seem a silly question because we all know what money is – it is the coins and notes which we have in our pockets! That is certainly true but the money you have in your pockets is not the only form of money:

> Money is anything which might be accepted in settlement of a debt or in exchange for goods and services.

If you wanted to sell your car and someone offered to buy it but gave you a pile of 'ringitts' for it, what would you do? The ringitt is the unit of money used in Malaysia. It is 'money' but, because it might be difficult for you to know the value of it and to change it into British pounds you probably would not accept the pile of cash for your car. Money can be almost anything but it must be **acceptable**.

Pacific Islanders have used shells, stones and even shark's teeth as money. In Europe, too, some very strange kinds of money have been accepted. In Italy, in the late 1970s, there was a shortage of small notes, so buses and railway stations used to give small amounts of change in sweets!

7 WHY DO WE NEED MONEY?

When people were farmers and lived in isolated communities, there was rarely any need for money. People grew or made everything they needed for themselves. After a time, however, people began to specialise, i.e. they began to make or grow just one thing or one type of thing:

▶ Some people chose to grow food.
▶ Some became hunters of meat and furs.
▶ Others became builders, carpenters, potters, spear-makers, etc.

When a spear-maker wanted some food, he simply swapped a spear for some food. This process of swapping is called **barter**.

The problem with barter is that it needs two people who want to trade at the same time – and for each other's goods! It also runs into problems with the fact that some goods are very valuable and not easily divisible. A man who builds a house for a spear-maker may not want a lot of spears! The answer is to find some *common* item which everyone will accept and which has a value known to everyone. This common item can then be used as **money**, i.e. the means of payment. Gold, silver and precious stones have all been used as money in the past and are still used as a store of wealth by some people.

Money has many uses:

▶ Money is a **medium of exchange** – it allows us to exchange different goods. A carpenter can make chairs, sell them to several different people and then buy a new hi-fi from someone totally different.
▶ Money is a **unit of account** – it allows us to make comparisons between different goods. Without money the value of a donkey compared to a set of furniture is difficult to establish.
▶ Money is a **store of value** – it provides a store of value for the future. In theory, money remains valuable over a period of time but this concept does not take inflation into account.
▶ Money is a **measure of debt** – it enables banks and individuals to keep a record of exchanges that have been made for settlement in the future. The technical term used for this function is to say that it is a **standard of deferred payment**.

8 THE QUALITIES OF MONEY

For money to be really useful it has to possess several qualities:

▶ It has to be **acceptable** – people must recognise that it is money and be prepared to accept it.
▶ It has to be **durable** – to be tough and to last a long time so that it can be passed from person to person, stored in a bank, and used in machines.
▶ It has to be **portable** – to be easy to carry around. Some Pacific Islanders used to use big stones as money (most were about a metre across!). They could not put many of those in their pockets!
▶ It has to be **scarce** – there must not be too much of it around. It might also, because it is scarce, have **intrinsic value** – i.e. be valuable in itself and not just as money. Gold and silver both have intrinsic value. They can be saved and sold in the form of bars or of jewellery, and both have been used as money.

Today, money is not just the coins and notes in our pockets, it is a wide variety of types of money. Some of it is in the form of actual cash while other types of money are **near cash**, i.e., in a form which is easy to convert into cash:

▶ current accounts (cheque accounts)
▶ deposit account books
▶ building society savings books.

As well as these forms of money, there is yet another type which has become very important over the past few years: **credit money**. The types of money and cash listed above are all 'real' in the sense that they have been earned or acquired in some way and have then been put into some form of bank account. Credit money, on the other hand, has not yet been earned – it does not yet exist but it can be spent.

Credit money is sometimes called **plastic money** after the plastic cards which are sometimes used to issue and control it. There are two things to note, here:

1. not all credit money is issued through plastic cards (some can be issued through traditional 'paper' transactions); and
2. not all plastic cards are credit cards.

Credit Cards

With a credit card, you are given a **credit limit**. You can spend up to that limit and pay back in regular instalments. (Visa and MasterCard are types of credit card.)

Charge Cards

With these cards, you may be given a credit limit but some allow you an unlimited spending total. The difference between charge cards and credit cards is that the credit is only extended for about one month. At the end of every month, the *whole* outstanding amount must be paid off. (American Express and Diners Card are examples.)

Debit Cards

Newer than credit cards, debit cards carry no limit because they can only be used to spend money which is already in your bank account. There is *no credit* involved. When you use a debit card your bank account is effectively debited straight away. (Switch and Delta are versions of such cards.)

Banks in Britain have grown from the old **goldsmiths** of the sixteenth and seventeenth centuries. There were about forty of them in London, offering banking services in the late seventeenth century. They kept people's money safe in strongrooms, gave loans, and even issued banknotes (until 1770). Gradually these goldsmith-bankers became known as **banks** and the number of banks in Britain grew until there were over 700 in the early 1800s. One of them was the original **Bank of England**, which was then a private bank (formed in 1694). Since the early nineteenth century, a series of mergers, takeovers and some failures have resulted in the number of individual banks falling until, today, there are only a few very large banks, including:

▶ Barclays
▶ Lloyds
▶ Midland
▶ National Westminster

together with the GIROBANK, TSB plc and several smaller ones.

The banking system has been revolutionised in the early 1990s by changes in the law which have allowed building societies to become banks and which have made mergers possible between banks and building societies. The Abbey National is now one of the largest banks in the country and some of the larger banks are pursuing mergers with building societies and other banks.

10 ▶ BANKING SERVICES TO BUSINESS

Modern banks offer a very wide range of services to businesses – both large and small – which we now consider.

A. ACCOUNTS

Businesses need to be able to keep their money in a safe place and to access some of it quite quickly. Banks, therefore, offer businesses four main types of account:

1. cheque accounts
2. deposit accounts
3. foreign currency accounts
4. money market accounts.

Cheque accounts

Cheque accounts normally pay no interest on the money kept in them but enable businesses to write cheques at any time (in other words, to be able to access their money at any time). These are usually called **current accounts**.

Deposit accounts

Deposit accounts pay interest on any money kept in them but make it less easy to draw money out. Usually there is no cheque book with this type of account, although some banks are now introducing interest-bearing cheque accounts.

Foreign currency accounts

Foreign currency accounts suit companies which do a lot of business abroad and which, therefore, receive a lot of money in foreign currencies. These companies can open bank accounts in which they can keep those foreign currencies. If they only had their British sterling (£) bank accounts, the foreign currencies would have to be changed into sterling before they could be banked. Some companies keep these foreign currency accounts so that they can pay their own bills from abroad without constantly having to change British pounds into other currencies.

Money market accounts

Money market accounts are special accounts which are really only for the largest companies which have very large amounts of money available for short periods of time. Various institutions – including the Government – need money for very short periods of time (often only overnight) and are prepared to pay for it. Banks can, therefore, arrange for companies' cash to be loaned overnight. This gives the company an income in the form of interest on money that it would normally have had to keep in a non-interest bearing cheque account.

B. ACCEPTANCES

Banks can help companies who are paid by **drafts** or **bills of exchange** (see p. 119) by arranging for them to be **accepted**, i.e. converted into cash immediately.

C. LOANS

Overdrafts occur when an account holder draws out more money than is actually in the account – they overdraw.

Companies can obtain various types of **loan** from their banks:

▶ overdrafts – short term loans (see p. 72)
▶ loans – medium- or long-term loans, with or without security
▶ mortgages – long-term loans secured against property.

D. ACCOUNT SERVICES

Banks offer business a number of services to help them to run their current accounts more efficiently. Two of the most important are standing orders and direct debits:

Standing orders

If a company has to pay a fixed amount of money every month, say to the electricity board, it can ask the bank to pay it by standing order. The bank will make a note on its computer and the company's account will have the electricity payment taken out of it automatically each month.

Direct debits

These are similar to standing orders except that, instead of the bank being ordered to pay a specific amount each month, it is asked to pay whatever the electricity board asks for. This is particularly useful if the amount to be paid varies each month.

E. BANKER'S DRAFTS

These are a way of making **guaranteed** payments from your bank account. Sometimes another person or company will not accept an ordinary cheque – cheques can **bounce** (i.e. fail to be honoured by the bank usually because there is not enough money in the account) or they can be **stopped** (a person who writes a cheque and thinks better of it can, if quick, ask their bank to refuse to pay it when it is presented by the person to whom it was given).

Both of these problems are avoided by the use of **banker's drafts**. Once you have asked your bank to make a banker's draft out for you and have handed it over to the person you are buying something from, the draft cannot bounce or be stopped. The bank would not have issued the draft for you unless there was enough money in the account, so that it must be honoured when it is presented for payment.

F. EXPORT SERVICES

Britain depends on its exports and British banks now give a number of different services to companies which export their products abroad. They will often provide finance for exports or will advise companies on the best way to set about selling their goods abroad.

G. OTHER SERVICES

These vary from providing insurance for business property and for business activities, to providing computer services for companies which are too small to be able to afford their own computers. Computer services are often provided by banks for the weekly or monthly payroll of companies.

Banks also provide **night safes**, which are often seen in the outside walls of banks. Customers of the bank who have paid for the arrangement, can deposit cash and valuables after the bank has closed. It would be dangerous for most retailers to keep the money from their tills in their own houses overnight – it might amount to many hundreds or even thousands of pounds – so most retailers have an arrangement to use their bank's night safe.

H. ADVICE

Bank managers are highly trained and knowledgeable people who are able to offer business people advice on many matters: setting up a company, finding premises, working out cash flows and money requirements, and dealing with accountants and the Inland Revenue. Most banks are proud of their ability to give sound advice.

11 ▷ THE CITY OF LONDON

People are often confused because the City is both a real place and an idea.

▶ It is *real*, because it is a unit of local government which dates from mediaeval times.
▶ It is an *idea*, because it is the term given to the collection of financial institutions upon which the wealth of the City of London (and a good deal of the wealth of the UK) is founded.

The City consists of:

▶ clearing banks
▶ currency traders
▶ stockbrokers
▶ discount houses
▶ insurance companies

▶ merchant banks
▶ commodity traders
▶ market makers
▶ finance houses
▶ unit trust managers.

The City is a **money market** in that all of these institutions together form a market for money. The City is also centred around several other important markets:

▶ the **Stock Exchange** for trading in stocks and shares
▶ **Lloyds** for all types of insurance from ordinary household to insurance for oil tankers
▶ the **Baltic Exchange** for shipping
▶ the **London Metal Market** for metal commodities.

The City is also the world's largest international banking and insurance market and forms a major part of the UK's **finance sector**.

12 ▷ INSURANCE

Insurance is simply a way of reducing the risks which are part and parcel of every business's existence. In the seventeenth century, many firms would go out of business if their offices or shops were to burn down. An accidental fire caused by a candle or spark would ruin the business person and put many people out of work. It was not practicable, of course, for the owner to keep enough money 'under the bed' so that they could set up again if anything happened. Also, the likelihood of fire was low. Gradually, it began to occur to people that they could share the risk of fire if they each paid a certain amount every week or month and if that money was used to help the very few people who actually experienced a fire. This is called *'pooling' the risks*.

Slowly but surely, an 'insurance' market began to grow in which each business paid a small amount every month and then the insurance company paid out to those who suffered a fire.

The insurers use *actuaries* who work out the chances of any event happening, and they then use these figures to set the premiums (the amount paid each month by people who join the scheme). For example, an actuary might work out that, in every 1,000 businesses, there is likely to be just one major fire costing around £100,000 each year.

If 1,000 customers want cover for fire then the insurance company will charge them about £150 a year each for their fire insurance cover. These 'premiums' will bring in £150,000 in a single year. £100,000 will cover the risk of a claim on the insurance company and £50,000 will represent 'gross profit' and a safety net in case – by chance – there is more than one claim in any given year.

It must be remembered that companies do not take out insurance only to help themselves. Frequently – today – insurance policies are paid for by the company to help the employee or their relatives. These policies – often life assurance or health insurance – are seen as a benefit of employment. (See chapter 15.)

A. TYPES OF INSURANCE AND ASSURANCE

There are lots of different types of insurance today but there is an important distinction between two major types: insurance and assurance.

▶ **Insurance** is usually a scheme which covers you for something which *might* happen. You pay premiums which are not repaid, so that you are insured if the event you fear happens.
▶ **Assurance** is a scheme which covers your life for something which definitely *will* happen, i.e. your death. Because the *only* certainty in life is that you will die (sometime), such a policy which provides for money to be paid out is called an assurance, i.e. you are *assured* that it will be paid on the event of your death.

Company insurance

A company normally tries to cover several different risks, by insurance or assurance as appropriate.

1. Assurance would be used to cover the risk of possible death of a senior manager, owner, or director and the adverse effect that this might have on the company. This is often called **Key Man Cover**.
2. The risk of an accident happening to any member of staff which requires them to be off work for any length of time, can be covered through **health insurance** which pays for prompt and speedy hospital treatment, or through **personal**

accident insurance which will help the employee and his or her relatives to cope with the effects of the accident.

3. The risks to the business through fire and other disasters (such as floods or storms) cannot be underestimated. These are normally covered through a policy which covers either or both of the company's buildings and 'contents' i.e. its equipment, furniture, etc. **Building and contents insurance** provides for payment in the event of a disaster happening, so long as it is specifically covered in the policy agreement.

4. Even if a company has insurance cover for fire it may not do it any good. If a bakery burns down one night it will not be enough that the baker is paid the value of the building and its contents. The money in hand is all very well but new premises will have to be found, new equipment bought, delivered and installed, and – eventually – business started again. This may be in a different part of town and without the 'goodwill' that had been built up with the bakery's old customers. Most business insurance policies have to include, therefore, something for **consequential loss**, i.e. losses which have occurred as a consequence of the fire, like loss of custom and loss of turnover, while the business is finding new premises and equipment.

5. **Fidelity insurance** covers a company for losses due to dishonest staff. Certain types of business are particularly vulnerable to losing money and goods to theft by the staff themselves. This can be covered in some cases by fidelity insurance. However, the company has to abide by very strict rules in the way it recruits its staff and it may also have its premiums increased significantly if it does not take care to try to avoid theft and pilfering by its staff.

6. Businesses are almost always places where employees and members of the public are constantly working or visiting. Should an accident befall someone while they are on the premises the company might be found to have been negligent in some way. If, for example, a warehouseman were to leave a box across a doorway and a customer was to fall over it and injure themselves, the company – as the warehouseman's employer – would almost certainly be found to have been negligent. In such cases, the courts would usually decide that the company should pay **damages** to the member of the public. These can be fairly significant in certain cases and, therefore, all companies are required, *BY LAW*, to have **public liability insurance** which covers them for such eventualities.

> 66 Policy Wording: It is vital for you to make sure that the insurance or assurance policy that you have purchased really *does* cover all of the risks you have identified. Many people each year are disappointed – and a lot poorer – because they did not check the policy. Some household contents policies, for example, do not have specific cover when you take, say, your walkman out of the house. Such **'all risks'** cover usually requires a special form to be completed and more premium to be paid. 99

B. ARRANGING INSURANCE

Insurance is sometimes arranged direct with the insurance company but this so-called **direct insurance** route is almost always confined to personal insurance. Companies usually use a specialist called an **insurance broker** who knows a great deal about the business and is able to recommend the best policies for particular situations.

Most insurance in the UK – and a large proportion of the world's insurance – is handled through **Lloyds of London** which is a very large 'market' for insurance.

Lloyds began back in the seventeenth century, in a London coffee house, and has grown to become one of the largest insurance markets in the world. Lloyds is not a single company but is simply a place where hundreds of insurance companies (called **underwriters**) have their offices. The presence of so many underwriters in one place makes the business of sharing risks much easier.

C. INSURANCE PEOPLE

We have already mentioned two types of people to be found in the insurance world but you will encounter several other names as well as different uses for the same job titles.

Broker

An insurance broker is someone who listens to what customers want in the way of cover and then uses their expertise and experience to find the right sort of company to carry the risk.

You are most likely to come across an insurance broker in your local town or city. They will arrange almost any type of cover from personal life assurance or possessions insurance to business fire and premises cover (and many more). Brokers also operate in the major insurance centres of the world to arrange high value cover and to 're-insure' risks when they have been pooled into large amounts.

Whereas life assurance cover for many thousands of people can be carried by just one company there is no company large enough to carry the insurance for, say, a North Sea Oil Rig or a fleet of modern aircraft. Risks such as these, which can exceed hundreds of millions of pounds must be 'laid off' among several companies and this is where the big insurance markets of the world come into play. The insurance brokers, in these markets, act to make sure that a very large risk – up to £150m for just a single jet transport aircraft – is shared by a large number of companies. Should such an aircraft crash or be destroyed in some other way, each individual company will carry only a relatively small share of the total loss.

In these technological times, however, whole insurance markets sometimes come under great strain if a number of rare events happen in the same year. Lloyds of London suffered just such massive losses in the late 1980s and early 1990s when a whole string of disasters – earthquakes, volcanic eruptions, unusual floods, and forest fires – happened in a very short space of time.

Underwriter

Up to now we have spoken of the broker finding 'companies' willing to take on specific risks. Those companies are called **underwriters** because they underwrite the value of the risk.

If a developer builds a new office building, the fire risk may be around £200m. The brokers look around to find groups of underwriters in Lloyds who are willing to take on part of the risk. Groups of underwriters usually specialise in certain types of risk: some will specialise in property cover, others in ships, some in aircraft, yet others in road vehicles.

Cover for very large risks will be shared between several groups of underwriters and may even be 're-insured' even after the original contracts have been signed.

If, for example, a firm of underwriters has signed a contract to take on part of the risk for a large building (say £20m out of a total risk of £200m), they may reach a point during the year when their 'exposure' to property risks is felt to be too high, i.e. they have taken on too much property risk and it now forms too high a proportion of their total risk or 'exposure'. In such circumstances, they may look around for another company willing to take on part of *their* risk. In other words, they will re-insure say £15m of the original £20m with another company. **Re-insurance** is a very big market these days.

Assessors

What happens if a disaster strikes and an insured building burns down or some vital business equipment is stolen or damaged? In such a case, the insurance company will send out an **assessor** who will 'assess' the damage and decide how much money the insurance company will need to pay out.

It is often not realised that insurance policies usually cover a business only for the *current* value of a piece of equipment. If your company's main computer is insured and someone manages to destroy it by dropping it on the floor you may not be given enough money from the insurance company to *replace* it.

This is because most policies only cover 'current value'. If the computer cost £3000 two years ago then its market value today may only be £500. If your insurance policy only covers current value then £500 is all you will receive from the policy after the assessor has been to see the damaged machine. If an equivalent replacement computer costs £1750 today (computer prices have been going down over the years) then you will have to find the extra £1250 out of your own pocket.

The way around such problems is to make sure that your company's insurance policies cover your equipment on an 'as new' basis. This costs a little more to insure, i.e. you will pay higher premiums, but if something happens, the assessor will arrange for you to be paid enough to buy an equivalent computer today.

Actuaries

Although the job of an actuary is not widely known it is one of the most vital jobs in the whole insurance industry. Actuaries are highly qualified and skilled people whose rôle is to work out for the insurance companies exactly what risks they are carrying.

If you wanted to set up an insurance company to cover your friends for the possible loss or theft of their stereos, how much would you charge them every year? Your 20 friends who want cover have stereo equipment worth a total of £10,000 and you could not possibly afford to pay out all that money!

However, it is clear that only a small proportion of stereos are lost or stolen each year so what you need to know is what the chances are of this happening. Insurance companies keep all of these records but, for your purposes, a visit to the local police station might show that, in your town, 200 stereos are stolen in an average year. If you know that there are 20,000 homes with stereos in your town it is a simple matter to work out the annual risk: 1 stereo is stolen for every 100 households.

If you are willing to accept that risk then you now need to calculate the risk of one of your friends' stereos being stolen. There are only 20 of them so the chances are that one of their stereos might be stolen once every five years.

Your risk is, therefore, that you might have to pay out £500 every five years. Your 20 friends might, therefore, be charged just £5 per year insurance premium.

However, this does not allow for any administrative charges, profit for yourself or – most importantly – for the chance that a claim might be made before the end of the five years. The real policy might, therefore, be nearer to £10 or £15 per year.

Actuaries work out these risks on a very large scale for the major insurance companies. For car insurance, for example, the actuaries know that accidents are much more likely for young, male drivers and it is these people who are, therefore, asked to pay much higher premiums. Although they calculate risks for property loss and car accidents, one of their main specialisms is in the life assurance market, where they work out the risks to insurance companies from providing life cover for individuals.

Mortality statistics (figures which show the reasons why people die) have been gathered for many years and provide the actuaries with a very good idea of the overall risk to their companies from certain accidents and diseases. The companies then know how much to charge people for cover.

Life assurance is now more expensive for smokers than for non-smokers, because the insurance companies know that more smokers die, younger, than non-smokers. If you engage in certain hazardous sports, your life assurance may also be more expensive to obtain. Hang-gliding, mountaineering and pot-holing are all examples of sports which would probably increase the cost of your life assurance (they are usually excluded from ordinary life policies).

13 ▷ THE STOCK EXCHANGE

Originally people sold their shares by going to a particular coffee house in London and simply asking around until they found someone who wanted their shares. With thousands of companies and millions of shareholders on today's market that method would be impossible. So, we have a **Stock Exchange** which is really a 'stocks and shares exchange'. It is composed of about 4,000 members who are specialists in finding buyers for stocks and shares. From 1908 until 1986, the Stock Exchange was divided into two different types of member who did very different tasks:

1. **Jobbers** were the people who actually traded in stocks and shares. They were prepared to buy from, or sell to, people who either wanted to buy or sell shares.
2. **Stockbrokers** were people who acted as middlemen between the public and the jobbers. They took orders from the public to either buy or sell shares and then found a jobber who was offering the right price for those shares. As a member of the public, it was impossible to deal with a jobber direct – you had to go through a broker.

A. THE 'BIG BANG'

Since the election of the Conservative Government in 1979, there has been a series of important changes in the City and in the Stock Exchange. The changes to the Stock Exchange are known as the 'Big Bang'. Most of these changes occurred in 1986.

▶ From March 1986, outside firms (which were not members of the Stock Exchange) have been able to take over Stock Exchange firms. Before that date, member firms were protected against takeovers from outsiders.

▶ From October 1986, the distinction between jobbers and brokers ended. Both jobbers and brokers can now exist in the same firm. A single person can now perform both functions, although in practice the firms are still divided internally into the two types of staff. In addition, there are now **licensed dealers** who can trade in stocks and shares without being members of the Stock Exchange.

▶ From October 1986, stockbrokers (and the firms who employ them) have been able to charge any commission they like on share purchases and sales. Up to that date, there were fixed scales for commission charges.

▶ From October 1986, all Stock Exchange firms have been able to offer a full range of financial services to their customers.

B. THE UNLISTED SECURITIES MARKET (USM)

Yet another change was the introduction of the USM. This is a sort of mini-Stock Exchange which has fewer regulations and is cheaper to join, and so has encouraged the shares of smaller companies to be traded.

C. WHY SHARE PRICES ARE IMPORTANT TO BUSINESS

The role of shares is to raise money for companies. We might think that, once the shares had been sold, the company would not really be interested in the price that they were fetching on the Stock Exchange. This is not, in fact, the case. Companies are interested in the share price for two reasons:

1. Shares are a form of ownership of a company; they represent votes and therefore control. Anyone who owns most of the shares or even a large percentage of them can influence what happens within the company.
2. If the company's share price falls, then it becomes easier for another person or firm to buy them and possibly to gain control of the company.

EXAMINATION QUESTIONS

QUESTION 1

Patrick McNab, who owns a manufacturing business, decides to acquire his own fleet of delivery vehicles instead of using independent road haulage contractors. He also decides to lease, rather than buy, the vehicles.

(a) Why do you think he chose to acquire his own fleet? (6 marks)
(b) How does leasing help to reduce the initial cost of the vehicles? (3 marks)
(c) What other advantages are there for Patrick in leasing rather than purchasing outright for cash? (6 marks)
(ULEAC)

QUESTION 2

Examine the following newspaper clipping which appeared on Friday, 18 April 1986 and then answer the questions below:

(a) What is the name of the market where these prices arise?
_____ (1 mark)

(b) What is being priced?
_____ (1 mark)

(c) What was the price for Rowntree in pounds sterling on Thursday, 17 April 1986?
_____ (3 marks)

```
┌─────────────────────────────────┐
│  FOOD, CATERING, ETC.            │
│  Argyll Grp      333    –5        │
│  AB Food         246    +5        │
│  Ass Dairies     140             │
│  Ass Fish        100             │
│  Bejam           179    –2        │
│  Brthwick         36             │
│  Cadbry Sch      151             │
│  Fitch Lovll     246    +1        │
│  Grand Met       351    –9        │
│  Kwik Save       224    –2        │
│  Nth Foods       272    –2        │
│  RHM             161             │
│  Rowntree        395    –8        │
│  Sainsbury       346    –2        │
│  Tate Lyle       493    –7        │
│  Tesco           280             │
│  TH Forte        139    –3        │
│  Unigate         206             │
│  Utd Biscuit     186    –3        │
```

(d) (i) Which of the above is priced highest?

_____ (1 mark)

(ii) Why do you think this is so?

_____(4 marks)

(4 lines for answer.)

(NICCEA)

QUESTION 3

Read the following information and answer the questions below.

Mary Thorpe has recently established an interior design consultancy business in premises (valued at £40,000) which she inherited. She also put £10,000 of her own savings into the business.

She has further savings of £5,000 in a bank deposit account and she also inherited some shares with a current market value of £4,000.

In the first year of trading, her income from business fees was £25,000 and her business expenses amounted to £10,000.

(a) State **three** features of a bank deposit account.
   1. _____
   2. _____
   3. _____(3 marks)

(b) At present, Mary pays most of her business expenses by cheque. Explain when **each** of the following would be a more suitable method of payment.
   (i) Standing order
      (3 lines provided)   (3 marks)
   (ii) Direct debit
      (3 lines provided)   (3 marks)

(c) (i) State three factors which a bank manager would consider before granting a loan to Mary's business.
   1. (2 lines provided)
   2. (2 lines provided)
   3. (2 lines provided)   (3 marks)
   (ii) Why might Mary prefer an overdraft for her business rather than a bank loan?
      (8 lines provided)   (6 marks)

(d) Mary has decided to install a new office computer, printer and appropriate software costing £12,000. She intends to finance this through a leasing company. Why would Mary choose to lease this equipment instead of buying it?
(8 lines provided)
(6 marks)
(MEG 1994)
(Commerce Option)

TUTOR'S ANSWER TO Q.2

(a) The Stock Market
(b) Shares
(c) On Thursday 17 April, the price for Rowntree shares was £4.03. The reason for is that on the following day the shares were priced at £3.95 having fallen £0.08.
(d) (i) Tate and Lyle are priced the highest at £4.93.
(ii) The reason for this could be that Tate and Lyle have announced a good dividend or have had a profitable period. Both these could have caused the price of their shares to increase as the demand for them increases. This increase in their share price is reflecting their success in the past. It could be, however, that they are likely to be successful in the future perhaps because they have developed a new product. This, too, could increase the price of their shares as buyers of the shares envisage larger profits and higher dividends in the future.

STUDENT'S ANSWER TO Q.1

66 Good. Another point is that the product will tend to be handled more carefully when it is his own fleet which is delivering; i.e. less damage. 99

66 This is a good point. 99

66 Another good point – but for 6 marks you need to mention other advantages. For instance, the money you would have spent on buying a fleet of delivery vehicles (if you hadn't leased) can be used somewhere else in the company. 99

(a) He may want his own fleet of vehicles because the haulage contractors are unreliable. His own fleet would always be ready whenever he wanted to use them. The haulage contractors may be too expensive over the long term. Having his own fleet means that he can advertise his company on them.

(b) Leasing helps to reduce the initial cost of the vehicles, because you lease over a long period of time, rather than pay all in one go at the beginning.

(c) Patrick can change the fleet of vehicles for something new/more up to date, rather than sell and buy new vehicles.

COURSEWORK

When you are working on your coursework assignments or looking for additional information on sections of this chapter, the following hints may be useful:

GENERAL COMPANY FINANCE

You will find out a lot about how companies are financed by looking through any *Annual Reports and Accounts* that you can obtain. The *balance sheet* and the *profit & loss account* contain information about how the company uses its profits or, perhaps, how it finances its losses. You will also be able to see how the share capital is made up.

The *Notes to the Accounts* are particularly useful if you do not understand any of the headings. Another important source of information is a quality newspaper.

FACTORING

For more information on what services are available, how they are arranged and how much they cost, see the factoring section in your local *Yellow Pages*, or write to one of the large, national factors, such as:

► Griffin Factors Ltd, 87, Queen Street, London, EC4V 4AP
► International Factors Ltd, 137–141, Regent Street, London, W1R 7LD.

LEASING

There will be several companies who specialise in leasing in your local copy of the *Yellow Pages* but you might also try:

► Lombard North Central PLC, 31, Lombard Street, London, EC3V 9BD.

BANKING & MONEY

► The **local branch** of any of the 'big four' clearing banks – Barclays, Lloyds, Midland, National Westminster – should be able to answer any question you have or, perhaps, branches of the TSB or the Cooperative Bank. The National Girobank can be reached by addressing letters to: The Public Relations Office, National Girobank, Bootle, Lancs.
► The **Banking Information Service** at 10, Lombard Street, London, EC3V 9AT has a wealth of booklets and other material for students.

THE STOCK EXCHANGE

Information can be had direct from the Public Relations Office, The Stock Exchange, London, EC2N 1HP. Do not forget, though, that your local stockbrokers might be able to tell you more and may even be prepared to come into schools to give short talks or to see small groups at their offices (by appointment only).

INSURANCE

The large insurance brokers in your local *Yellow Pages* will be able to give you information on what is available for business insurance and how much it costs.

It might also be possible to obtain some information from the local offices of the larger insurance companies such as:

► Commercial Union
► Eagle Star
► Legal & General
► Provincial
► Royal Insurance

► Cooperative Insurance
► Guardian Royal Exchange
► Norwich Union
► Prudential
► Sun Alliance

You will find their addresses and telephone numbers in the local telephone directory or the *Yellow Pages*.

<table>
<tr><td>

**FINANCE
ASSIGNMENT**

</td></tr>
</table>

CAPITAL STRUCTURE OF FIVE COMPANIES

1. Obtain the **Annual Reports and Accounts** for five public limited companies (PLCs) from different industrial sectors. You can write away for them, look them up in a local library or perhaps your school has a resource bank of them.

2. Use the **balance sheet** to identify for each company:

    ▶ loans – under 'liabilities' (long-term) and including debentures (sometimes called 'loan stock');
    ▶ share capital – ordinary and preference;
    ▶ reserves – money set aside out of profits each year to provide for a 'rainy day'.

3. Use the **profit & loss account** to identify for each company:

    ▶ profits – distinguish between profits *before* tax and those *after* tax;
    ▶ retained profits – compare them with last year's to see how well, or badly, the company is doing.

4. For each company, calculate:

    ▶ the retained profits as a percentage of turnover (total sales)
    ▶ the profits after tax as a percentage of turnover
    ▶ dividends as a percentage of profits after tax
    ▶ long-term loans as a percentage of share capital plus reserves (this is called the **gearing** of the company).

5. Write a report for your school magazine which:
    (a) presents all this information clearly and usefully;
    (b) explains all the important terms used;
    (c) comments on the differences between the companies in
        (i) the way they have raised their capital between equities (ordinary shares) and loan capital;
        (ii) the proportion of profits paid out as dividends to shareholders, interest on long term capital and retained profits.

A Review Sheet for this chapter will be found on p. 239.

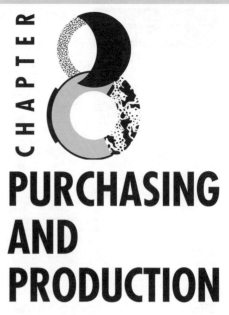
GETTING STARTED

Production means actually making the goods or products, and involves many stages in modern manufacturing.

Perhaps the easiest way to think of production is to see, in your mind's eye, the long car production lines which most of us have seen in films or on the television.

The basic bits and pieces (known as **components**) enter the factory at one end and are then put together, bit by bit, until the finished article leaves at the other end. This is known as **line production** and was one of the very earliest methods of **mass production**.

Before the Industrial Revolution, most goods were produced by individual craftsmen in their own homes or in small workshops. This was an early form of production which required the craftsman to be very organised about his work. A carpenter who was going to make a set of chairs would have to think about all the major production stages which we have today – except that he probably would not recognise them by the same terms.

1. He would have to choose and buy the wood, making sure that it was of the right quality and that it was delivered to his workshop at the right time.
2. He would have to make sure that all his tools were laid out in the right places in his workshop so that he could work easily. It would not help for him to leave his saws and planes at the other end of the workshop from the door at which the heavy timber arrived.
3. He would have to do the work in the right order. Sawing and turning all the legs first; steaming and bending all the backs next; sanding and smoothing all the pieces; then gluing them all together and clamping them; and, finally giving them a final smooth before varnishing and polishing all the finished chairs.

The things which the old carpenter would have done by experience (because he had learned them all during his apprenticeship) have, today, become an extremely complex part of management.

PURCHASING

PRODUCTION

TYPES OF PRODUCTION

ECONOMIES OF SCALE

PRODUCTION ENGINEERING

PRODUCTION MANAGEMENT

CHANGE IN ENGINEERING AND PRODUCTION

ESSENTIAL PRINCIPLES

1 > PURCHASING

The first stage in any business which is producing goods is the **buying** of the raw materials needed. Whether the firm is going to produce 'home-baked' cakes or machine tools it is going to need to buy the basic raw materials.

Purchasing is, therefore, an extremely important part of the activities of a firm. A good buyer can save the company substantial amounts by sensible buying policies, and lower costs can mean extra profit for the firm.

The role of the Buyer or Purchasing Officer is to know exactly where to obtain a wide range of raw materials; how much to pay for them; what sort of contracts to enter into; and how to deal with suppliers who do not deliver on time or in the right quality or quantity.

The job can be summed up by '*double P; double Q; double T (P P Q Q T T)*':

- ▶ Price
- ▶ Place
- ▶ Quality
- ▶ Quantity
- ▶ Times
- ▶ Terms

A. PRICE

The purchasing officer must know the prices at which the materials can be bought – what is too low a price (because, possibly, the quality will not be good enough) and what is too high a price.

B. PLACE

Components are of little use if they are delivered to the wrong location or, even, to the wrong unloading bay at your factory. The buyer must specify exactly where the materials are to be delivered.

C. QUALITY

> Buyers have to be experts, not only in the items to be bought but also in the product in which the items are to be used.

It is vital that the quality of the components be exactly as required by the designers or production engineers. Obviously, the quality must not be poor because the finished goods will then be faulty, giving the company a bad name which will be very difficult to live down. It is not so obvious, but just as true, that the materials must not be of *too high* a quality. Goods are designed to last for a specific time. If they last too long then they are overtaken by newer designs. An article which has parts which are of too high a quality may last longer than the makers want it to last – in effect they will have paid for too much quality! The buyer must buy exactly the right quality of components.

D. QUANTITY

The purchasing officer must buy the right *amount* of the components. Enough must be bought to be able to take advantage of *discounts for large orders* but the buyer must not buy too much.

If a firm buys too much of a component then it will have to pay extra storage costs.

E. TIME

It is the duty of the purchasing officer to make sure that the components arrive at the right time: too early and the firm will have to use up valuable storage space in storing them; too late and the whole production process might be held up.

F. TERMS

This means the agreement between the firm and its suppliers for a certain component and includes all the terms of the contract for the supply: how many are to be delivered;

at what intervals; to what quality; and at what price. The buyer must make sure that his company pays only as much as it absolutely has to for the components.

For many years, the Purchasing Department was very much underrated. Glamour has tended to be attached to the people in Sales and Marketing. However, the purchasing officers are vitally important to modern industry – they have to carry in their heads a mass of complex information about the materials which the firm needs; they must be good negotiators; and they must know a great deal about the law of contract.

The role of the purchasing officer has become even more important over recent times as companies have tried to reduce the amounts of expensive stock they hold. **'Just-in-Time'** systems put great pressure on buyers to make sure that materials and component deliveries are linked very closely to production schedules. The closer they can be linked, the more efficient and potentially profitable the company can be.

Car dealers, today, operate such systems. When cars are bought by a member of the public, the chances are that they will be supplied direct from the factory against a pre-agreed delivery schedule. In the past, it was all too common for your new car to have been stored for several months at a dealer's premises.

2 ▷ PRODUCTION

In the discussion at the beginning of this chapter, we talked about a carpenter needing to be well organised in order to produce chairs. It is also true that, if the carpenter is *not* well organised, he will produce the chairs very inefficiently, i.e. late, or to a poor quality. In the same way, modern industry needs to be very well organised to produce its products efficiently. Any company which is not, will find it very difficult to sell its goods and may well go out of business.

There are a number of ways of producing goods today. An easy way to remember these types of production is by using the letters *JMB* – standing for *job, mass* and *batch*.

 Remember: JMB

3 ▷ TYPES OF PRODUCTION

A. JOB PRODUCTION

This applies wherever a firm has to produce individual items to a special specification (set of requirements). High quality pottery, made-to-measure clothes, bridges, and ships are all made using *job production* techniques. With job production, every item produced is different and the firm has to rearrange its production floor to meet the special requirements of each job. Because they are individually produced, job-production items usually require a large amount of human labour. The experts call this a **high labour to capital ratio**. This simply means that the production technique requires more labour than machines – the production is **labour intensive**.

B. MASS PRODUCTION

Most of us are familiar with the long production lines which produce everything from television sets to tinned peas, and from cars to sweets. The idea of **mass production** is to make a very large number of identical products as cheaply as possible. It is often said that the idea was invented by Henry Ford in the USA. This is not so, although it is true that Ford was the first in *modern* times to put the principle into business practice. The *idea* was actually used to good effect by the Royal Navy during the Napoleonic Wars, a hundred years earlier, when they established a block-making factory at Portsmouth on mass production principles.

Anything which is needed in large numbers, and in identical form, can be produced using mass production, e.g. light bulbs, soap, sweets, cars, vans, and hi-fis. The same techniques are used to produce large amounts of liquids and semi-liquids. When the production process is fully integrated, so that one activity merges smoothly into another, it is called **continuous flow mass production**. In theory, with such production methods, the product should never have to be delayed during the production process to wait for parts or components to be brought to it. Most car manufacturers, these days, use a system of continuous flow which allows the body shell to be pressed, welded together, painted, and then moved at a slow speed along the production line while components are attached (including wheels, tyres, axles, seats and fittings, and even the whole engine, electrics and gearbox. The 'flow' of the production line never stops.

There are two other things which need to be said about mass production techniques:

1. They are almost always high in capital (machines) to labour ratio. Today, some mass production lines are fully automated and require virtually no human operators at all.
2. To be most efficient, i.e. to produce goods at the lowest cost, the production lines need to be kept going most of the time. Stopping and starting them costs more than continuous production. Therefore, planning has to be good. Demand for your product has to be anticipated well in advance. If demand falls off for some reason, the lines are usually kept going for quite a while afterwards.

C. BATCH PRODUCTION

This third production technique falls somewhere between the first two. Any product which needs to be made in reasonably large but limited numbers is usually made using batch production techniques. Many cargo ships these days are built in a series of identical units (perhaps three or four). They cannot be made using mass production lines because there are not enough of them but they do require *some* of the same skills as mass production. Most modern furniture is not mass produced because the designs are only released in hundreds rather than the tens of thousands or millions to which mass production is suited. The designs are, therefore, made in batches. The same applies to things like high-quality motorcruisers, some clothes, etc.

ECONOMIES OF SCALE

Why is it that an ordinary family car in the 1930s used to cost the equivalent of five years' pay for the working man while, today, a much better vehicle can be bought for less than one year's salary?

There are a number of factors which have resulted in this fall in 'real cost' but the main one is **economies of scale**. Economies of scale exist where companies are able, by making large quantities of a particular product, to reduce its price. To make just one car, a modern car firm would need designers, testers, metal working machines, presses, paint shops and robots. If it only ever made that single car then it would be extremely expensive. As the *scale* of production increases, however, the process becomes more efficient and the overheads are set off against more and more production. Economies of scale mean that large quantities of goods can be produced relatively cheaper than small quantities.

Scale effects, as they are sometimes called, are one reason why it is very difficult for new companies to break into certain industries. A small car manufacturer might make very good cars but they will also cost quite a lot because the company has no advantages of scale to help them keep costs down. The larger car manufacturer will almost always be able to undercut the price of the smaller one and, thereby, keep its customers. You should note, however, that this applies only to similar vehicles, e.g. if a small company tried to produce a direct competitor to the Vauxhall Corsa. The argument does *not* necessarily apply when the small company does not compete 'head-on' with the larger one but, instead, identifies a 'niche market'.

Niche Markets are those small market areas that are not served by the major producers. High-quality sports cars are such a market. In a totally different sector, ecological washing-up products are another 'niche' market. In both cases, the *main* market is served by large manufacturers who keep costs down through *economies of scale*. However, there are a number of people who have the money and the 'demand' for sports cars and this is an area which large manufacturers do not serve. Smaller car manufacturers are, therefore, able to achieve profitable sales – *as long as they have correctly identified the exact niche that they are trying to serve*. In the same way, there are many people who are willing to pay more for an ecologically friendly washing product which the larger companies do not produce. Smaller companies can enter markets in this way.

If there is real money in a niche market, then it will not stay a 'niche' for long. The larger manufacturers will very quickly gear up to meet the demand and can usually – through massive economies of scale – begin to dominate the niche.

PRODUCTION ENGINEERING

It is the job of the Production Engineer to make sure that the product is manufactured in the most efficient way.

A. SITE

The first thing to be done is to choose the right **site** for the factory. This has been discussed in some detail in Chapter 6 but it involves the correct choice of site with respect to:

► land
► labour
► raw materials
► climate
► transport
► social facilities.

B. LAYOUT

It is extremely important that the factory is laid out properly so that work can progress easily from stage to stage. In the case of the carpenter (see the beginning of the chapter), all that was needed was for him to ensure that his tools were on the right side of his workshop. In a modern factory, every machine, and its various tools, has to be in the correct place. Otherwise, the product might have to be moved *back* down the factory, which would be inefficient and time consuming.

There are three basic types of factory layout: process, product and group work.

Process layout

> ❝❝ The difference between process and product layout is highlighted by the fact that 'process' layout can almost always make many *different* types of product. In contrast 'product' layout usually has to be radically altered before it can deal with a different product. ❞❞

In this type of layout each part of the production of a product is separated out and placed in a different part of the factory. In the case of a boat manufacturer, the factory may well be set out as in Fig. 8.1.

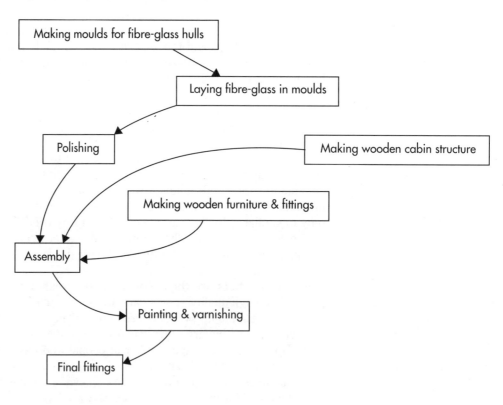

Figure 8.1 Process layout

Product layout

Here, the manufacture is done in stages along a single production line for each product. This is the type of production with which we are all familiar for things like cars and confectionery.

The manufacture of a chocolate bar might take place on one product line while a different type of sweet is produced on another line running alongside; see Fig. 8.2.

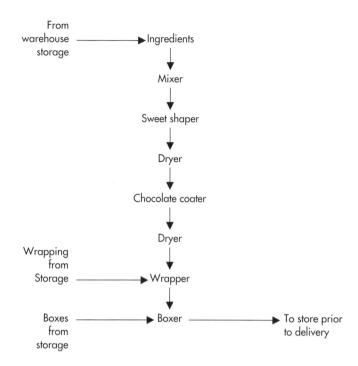

Figure 8.2 Product layout

Group work

In this type of layout, the machines are all grouped together so that each member of a group of workers can take part in *every* stage of the production of the product. The object is to try to avoid the boredom which can result from production-line methods. On a production line, each worker – in theory – only does one job: it could be checking sweets to make sure they all have wrappers on; or it could be adding a certain part to the wheels of a car. These jobs do not change very often and workers often become extremely bored.

The result of this boredom is often **absenteeism**, i.e. the workers take time off work for any minor sickness which, in other circumstances, would not prevent them from working. It may also increase the staff turnover rate – the speed with which people leave the company and have to be replaced (the replacement and training of new staff being very expensive).

So, to try to avoid high rates of staff turnover, the idea of 'group work' was born. Each self-contained group is a factory in miniature making the *whole* product. The workers in the group have to decide their own methods of work and allocate the tasks among themselves. When this was tried by Philips, the electrical firm, for workers making electric light bulbs, they found that it had a remarkable effect; it stopped many workers becoming bored, it reduced staff absenteeism and it slowed down the rate of staff turnover.

There are undoubted benefits to the workforce from this method of manufacture but it can only be used in certain types of industry and it is sometimes not economic.

Production Management includes many aspects of production and each of them has its own experts: production engineers, planners, controllers and inspectors.

A. PRODUCTION ENGINEERS

These decide on the best way to actually make all the parts of the product:

▶ how the product will be made
▶ what machines will be needed
▶ what the quality of the final product will need to be
▶ what special **tools** or **jigs** will be needed.

Note that 'tools' means anything which has to be attached to a machine to allow it to do its job. Most machines these days are general purpose machines which do things like turning or drilling. To do a *specific* job, those machines will need special tools attached to them, e.g. to drill exact holes or to create exact shapes.

A 'jig' is a framework which helps the engineers to build or make something. Before furniture is put together the engineers create a metal jig into which the bits can be slotted and glued. The jig gives them shape and keeps them together until the glue is fully set.

Production engineers also undertake method study and work study.

Method Study

The idea of method study is to try to find out the very best way of doing any particular task. The engineers will, for example, try to find out in which order the job needs to be done and what tools will be required.

Work Study

Work study used to be called **time and motion study** and is still the subject of much suspicion by workers on the shop floors of many firms. As many workers are paid a bonus based on how much they produce in a week, it is necessary for companies to know how much they would produce if they were working 'normally'. The work is therefore, measured; a time-and-motion man will stand by the worker with a stop-watch and time exactly how long it takes for him to perform a certain task. After lots of adjustments are made the result is a **base time** for the job. From then on, the worker who does better than this base time will earn a bonus. Work study today is often more sophisticated than this, but the principles are still the same.

B. PRODUCTION PLANNERS

These, as their name suggests, are people responsible for making sure that the production of an item is properly organised. They decide where and when to begin production; they make sure that the materials which are needed will be on hand and that there will be enough workers to do the work; and they plan which machines will be needed and for how long.

C. PRODUCTION CONTROLLERS

These are responsible for making sure that the plans made by the Production Planners are kept to. At one level, they are called **progress chasers**; they spend their time making sure that everything is following the original plan. As the work passes each machine, or each stage in the production process, the operators will hand in a slip to the Production Controller's office. By keeping an eye on these slips, the progress chasers can see exactly how far each job has progressed and whether any delays are occurring.

D. INSPECTORS

These people are responsible for making sure that the materials which go into the product are of the right quality. They are usually, although not always, part of a **quality control system**.

> ❝❝ Quality control is not simply a matter of trying to ensure that each product is of the correct quality. Today, most British firms are working towards a complete structure, or system, to ensure quality throughout every aspect of the firm's management and production system (the guidelines for this are laid down in an International Standard ISO9000). ❞❞

7 ➤ CHANGE IN ENGINEERING AND PRODUCTION

A. ROBOTS

Production lines have been partially automated for many years. This means that certain machines can automatically perform tasks which humans had previously to do by hand.

The first **semi-automatic machines** were probably watermills which carried on milling grain under water-power even when the miller was doing something else. During the nineteenth century, most factories in Britain had semi-automatic machines which, using steam power, would happily stamp, drill or turn metal all day.

True **automation**, in which the machines do not need to be tended by a human being, did not arrive until the twentieth century. However, semi-automated production lines have been in operation for many years making various components or chemicals without people having to 'feed' them or reset them.

But none of these early attempts at automation were robots. A **robot** is an automatic machine which is able to do more than one job. The automatic machines of the past were only able to do one job; a machine for filling milk-bottles would need to be extensively changed if it was to be used to fill wine bottles; and a machine for drilling holes in a specific piece of metal would have to be almost completely changed if you varied the shape of the piece of metal or the number of holes to be drilled.

A robot, on the other hand, contains one or more computers and can be reprogrammed to do different tasks. A good example is the team of welding robots which Rover use to weld car bodies. This year, the robots are programmed to put, say, twenty welds in twenty different places on the body of a Rover 600. Next year, without changing the robots themselves, they could be reprogrammed to put 17 welds, in totally different places on a totally different car body – the Rover 100 series, for example.

The advantage of robots therefore, is that they can be reprogrammed to do different jobs quite easily. They are also very accurate and, of course, do not tire. A robot in a welding or painting shop can work 24 hours a day without breaks for tea or lunch. Although robots do break down every now and then, they are 'off work' for less time than humans tend to be.

On the one hand, then, robots bring a great many benefits by allowing firms to achieve quite high levels of production with fewer human operators. On the other hand, there are people who accuse robots of 'doing humans out of jobs'. The evidence from the countries which use robots the most, however – Germany and Japan – is not so clear cut. Those countries have managed to employ very large numbers of robots while still keeping their rate of unemployment quite low (compared to the UK).

B. AUTOMATIC HANDLING SYSTEMS

These are simply highly computerised systems for handling all the various materials and products of the firm:

Automatic materials handling

This uses a series of tubes, conveyor belts, and lifts to bring the material directly into the factory without human operators having to unload it.

Automatic warehousing

This uses a similar set of conveyors to take finished goods straight off the production line and directly into the warehouse where they will be stored to await shipment to shops or customers.

Automatic transport between workstations

This is a system of computerised trucks or trolleys which take the half-finished product from one work area to the next – again, without humans having to load and unload it. The best known example of such a system was the one seen in the TV advertisements for Fiat cars in which robot trolleys transported cars around without a human in sight.

C. COMPUTERISED DESIGN AND MANUFACTURE

In many processes these days, especially in the high-tech industries of electronics, the whole production process from the design of the product through to its planning and production is aided by computers. The key ideas are those of:

► CAD – computer aided design
► CAM – computer aided manufacturing
► CIM – computer integrated manufacturing.

With CAD designers can use the computer screen to help them to design products. The computer allows the designers to draw the product, see it from many different angles, and experiment with different changes, without the need for the hundreds of detailed technical drawings which would have occupied the time of ten or twenty designers, ten or fifteen years ago.

With CAM parts of the production process are linked into one or more computers. These computers do many of the tasks which would have taken human beings many hours in the past. The computers can establish the production plan, timetable the machines needed, do the progress chasing and, in some cases, even keep an eye on quality.

With CIM the whole production process is overseen by a computer system. Such systems are only just being developed but they offer significant improvements in efficiency because the computers can spot problems, communicate them to each other, and remedy them much faster than human operators and systems can.

Outside the systems mentioned above, many machines, these days, are controlled by computer but are not actually robots. These machines are controlled by fairly simple computers which accept instructions by numbers and are, therefore, called **numerically controlled machines**. **Computer Numerically Controlled (CNC)** machines are gradually being replaced by robots and by CIM systems but there are many still in operation.

EXAMINATION QUESTIONS

QUESTION 1

State three reasons why a manufacturing company might benefit from employing a purchasing department. (3 lines provided)   (3 marks)

QUESTION 2

Outline what is meant by 'job production' and 'batch production'.
(4 lines provided)   (4 marks)

QUESTION 3

Filby Wholefood Ltd manufactures biscuits. They are mass produced with part of the workforce involved in packaging the biscuits into boxes on an assembly line.

(a) What is meant by the term 'mass production'? (2 lines provided)   (2 marks)
(b) Give two reasons why Filby Wholefood Ltd might benefit from mass production.
    (2 lines provided)   (2 marks)
(c) Explain briefly what you view to be the disadvantages to the workforce of mass
    production. (4 lines provided)   (3 marks)
(d) How might Filby Wholefood Ltd aim to overcome these disadvantages?
    (4 lines provided)   (3 marks)

QUESTION 4

JMV-UK is the British division of a large multinational car manufacturer. Production at JMV-UK involves three operations:

▶ engine machining and assembly;
▶ body pressing and welding;
▶ paint, trim, electrics and final assembly.

Each operation is a continuous flow process with all the parts put together in order.
(a) What do you understand by a continuous flow process of production? Use
    examples to help explain your answer.   (6 marks)
(b) Why is this method of production particularly suitable for the manufacture of
    cars?   (6 marks)

The company has introduced a new production system called 'just in time' (JIT) for some of its operations. As the car body shell begins its three-hour journey down the assembly line, the seats are being manufactured in a nearby factory. The finished seats are delivered at the right point on the assembly line, just in time to be fitted into the car body. This allows JMV-UK to select from over 100 varieties of seats to meet the special requirements of each customer.

Close co-operation and detailed planning are required between JMV-UK and its suppliers. As JMV-UK does not hold stocks, any problems at the suppliers could cause

JMV's production line to stop. On the other hand, JMV needs less storage space and defects in parts may be spotted quickly.

(c) What is meant by a 'just-in-time' production system? Use examples to help your explanation. (6 marks)

(d) Explain the advantages and disadvantages to JMV-UK of using the 'just-in-time' system. (12 marks)

JMV-UK aims to build a high quality car that really satisfies the customer. To achieve this, and make a profit, JMV operates a quality control system based on teamwork. There are no quality inspectors on the assembly line to check on the finished car. Instead, all staff are encouraged to check for quality as they complete their task. In this way, JMV builds in quality control rather than having to correct numerous defects once the car is completed.

(e) Why is quality control important to JMV-UK? (10 marks)

(f) JMV builds in quality through teamwork. Why might this system be better than checking after the car is completed? (8 marks)

(NEAB)

TUTOR'S ANSWER TO Q.3

(a) Mass production means the production of a very large number of identical products as cheaply as possible, normally through components being assembled on a production line.

(b) One reason for using mass production techniques might be to increase the output of labour. The employees of the company will be able to concentrate on one job, such as packing the biscuits into boxes. This, therefore, means that they can become expert and efficient in one particular area. A second reason could be to produce a more standard product for the market, so that the consumers would know exactly what they are buying.

(c) One disadvantage, to the workforce, of mass production is that by doing the same tasks the job may become boring. This boredom could lead to frustration and a low morale among the workforce. If the company has difficulty in selling its products then it may have to make some of its workforce redundant. Many of those made redundant may find it difficult to obtain further employment because they are specialised in a small area.

(d) To relieve the boredom the company could rotate the workforce from one type of job to another every three months or so. This would ensure that the tasks they are engaged in do not become too repetitive. It would also allow the workforce to develop other skills.

STUDENT'S ANSWER TO Q.3

❝ This does not really answer the question. Mass production involves producing large numbers of an *identical* product (here a type of biscuit) on an assembly line. **❞**

❝ Some good points. Because mass production techniques give high output per person employed, or per pound spent on capital equipment, the firm can produce more cheaply. **❞**

❝ A good answer. **❞**

❝ Again, a good answer which deals with the main point. **❞**

(a) Many different types of biscuits are manufactured before being packed on an assembly line.

(b) It is cheaper to buy the ingredients in bulk. You can produce cheaper, can sell cheaper and gain a large share of the market.

(c) The work becomes boring very quickly, which makes it tedious for the workforce who may not produce as much, leading to poor efficiency within the company. The workforce are dependent on one another. If one group of the workforce is slow, this leads to a hold up in production. The workforce may not realise the role they play in the firm, as most will not see the final products.

(d) They could introduce job rotation so that the workforce perform a variety of jobs, which helps to reduce boredom. Attempt to improve communication between the management and subordinates, so that subordinates have greater participation within the company.

COURSEWORK

ASSIGNMENT –PRODUCTION

1. Choose a product from the list below:

   ▶ small wooden rowing boat
   ▶ snow sled
   ▶ summer dress for nurses' uniform
   ▶ bird table for feeding and drinking – with shelter
   ▶ a special cake for young children.

   If you can think of anything else you would like to 'make' ask your teacher whether it would be a suitable subject for a project. The product you have chosen is to be your subject for 'production'. (Nothing actually needs to be produced, however.)

2. You must **design** the product – and produce drawings which can be used by the people who will eventually have to make the bits and pieces and put them together.

3. You must produce a **production plan** which shows how the product will be made, in what stages, and how long you think it will take. You should also indicate what tools or machines will be needed.

4. The production plan should also list the **materials** which will be needed, how much they will cost, and where they should be bought.

5. Finally, estimate how long it will take to make each one of your products and whether there are any ways in which the job could be made more efficient. Could more machines be bought or could the job even be automated?

A Review Sheet for this chapter will be found on p. 240.

GETTING STARTED

Most people think they know what 'marketing' involves but very few are fully aware of the sheer scope of this management skill. It is often confused with sales or with advertising but it is these and much more.

Marketing is a complete process within the business which includes:

▶ finding out what the customer wants – this is called **market research** and involves finding out what types of products are wanted (**product policy**) and what prices consumers are prepared to pay.
▶ helping to produce the **right product** at the **right price**.
▶ persuading customers to buy the product – by means of **advertising** and **packaging**.
▶ transporting the product to the customer in the most convenient and efficient way – **distribution**.

Within these broad areas there are many other aspects to marketing – some of which are looked at in greater depth in this chapter.

CHAPTER 9
MARKETING

MARKETS

TYPES OF MARKET

THE MARKETING MIX

PRODUCTS

PRODUCT POLICY

PRODUCT LIFE CYCLE

PRODUCT DIFFERENTIATION

PRODUCT DEVELOPMENT

PRICING

COSTS

DEMAND

PROMOTION AND ADVERTISING

MARKET RESEARCH

PLACE

DISTRIBUTION

TRANSPORT

ESSENTIAL PRINCIPLES

We all have an idea of what a **market** is, the most usual variety being the one which has many stalls set out in the town square on a specific weekday. Everyone knows this local market. At one time, these markets were the only way in which goods were bought and sold. The open-air markets we are all familiar with are places where people with goods to sell can find people who want to buy them. Both types of person benefit because they know exactly where and when the market will be.

The markets which Marketing Managers are concerned with are just larger versions of the open-air market. All markets have:

▶ **sellers** who have goods or services to sell
▶ **buyers** who need the goods or services and have the money to pay for them.

There are three main types of market:

1. **Open-air markets:** These are the simplest because all the buyers and sellers are together in one place at one time.
2. **Consumer markets:** Most goods and services, these days, are not sold in one place but across the entire country (or even the whole world). These 'consumer' markets are usually divided up into:

    ▶ **Single-use consumer goods**, e.g. food, gas, newspapers
    ▶ **Consumer durables**, e.g. televisions, freezers, refrigerators
    ▶ **Consumer services**, e.g. post, photocopying, hairdressing.

3. **Industrial markets:** These are for the goods and services bought by organisations such as companies, schools, local authorities, etc. Industrial markets include:

    ▶ **Industrial capital goods**, e.g. machinery, buildings
    ▶ **Industrial services**, e.g. parcel delivery, printing, cleaning.

> ❝ Note that only the simplest of markets – the open-air or enclosed ones – can be visited. The other types – consumer and industrial – are happening all around us, all the time. ❞

The easiest way to remember what marketing is all about is to remember what the marketing people call the **marketing mix**, i.e. the four Ps:

▶ product
▶ price
▶ promotion
▶ place

Product

Product involves decisions about the product's quality, its style and design, the branding policy (what to call it and how to ensure that customers recognise the 'brand name'), how to package it, and what guarantees to offer.

Price

Price means the need to set not only the price itself but also any discounts which might be given and any allowances permitted, e.g. £50 for your old cooker when you buy a new one.

Promotion

Marketing involves the choice of how the product is promoted – the advertising and the publicity it is given.

Place

Place refers to how the product is distributed and through what types of shop or other organisations.

Consider the following two companies and the **products** – both toasters – which they want to sell:

1. **Excello-Toaster Company Ltd**
   This company has taken several years of technical development to design their 'Supatoast, Mark 2'. It is very well made, of the highest quality materials and has many built-in additions. As well as toasting bread and rolls, it has a built-in clock, an adapter for browning cakes and pies, and an electric can opener. The company estimates that they can make a reasonable profit if they can sell the new toaster at £47 each.

2. **Toast-Easi Ltd**
   After a thorough period of market research, during which this company found out exactly *what* users of electric toasters want, this company has produced the 'Easi-Brek'; a basic toaster with no extras on which they can make a reasonable profit if they can sell it at a price of £17 each.

Which of these companies is more likely to be successful in the 'market' for electric toasters?

The answers you have arrived at in response to the above example should already have told you a great deal about product policy. Most firms fall into one of two categories when it comes to product policy:

1. **product-oriented** firms invent new products and then try to sell them
2. **market-oriented** firms find out what people want, find better ways of producing it and then sell it.

With very few exceptions, it is the second type of firm which does better in the real world.

5 ▷ PRODUCT POLICY

Product policy in marketing involves:

▶ finding out what people want in a particular product and what they use it for – there is very little point in producing a radio for the mass market which has 12 different wavelengths on it if people only ever really use two or three;

▶ deciding what the product should look like – this involves making sure that the design is not only up-to-date, but that it is suitable for people to use, i.e. has no sharp edges, is easy to hold, etc.;

▶ making sure that the price is right for the people who the company thinks will be likely to buy the product;

▶ selecting the appropriate 'slot' in the market with regard to other factors, such as status.

6 ▷ PRODUCT LIFE CYCLE

Although it is possible to consider the life cycle of a complete product (e.g. the television) the length of time involved is extremely long. It is more usual and useful to consider the life cycle of *individual products within the broad group*, e.g. the 'Supercol 3400 TV'.

Almost all products have a lifetime during which they are used. During this lifetime, the product will first be very new to the market and only a few people will know about it. After a while, the product will become widely known and, its producers hope, popular. Then, towards the end of a product's life, it will become less popular and will be replaced by other newer products.

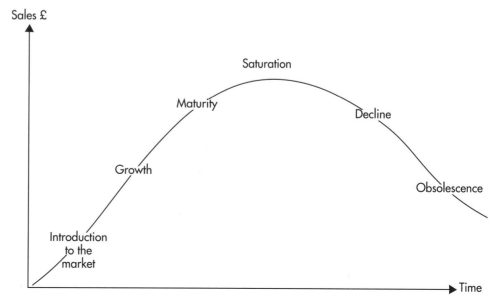

Figure 9.1 Product life-cycle

Different products have different life cycles – both in length and shape, but every life cycle goes through a series of common stages. These are shown in Fig. 9.1.

The length of the life cycle will differ for different types of product; a television may have a very long life cycle, whereas an item of fashion-wear may have a relatively short one. The length of a product life cycle can be extended by improving the product or by changing the way it is marketed, e.g. the way in which it is advertised, packaged, or presented to the customer.

Product differentiation means 'making the product different'. It would be difficult to sell a new light bulb on today's market for light bulbs unless you could convince consumers that it was, somehow, different to all the others on the market. In terms of shape, light output, technology and life expectancy your light bulb would probably be the same as those of the other companies. To sell it, you would have to **differentiate** it. This could be done by attractive packaging, competitive pricing, incentive offers (e.g. free coffee mugs with 10 labels returned) or by creative advertising.

Product policy will determine how a company develops a particular product. Market research may reveal, for example, that a product is perceived as being 'old fashioned' in appearance. Without changing the way it works or is built, product development may then focus on changing the design and colour. The new designs may then help to differentiate the product from similar ones.

Many products are so mature and allow for so little new technology and additions that good design and packaging are often the *only* way that they can be differentiated. A good example of this is domestic electric kettles. The technology is almost totally fixed and no 'extras' (except for, perhaps, water level indicators) are possible. The only way a manufacturer can differentiate their own kettle is through excellence in design. Tefal and Russell-Hobbs have both done this so successfully that they are actually able to charge a 'premium' (i.e. a higher price) for their kettles.

Before a product can be **priced**, you have to find out how much it is going to **cost** you to produce and how much profit you require from it. The next section considers costs in more detail.

The cost of a product may be worked out from two separate calculations:

1. How much does it cost to make the product?

This is the **direct cost** including such things as raw materials, pay and energy; these can also be called **variable costs**.

2. What does it cost to provide the firm in which the product is to be made or, simply, for the firm to remain in existence?

These are called **indirect costs** (or sometimes **fixed costs** or **overheads**) and consist of rent for offices and factories, management salaries, and administrative costs, all of which have to be paid whether or not a product is made.

Indirect costs are usually the same however many units of the product are made, whereas the direct costs increase as the number of units produced increases.

These separate costs are then added to find the total cost:

$$\text{total costs} = \text{direct costs} + \text{indirect costs}$$
or
$$\text{total costs} = \text{variable costs} + \text{fixed costs}$$

Break-even analysis

Companies need to know at what point in the production of a product they will begin to make a profit. This is called **break-even analysis**, which involves plotting a graph of costs against revenue. First, the **indirect costs** which are fixed are represented on the graph by a horizontal line labelled (TFC) total fixed costs. The **direct costs** increase as the amount produced increases, so their line will be an upward sloping one labelled (TVC) total variable costs. Both sets of figures are then added together and a line drawn representing total costs (TC).

Finally, lines are plotted on the graph representing the money which would come in from sales at various prices.

Figure 9.2 shows:

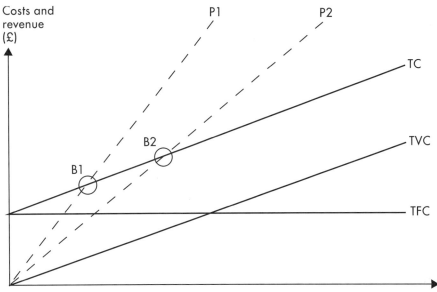

Figure 9.2 Calculating the break-even point

- ▶ indirect costs (line TFC)
- ▶ direct costs (line TVC)
- ▶ total costs (line TC)
- ▶ the income from pricing the product at one price (line P1)
- ▶ the income from pricing the product at another price (line P2)

There are break-even points (B1 and B2) which show that P1 will result in the firm making profits earlier than P2.

Example

Try to do the following example yourself: The Sick Parrot Record Company has decided to release cheap CDs of the group Over the Moon, Brian. They have several people working for the group on a full-time basis and have rented an office from which the CDs can be marketed. The first CD will have to be produced (using an expensive recording studio and several very expensive sound engineers and producers) and then manufactured (by another company). The final product will then have to be sold to the record trade, advertised to the general public and promoted to the television and radio companies for 'air-time'. Even without producing a single CD the company will have to bear weekly costs of £500 in rent, salaries and administration. Table 9.1 shows the costs, once production begins.

PRODUCTION (PER WEEK)	DIRECT COSTS (VARIABLE) £	INDIRECT COSTS (FIXED) £	TOTAL COSTS £
0	0	500	500
100	200	500	700
200	400	500	900
300	600	500	1100
400	800	500	1300
500	1000	500	1500

Table 9.1 Pricing of Sick Parrot CD

The Sick Parrot Record Company want to know at what point they will begin to make a profit.

Draw a graph of the three lines for direct, indirect and total costs using the data given in Table 9.1, and plot extra lines to show what sales revenue would be if Sick Parrot were to charge:

(a) £3
(b) £4

for their CDs. How many CDs per week would they have to sell to break even? Which price would you advise them to charge?

This process of break-even analysis shows a company at what point they can begin to make a profit at a given price but it does not tell them what prices to charge. What would happen to the Sick Parrot Record Company, for example, if the price you have advised them to charge is one that the record buying public is not prepared to pay for a new and untried group?

11 ⟩   DEMAND

A. ESTABLISHING DEMAND

It is important for a company to know what the demand for its product will be at a whole series of prices. In the case of the record company, they will conduct a survey to find out. People will be asked whether they would buy a Sick Parrot CD at a variety of prices ranging from, say, £6 down to £2. The survey might show that:

▶   at £5 per CD, 300 people would buy them
▶   at £4 per CD, 400 people would buy them, and
▶   at £3 per CD, 500 people would buy them.

It should be expected that Sick Parrot fans will be prepared to pay as much as £6 while many other people would not buy their CDs unless they were quite cheap, say £2. You would almost certainly find that the higher the price, the less people would be prepared to buy, and the lower the price the more people would buy.

B. DEMAND CURVE

This data could be presented as a **demand curve** for the CDs on a weekly basis; see Fig. 9.3.

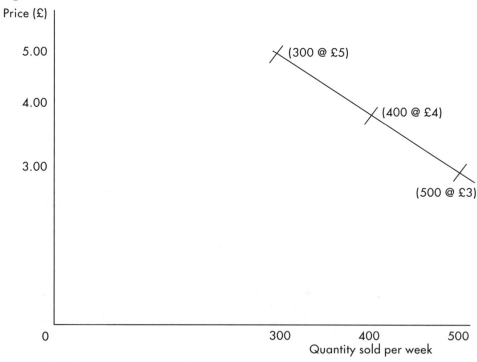

Should the company aim to produce 300 CDs a week because they can get £5 each for them, or should they aim to produce 500 CDs a week at £3 each? The only way this question can be answered is to find out what the size of the profit is at each level of demand.

Using all the data you now have for the Sick Parrot Record Company Limited, complete the chart in Table 9.2.

SELLING PRICE £	NUMBER SOLD (PER WEEK)	TOTAL SALES REVENUE £	TOTAL COST £	PROFIT £
5.00	300	1500	1100	
4.00	400			
3.00	500			

Table 9.2 The Sick Parrot Record Company Limited – profit statement

What would be the most profitable production figure for this company and how much profit would they make per week? Remember the formula:

total profit = total revenue – total cost

(The answers to this question are given at the end of the Tutor's Answer section in this chapter.)

You should note that changing the price or the amount of production will not necessarily make a firm more profitable.

C. LOSS LEADING

Sometimes a firm will deliberately ignore the pricing techniques described above and will sell a product at a very attractive, low price on which the firm actually makes a loss. The idea is usually to interest people in the product and to attract their attention to other products in the range. It is called 'loss leading' and is most common in supermarkets.

Customers are attracted by a very low price for one product – say, sugar or potatoes – and once in the store tend to buy other things. The supermarket hopes to make up on all the other purchases what it loses on the sugar or potatoes.

12 ▷ PROMOTION AND ADVERTISING

Some products do not need to be advertised, as such. If they are very specialised products made in small numbers, the customers can simply be informed by letter that a new or different product is available. Most products, however, are designed for the mass market and people need to be informed that a new product is available. That was the way advertising began – simply as a way of informing a large number of people that a new product was on the market:

Today, advertising is about much more than merely giving information. Most advertising also performs at least one other function – the promotion of a company image – and, of course, persuasion. So:

> ### Mr Jeremiah Postlethwaite
> begs leave to inform his many
> esteemed clients that he has,
> *AT GREAT EXPENSE,*
> developed a new
> and completely efficacious cure
> for the common cold
> and other diverse ailments.
>
> ———●———
>
> The patented *Postlethwaite Curative*
> may be purchased from Mr Postlethwaite's
> elegant new premises in the High
> Street for the sum of just
> *one shilling and sevenpence halfpenny*
> per large bottle.

Figure 9.4 An old fashioned advertisement (1870)

▶ advertising **informs**
▶ advertising **persuades**.

Both of these objectives can apply to the same product but at different stages of its life cycle. When a product is new, the advertising is mainly concerned with telling people what it is, how much it costs and where it can be bought. Later, when the product is mature, advertising may be directed towards increasing, or defending, its market share.

A. THE ADVERTISING AGENCY

Designing advertising campaigns and writing advertisements is something which usually requires the skills of **advertising agencies**. Within an agency, there are people such as **copywriters** (who actually write the text of the advert), **artists** (who draw any illustrations or who draw a series of frames to represent different stages of a TV advert), and **designers** (who design the overall look of the advert).

The agency is responsible, therefore, for two main functions:

1. the **message** – the design and wording of the actual advertisement or the same functions for a TV or radio advertisement; and
2. the **medium** – the way in which the message is transmitted to the people who are supposed to receive it.

$$medium + message = advertising$$

The medium used can be any one, or a combination, of the following:

▶ posters
▶ cinema
▶ newspapers (national dailies and sundays; regional and local)
▶ free newspapers (often called 'free-sheets')
▶ magazines
▶ leaflet 'drops' (circulation of leaflets, through special organisations, direct into the home or business)
▶ television
▶ teletext
▶ radio
▶ direct mail (by leaflets posted direct into the home or business)

Within each category above, the actual medium chosen will depend upon requirements.

B. POSTERS

Poster sites will have differing values for advertisers depending upon where they are and who will see them: hoardings outside airports are ideal for advertising airlines; those in railway stations are good for advertising snacks or magazines.

Poster sites are graded by the 'OTS' (opportunity-to-see) score and potential advertisers can choose their poster site depending on how much they have to spend, how many people they want to see the poster and how quickly. Buses, trains and tube trains are forms of 'mobile' poster sites. The outside posters on buses are often seen by a great many people and can be very effective advertising.

Poster sites are handled by about six national companies who divide their sites into bus stops (such as Adshel), rail sites (Adrail), city sites (Advantage, Mills & Allen), etc. Each group of sites is then graded according to approximately what proportion of the adult population could be expected to see them in a given period. Motorpak, for example, offers poster sites on 34 motorway service areas which would be expected to be seen by around 2 million people at a cost of around £12,000 per package. The power of poster advertising in certain sites is reflected in the cost; a single panel which would be seen on the top side of 500 London buses would cost around £70,000 per month and 300 full-size posters spread across the nation might cost in excess of £120,000 per month.

C. CINEMA

Cinema advertising reaches an increasing audience and adverts can be tailored to a broad range of ages and socio-economic backgrounds. Predominantly, however, the audiences are composed of the young (in 1993 74 per cent of cinema audiences were between 15 and 34). More and more, cinema attendance is dominated by the middle and upper socio-economic groups (65 per cent of audiences are from these groups).

Most cinema adverts are for those products which are bought most by the 15–34 age group, e.g. motorcycles, clothes, soft-drinks. Cinema advertisements are expensive to make and, therefore, tend to be screened for long periods. The screening of a cinema advertisement can cost between £700 and £40,000 for a 60-second advertisement shown for one week; £700 would buy a week's showing at the 19 cinema screens in the Border region (between England and Scotland); £40,000 would buy the same advertisement showing at the 400 screens in London.

D. NEWSPAPERS

Newspapers vary, from the quality national press to small specialised local papers. The type of advertisement has to be chosen very carefully according to what is being sold. The **daily nationals** can be divided into two types: tabloids and quality dailies.

1. The **tabloids** are popular newspapers which have a small size and generally have a high proportion of photographs to text. The tabloids rely on high circulation, and the advertising which this draws, to make them profitable. At the moment, there are a large number of national tabloids:

   ► *The Sun*
   ► *The Daily Mirror*
   ► *The Daily Mail*
   ► *The Daily Express*
   ► *The Star*
   ► *Today*

2. The **quality dailies** are usually much larger in size and contain much more written material than pictures. The amount of detail is greater and the people who buy them are usually interested in knowing a lot about what is happening. Five papers fall into this category:

   ► *The Times*
   ► *The Guardian*
   ► *The Financial Times*
   ► *The Independent*
   ► *The Daily Telegraph*

There are also the **Sunday nationals**. These papers are only printed for the special Sunday newspaper-reading audience. The readers are special to advertisers because Sunday newspapers tend to be read for longer and by more people in the household than the daily papers. Sunday newspapers, too, fall into 'quality' and 'mass circulation' groups:

> You can work out 'value for money' so far as newspaper ads are concerned by finding out how many copies the paper sells and what its average readership is. Both figures are available through the Audit Bureau of Circulation (ABC). Then divide the cost of the ad by each of these figures to calculate, respectively, the 'cost per copy' and the 'cost per reader'.

► **Mass Circulation**
The News of the World
The People
The Sunday Express
The Mail on Sunday
The Sunday Mirror
Sunday Today

► **Quality**
The Sunday Telegraph
The Observer
The Sunday Times
The Independent on Sunday

Advertising in national newspapers can be very expensive. The cost, like all newspaper advertising, depends on how much space is taken, where it is in the newspaper (on the front page or tucked away at the bottom of an inside page, for example), and whether it is a **classified** advertisement (which means that it is all words and placed together with lots of other advertisements in a 'classified column', under a particular heading or classification such as 'Holidays in France' or 'Houses for Sale') or a **display** advertisement (one which takes up more space, is specially laid out, and usually has pictures or photographs).

In the national dailies and the Sunday newspapers a single, full page insertion (in black and white) can cost between £10,000 and £50,000. The same advertisement, in colour, might cost between £15,000 and £55,000. Smaller ads cost less, of course, but even a very small advertisement such as one centimetre in one column of the classified section usually costs between £80 and £120 for a single insertion.

Against these national costs, the local newspapers seem very cheap. In most local papers, a full-page advertisement costs between £800 and £2,000, and a single column centimetre (SCC) in the classified section would usually cost between £5 and £10. It must be remembered, however, that it is not the total cost which really matters but the 'cost per issue' or 'cost per reader'.

Deciding which newspaper to use for your adverts can be very difficult. It depends not just on their total circulation but on whether they are being bought and read by the people you want to reach. Look, for example, at the table below. Which paper would you use to advertise a new business computer?

NEWSPAPER	ADULT READERSHIP (MILLIONS)	% OF BUSINESS PEOPLE READING THIS PAPER
The Daily Mirror	7.5	9.7
The Sun	9.5	7.7
The Daily Telegraph	2.7	16.9

Table 9.3

E. 'FREE' NEWSPAPERS AND MAGAZINES

The traditional national, regional and local newspapers depend for their income on a combination of advertising revenue and what they call the 'cover price' (what the customer pays for the newspaper in the shop). The newspaper receives only a small proportion of the cover price because there are distribution costs to pay and the newsagents need to take a small amount for their trouble in selling the papers.

Free newspapers – which began in the US in the 1960s and were called 'free-sheets' – tackle the problem in a totally different way. Instead of relying on people to buy their paper in the shops they deliver it directly into people's homes. Their revenue comes entirely from the advertising which they sell in their pages.

F. MAGAZINES

Magazines also vary a great deal in the markets they are aimed at. One has only to look at the magazine display in a good newspaper store to see that it is possible to direct advertising very carefully to almost exactly the group of people for which your product is designed – from fishermen to footballers, and from computer buffs to collectors of stamps.

Magazines are not only better able to direct advertising at specific groups of people, they also tend to be read by more people, and for longer, than newspapers. Newspapers are usually read for a very short time and only rarely for more than one day. Magazines, on the other hand are kept by their readers for weeks and months (depending on what type of magazine it is). A good example of this is the radio and television magazines: *The TV Times* and *The Radio Times*. Both of these magazines are kept in the homes of their readers for at least one week, and are usually looked at each day. Research has shown that they both have a 'reading life' of about 8–9 days.

MAGAZINE	APPROX CIRCULATION (MILLIONS)	APPROX READERSHIP (MILLIONS)	APPROX ADVERTISING RATES*
The Radio Times	1.5	5.4	£16000
The TV Times	1.1	4.9	£14000
Readers' Digest	1.7	6.1	£19500
Marie Clare	0.3	0.9	£6500
Car	0.1	0.8	£6000

*Rates are an approximate indication only and are based on mid-1993 figures for a full-colour page.

Table 9.4 Selected magazine circulations and advertising rates

There are also such things as **free circulation magazines** which are distributed to their readers free of charge and which, like free newspapers, survive on their advertising revenue alone.

G. TELEVISION

Television – specifically the commercial channels which come under the control of the the Independent Broadcasting Authority (IBA) – is one of the most powerful advertising media. The advertisement costs a great deal to make and must be prepared by experts. Once made, however, it can be shown to an audience which will be very close to the one for which the product is designed.

Television companies divide the advertising day up into special **time zones** which are priced according to the numbers of people who will be watching at the time. In addition, they can provide detailed information on the composition of the television audience at any particular time of the day; see section L. Social Grouping below.

There is now a wide variety of television advertising opportunities:

▶ the independent stations including Yorkshire, Granada, Anglia, Borders, Grampian, Ulster and HTV (Wales)
▶ Channel 4
▶ GMTV
▶ cable
▶ satellite television

> The advertising costs quoted do not include the cost of actually making or producing the ad in the first place. To be effective, newspaper and poster ads have to be professionally designed and laid out, while TV and Cinema ads cost a great deal of money to design, script and film.

The cost of television advertising is priced on the basis of when the advertisement is to be screened and how long it will last. The 'when' really refers to how many people are expected to watch a particular programme so the television companies usually quote their rates as being a certain amount for each 1000 viewers and for a 30-second advertisement. The rate for Carlton, during early 1993, was about £6.50 per 1000 viewers and that for Tyne Tees Television about £2.20 per 1000 viewers.

If you were to place an advertisement during a programme on Carlton that attracted 7 million viewers, for example, you would expect to have to pay about £45,500, plus, of course, the cost of making the advertisement in the first place. This is why television advertising is so expensive. However, if you have the resources the cost would work out at much less than 1p for each viewer who you would expect to see your advertisement.

H. RADIO

Modern commercial radio provides the same sort of advertising as television and requires similar specialisms from the advertising agencies. There are now around 60 commercial radio stations selling advertising time for varying rates. On some small stations a peak time 30-second advertisement can cost £12–100, while the same length slot on Capital Radio in London can cost around £2000.

The first national commercial station, Classic FM, began operating during 1992. It has since been joined by Atlantic 252 and Virgin 1215.

In addition to the normal radio stations it is also possible to advertise on taped radio in hotels.

I. DIRECT MAIL

Direct mail is now becoming a very popular form of advertising. The average British household receives about 6.5 items of direct mail per month. A company can buy or rent detailed mailing lists from specialised agencies and can, therefore, be sure of details of their products reaching the homes of the sort of people who will be interested in them. Most direct mail shots, these days, include some sort of 'sweetener' to attract the buyer. The most common is for the order form for the goods to double as an entry form to a competition which offers attractive prizes.

J. OTHER ADVERTISING

The traditional forms of advertising, discussed above, are not the only possible media. Of growing importance are a number of different approaches including airship and aerial banner advertising, putting your message across on the back of cinema tickets, ads in taxis, pages on Teletext, Post Office queue advertising, and even ads on the television and video shows on aircraft and in doctors' surgeries.

K. SOCIAL GROUPING

Newspapers, television and radio all categorise their readers as shown in Table 9.5 to assist advertisers in choosing the medium which will reach almost exactly the sort of people who are likely to want to buy their product. *The Times*, for example, is read mostly by people in the AB range, whereas *The Daily Telegraph* has a wider spread of readers from A to C1: 87% of *The Times* readers, for example, are in the ABC1 categories while only 24% of *Sun* readers are in the same group.

REGISTRAR GENERAL'S LIST	NATIONAL READERSHIP SURVEY LIST	OCCUPATIONS
I	A	Higher managerial; administrative & professional
II	B	Intermediate managerial, administrative & professional
IIIn	C1	Supervisory, clerical & junior managerial
IIIm	C2	Skilled manual
IV	D	Semi-skilled & unskilled manual
V	E	State pensioners, casual earners, low-grade earners, widows, etc.

Table 9.5 Social divisions for advertising and marketing

Before any product can be marketed properly, its producers or sellers must know a great deal about:

- ▶ the market it is to be sold into
- ▶ the demand for the product itself
- ▶ the needs of the buyers for design, quality, colour, etc.
- ▶ the best media in which to advertise the product
- ▶ the best way of transporting the product to the buyer
- ▶ the price which people are prepared to pay for it.

Most of this information is obtained by specialist marketing people who arrange for two types of research to be carried out: desk and field research.

1. **Desk research** involves finding out what has been written already about the product and the market for it. It is highly-skilled work and requires patience and the ability to know which facts are useful and which are not.
2. **Field research** is the testing of the product idea by asking people what they think of it and by looking at the competition (how good are competitive products and how much is being charged for them). It requires skill in writing questionnaires and in arranging samples of the public to try out the product.

The results of market research for a product or a service must be interpreted with extreme care. To take an extreme example, a survey might show that only 5% of adults would be interested in taking a holiday specially designed for the under 25s. If the survey asked a sample of *all* adults, this result is not surprising. The survey should have been more carefully structured to ask the question only of those aged between, say, 18 and 25.

LIFE STYLE MARKETING

The old distinctions between consumers – age, sex, income and where they live – are becoming less and less useful to modern companies. The reason is that people do not buy products and services purely as a result of how much they earn or how old they are. A much more useful way of seeing consumers is by means of what *life style* they adopt. In this way, products can be targeted much more closely at the precise groups who would be interested in the products – and products can be designed to meet very specific needs.

Much market research is now concerned with identifying these life styles and with developing **life style marketing strategies**.

Life style marketing is based on very accurate statistics about the way people lead their lives: figures on level of education, cohabitation and divorce, life expectancy, career progression, travel trends, use of credit cards, and many others are all put together to arrive at different groupings of the population.

One well-used system was developed by CACI International and is called ACORN (a classification of residential neighbourhoods). ACORN divides the country into categories ranging from 'striving' to 'thriving'. One of the categories, for example 'aspiring', includes, as subcategories, groups called:

- ▶ new home owners
- ▶ mature communities
- ▶ white collar workers
- ▶ better off multi-ethnic areas.

These categories, each of which is a known number of the UK population, enable companies to target their products more precisely.

If, for example, you were thinking about publishing a new magazine for those who belong to youth organisations, it would be useful to know how many people belong to such organisations and to be able to take a sample of them to test your product.

14 ⟩ PLACE

For most people, **distribution** means two things:

1. how the goods are **transported** to the point at which the customer will be able to buy them
2. the **type** of organisation which will sell the goods to the customer.

In marketing, these are usually kept quite separate by calling the first **transport** and the second **distribution**. For example, a company which manufactures clothes will first want to decide what type of organisation it will use to distribute its clothes, and then it will decide how it will transport them to the final destination. We will deal with these two aspects below.

15 ⟩ DISTRIBUTION

A. DISTRIBUTION VIA WHOLESALERS

A clothes manufacturer is in the business of making clothes. As long as it decides not to move into the business of selling clothes then the avenues of distribution might be as shown in Fig. 9.5.

The advantage of this type of distribution is that large amounts of clothes can be transported at once to only a few wholesalers in separate regions. Then the wholesalers can break down the supply of clothes into smaller collections which the wholesalers' own transport can deliver to the many clothes shops. (See Fig. 9.6.)

Figure 9.5 Simple distribution

Figure 9.6 Complex distribution

B. MAIL-ORDER AND DIRECT SELLING

Another possible avenue of distribution would be for the manufacturer to sell its products to one or more **mail-order catalogues** which would then sell them direct to the public. The manufacturer might even decide to sell direct to **large retail stores** but to keep several wholesalers as well to supply the smaller clothes stores.

It may even decide to sell direct to the public by **direct mail** – a method of distribution which is growing in popularity because it gives the manufacturer control over the whole process, from actually making the clothes to seeing them into people's homes. It can also be more profitable.

The avenues of distribution are many, therefore, and it will depend on the needs of the manufacturer as to exactly which ones are chosen.

16 ⟩ TRANSPORT

Transport of goods can be achieved in many ways:

▶ road haulage
▶ railway freight
▶ canal and river
▶ air freight
▶ sea freight.

These methods are well known to most people but the major revolution in transport over the past 20–30 years is less well known: the use of containers.

A. CONTAINERS

Containers are a **standard shape** and have special hooks at each corner, they can simply be lifted by crane from one form of transport to another without the cargo itself being unloaded. This has made transporting goods much quicker and easier.

For example, once sugar was transported in 'hundredweight' bags – about 50 kilos – and a ship load of, say, 5,000 tonnes of sugar would be carried in 100,000 bags, each of which would have to be separately loaded and unloaded. Today, the same amount of sugar would be carried in about 200 containers and these would be loaded and unloaded by special crane. Containers are used on almost every type of transport: lorries, railways, ships and aircraft.

B. PIPELINES

Although they are not seen, because they are buried under the earth, pipelines carry a large amount of cargo these days. Most of it is oil and gas but, in some places, liquified coal is transported in this way.

C. CANALS

British canals are narrow, and shallow. This means that progress is very slow and thus they are unsuitable for much cargo. In fact, except for certain river-linked modern canals like that for the River Severn, the cargo-carrying days of British canals are virtually over. On the continent of Europe, however, this is not the case. European canals are much wider and deeper than the British ones and so carry a great deal of cargo – especially where they link up with the great river systems of the Rhine and the Rhône.

EXAMINATION QUESTIONS

QUESTION 1

The life expectancy of a branded article is known as a product life cycle and generally it has five phases:

(a) Introduction   (b)_____   (c) Maturity

(d)_____   (e)_____

(ULEAC)

QUESTION 2

Name three reasons why a manufacturer might carry out market research.

(i) _____(2 marks)
(ii) _____(2 marks)
(iii) _____(2 marks)

(NICCEA)

QUESTION 3

Franco's is a small firm making ice-cream in a variety of flavours. The ice-cream is sold from vans in nearby seaside resorts. Their sales vary a lot throughout the year. This means that they have a number of production and financial problems which they would like to reduce. The most they have sold in any one month is 20,000 litres.

(a) (i) Draw a graph to show how their sales might vary from January to December.
    (ii) Explain your reasons for drawing the graph in the way that you have.
(b) Explain what 'production and financial problems' the firm might suffer from because 'their sales vary a lot throughout the year'.

At the moment Franco's sells only ice-cream. The sales have not been increasing as much as they would like. They want to expand the business but are not sure of the best way to do it. These are the choices they are considering.

1. Sell ice-cream in containers to shops and supermarkets.
2. Make and sell iced lollies as well as ice-cream.
3. Buy in and sell soft drinks as well as ice-cream.
    (c) Consider these three options and advise the firm on the choice they should make. Give reasons why this choice of action would be best.
    (d) How useful do you think market research would be in helping this firm?
    (e) What factors must the firm take into account before launching an advertising campaign to sell their new line?

(NEAB)

QUESTION 4

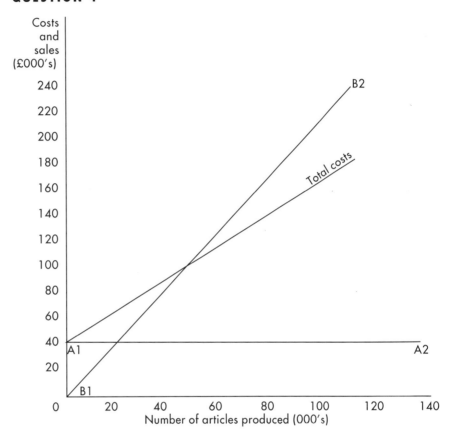

Figure 9.7

The graph (Fig. 9.7) was prepared for the marketing manager of Mammoth Enterprises Ltd. It is used as part of a test given to applicants for a job vacancy in the marketing department. Complete the test as best you can.

(a) What do the following lines on the graph represent?
    (i) A1 to A2 _____ (1 mark)
    (ii) B1 to B2 _____ (1 mark)
(b) What is the level of output at the break-even point?
    _____ (1 mark)
(c) What is the income from sales at the break-even point?
    _____ (1 mark)
(d) Use the graph to find:
    (i) the profit and loss if 100,000 articles are sold.
    _____ (1 mark)
    (ii) the total revenue if 80,000 articles are sold.
    _____ (1 mark)
    (iii) the output if total costs are £88,000.
    _____ (1 mark)
(e) What is the selling price of an article produced by Mammoth Enterprises?
    _____ (1 mark)
(f) Explain why total costs increase as production increases. (4 lines for answer)
    _____ (2 marks)

(ULEAC)

TUTOR'S ANSWER TO Q.4

(a) (i) Fixed costs
   (ii) Sales revenue
(b) 50,000 articles produced. The break-even point is where total costs equal sales revenue (total revenue).
(c) £100,000.
(d) (i)   If 100,000 articles are sold the total costs are £160,000 whilst the income from sales is £200,000. The difference between the two gives a profit of £40,000.
   (ii) If 80,000 articles are sold then the total revenue is £160,000.
   (iii) If total costs are £88,000 then the output level is 40,000.
(e) To find out the selling price of an article you have to divide the total revenue from sales by the total production, i.e.

$$\text{price} = \frac{\text{total revenue}}{\text{total production}}$$

So, referring to the graph, if you take any level of production the price will be the same, e.g. for a total production of 100,000 articles there is total revenue of £200,000, so the price is £2.

(f) The total costs of Mammoth Enterprises Ltd will consist of both fixed costs and variable costs. If the business produces nothing then it will still have the fixed costs to pay. These costs will include the rent and rates on the premises and interest on any loans they have obtained from a bank and, as the graph shows, they are fixed at £40,000. Variable costs, on the other hand, vary with how much is produced and include such things as raw materials, lighting and heating and the wages of labour. Total costs will therefore increase because variable costs increase as production increases.

Answers to the Profit statement (Table 9.2) for Sick Parrot Records.

Sales price	No. sold	Total revenue	Total cost	Profit
£5.00	300	1500	1100	400
£4.00	400	1600	1300	300
£3.00	500	1500	1500	0

COURSEWORK

**ASSIGNMENT –
PRODUCT POLICY**

Most companies conduct regular surveys to find out how their products are faring in the marketplace and to see whether any changes will have to be made. Choose an everyday product from the range of consumer products on the market today, e.g. toasters, washing machines, microwave ovens, cars, motor-cycles, computers, televisions, stereos. Make up a questionnaire in order to find out what people around you – your family, neighbours, friends, teachers, etc. – feel about this product. The questionnaire should cover at least the following points (but you will be able to think of more):

1. What is the main use of the product? Are there any other uses to which it is put?
2. Where is it used and at what times of day? how often is it used?
3. What do people think about the design of the product? Is it awkward to use or dangerous?
4. Is the price right, or is it too high or too low?
5. What do people think of its colour, packaging, etc.?
6. What improvements would people want to make to it?

When you have finished the questionnaire and have surveyed a reasonable number of people, put all the results into a chart or written report so that they will be of use to 'Product Planners'. Add to that chart your own detailed recommendations for the development of the product.

A Review Sheet for this chapter will be found on pp. 241–2.

CHAPTER 10

INTERNATIONAL TRADE

GETTING STARTED

You may have seen articles like those shown in Fig. 10.1 on p. 116 in the newspapers or on the television news and most of us assume that these exports are good for Britain. Likewise, most people seem to believe that imported goods are somehow bad. In the past, governments have spent a great deal of money trying to persuade people to '**buy British**' and even today, the Government spends many hours negotiating limits on the number of Japanese cars which may be imported.

If exports are good because they earn us lots of money from other countries, can imports be bad? After all, every export is someone else's import!

Most economists today agree that trade is almost always good for the whole world because everyone benefits from it in the long run. The simplest reason for trade is that countries sell goods to each other because they produce goods which other countries want at a price which is cheaper than they can make them themselves.

The case of Japanese cars illustrates this point. Although cars are made in the UK, the Japanese manufacturers are very efficient and can make them cheaper and then, in theory, sell them cheaper in Britain. If a British consumer can choose between having a British car for £9,000 or a Japanese car of the same quality for £8,500 then it is likely that the car from Japan will be chosen. In doing so, a saving of £500 is made which can be spent on something else. Trade allows these sorts of savings to be made all over the world and, if each country specialises in making those goods which it can make cheapest and best, this trade brings benefits to everyone.

ESSENTIAL PRINCIPLES

The size of British trade is staggering: Britain is one of the countries in the world which relies on trade for a large proportion of its economic activity.

BRAZIL
A beam on the Brazil market

Sheffield-based Land Infrared has sold five thermal imagers to the state-owned Brazilian electricity company, Furnas Centrais Electricas, to monitor electrical connections on its power plants and sub-stations.

Furnas generates and distributes power for south-east and central west Brazil.

The imagers are replacing a 20-year-old instrument and are being used to inspect connections and carry out repairs on a programmed system.

CZECH REPUBLIC
UK computers branch out

ROCC Central Europe, based in Prague and part of ROCC Computers, has won contracts worth more than $750,000 from the Czech Savings Bank for computer systems at branches at Ceske Budejovice, Usti Nad Labem, Brno and Plzen.

ROCC has had a presence in Central Europe since 1974.

SLOVENIA
Fastening on to an old market

A £3.8m contract to supply resilient railway track fastenings to Slovenian Railways has been won by Pandrol UK, whose products are used on more than 200 railways in 70 countries. Funding comes from the European Bank for Reconstruction and Development.

Pandrol says it has been cultivating the market for a long time, carrying out a series of successful test installations – the first 19 years ago. The contract includes local manufacture of half the components.

Figure 10.1

Source: Adapted from *Overseas Trade*, January 1995

> ❝ Note that a thousand millions is ONE BILLION while a million millions is ONE TRILLION. Although these differ from the old-fashioned British versions they are now the internationally recognised definitions of the terms billion and trillion. ❞

Almost 30% of everything we earn comes from trade. In value, it amounts to well over £100,000,000,000 (£100 billion) every year. Almost two-thirds of British exports go to Europe – some 65% – and half of our exports go to other members of the European Union (the EU). Of the rest, about 13% of UK exports go to the US, and 2% to Japan.

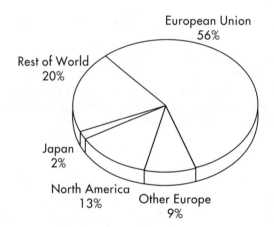

Figure 10.2

Since 1960 there has been a substantial change in the countries with which Britain trades most (see Table 10.1). In 1960, only 21% of British trade was with the EU; today it is 56%. In 1960, over 30% of British trade was with the 'developing world' (the countries of Africa, South America and the Middle and Far East). Today, the proportion of trade taken by these countries is only 9%. Britain did not really begin to make its Empire independent until the 1960s and, during that decade, was still trading a great deal with the colonies and with the new members of the Commonwealth. By the mid 1970s, Britain had joined the EU and had made most of its former colonies independent. Trade to and from Britain has, therefore, changed from being mainly worldwide to being mainly European.

AREA	1960	1991	1993
European Union	21	58	56
Rest of Europe	11	10	9
North America	10	11	13
Japan	1	2	2
Rest of World	57	19	20

Table 10.1 The changing nature of British trade (% of total UK trade)

THE GEOGRAPHY OF UK TRADE 1960 TO 1993

Most of the exports leaving Britain used to be manufactured goods, e.g. cars, machines, clothes and washing machines. Today, that has changed. With the discovery of large amounts of oil in the North Sea in the late 1960s, oil has become one of Britain's most important exports. In 1960, oil and fuel accounted for just 4% of British exports; by 1993, this rose to almost 10%. Similarly, whereas manufactured goods used to make up half of our exports in 1960, they accounted for only 34% in 1993. Unfortunately, Britain has been losing her place as a major trading nation. In the late nineteenth century, half of all world exports came from the UK. In 1960, our share had dropped to just 17% and, by 1993, it was only 7%. In 1993, the world's greatest trader was Japan, closely followed by the US and Germany.

There are many reasons for this decline, but the following would appear to be the main ones:

1. Other countries throughout the world have become industrialised and have competed against Britain in the world markets.
2. Many of these new competitors have had an initial advantage of having relatively cheap labour costs (compared to wages in the UK).
3. Britain's industry has been very slow to compete in world markets.
4. The quality and the design of goods made in Britain has been poor for many years.
5. Britain may have had too few qualified managers — especially in the field of marketing.
6. Most British managers do not speak foreign languages.
7. The value of the pound may have been 'too high' for most of the 1950s and 1960s. The result of this would have been that British exports would have been very expensive for people in other countries to buy.

2 THE BALANCE OF TRADE

Tourism is an export even though the money is spent in this country. We are really selling £s abroad – exporting our currency in return for other currencies – in exactly the same way as we sell clothes abroad in return for other currencies.

There are two types of exports and imports: visible and invisible.

1. **Visible trade** consists of all those goods which can be seen and touched such as machines, televisions, motorcycles, refrigerators, food and, of course, the raw materials which Britain exports, mainly oil.
2. **Invisible trade** refers to all those items which we export, which cannot be seen or touched, such as sales of insurance, banking services, airline seats, or sea cargo space.

One of Britain's fastest growing invisible exports is **tourism**. Every year millions of visitors come to visit Britain. Unfortunately, British tourists abroad spend more money than do foreign tourists in Britain, so we have a *deficit* in our tourist trade.

The **balance of trade** is obtained by taking all visible imports away from visible exports. If the result is negative then it is said that there is a *deficit* in the balance of trade. If the result is positive, then there is a *surplus*. In 1994, Britain imported more goods than we exported, which is referred to as a deficit. The balance of trade for 1994 was a deficit of £10,594 millions.

3 BALANCE OF PAYMENTS ON CURRENT ACCOUNT

The **balance of payments** is similar to the balance of trade, but takes more information into account. Whereas the balance of trade takes only *visible* exports and imports into account, the **current account** includes the balance of trade *plus* any invisible transactions which have been undertaken between Britain and other countries during the year. In 1994, Britain had a current account deficit of £1,684 million; see Table 10.2.

1994	£(million)
Visible export	134465
Visible import	145059
Visible balance	–10594
(Balance of trade)	
Invisible export	123046
Invisible import	114136
Invisible balance	8910
Balance of current account	–1684

Table 10.2 The balance of trade and the balance of payments on current account (1994)

Selling a new car within the UK is a relatively straightforward affair: the manufacturer transports the car to the garage and the garage sells to the customer. The only taxes to pay are motor tax and VAT to the British Government.

Barriers to trade

Selling the same car in a foreign country is a different prospect entirely. The foreign government will have to be assured that the car is fit for use on the roads (and they may have different laws on lights, indicators, seat belts, exhaust emissions, etc.). They may also charge a tax before you can take the car into the country to sell it. This tax, payable at the border, is called a **tariff** (or customs duty). Such tariffs are called a **barrier to trade**, since they increase the price you will have to charge for your new car in the foreign garage and make it easier for the native manufacturers to sell their cars instead.

A. EXPORTING

Export procedures and documents

The process of exporting can be extremely complex. The goods have to be transported to the docks or airport, passed through British customs, cleared through another set of customs on arrival overseas and eventually presented to the correct customer. In addition, if the goods are dangerous or are composed of chemicals or drugs, or are perishable foodstuffs, then certificates will be needed to show that various health or safety checks have been made. For certain countries, a licence may be needed before a particular product can be sold to the customer.

Many different forms and documents might be needed:

1. A **bill of lading** contains details of the goods being shipped, their destination and which ship they will be travelling on, etc.
2. The **export invoice** is the 'bill' to the customer, requiring payment once he has received the goods.
3. The **certificate of origin** proves that the goods have come from the UK and are not being imported under false pretences from a different country whose goods might be prohibited from entry.
4. The **certificate of value** proves the goods are worth what the invoice says they are worth — usually, so that the correct duty can be levied.
5. The **HM Customs declaration** is a signed statement of what the parcels, packages or crates contain.
6. A **declaration of dangerous goods** is required by international law for certain classes of goods such as explosives or volatile chemicals.
7. A **certificate of insurance** is needed by the shipping company, or airline, or by your customer, so that they can be assured that the value of the goods is covered should an accident happen.
8. A **health certificate** is needed for drugs and similar products and for transport of animals.

9. An import licence grants permission to import your goods, and is needed for certain countries and products. In some cases, for example high technology goods, an **export licence** might be needed.

On January 1st 1993, the countries of the **European Union** introduced the *single market*. This means that, for trade within the EU the terms 'export' and 'import' have ceased to have a real meaning. For official purposes, all movements of goods within the EU are know as **despatches**.

One would think that these changes would make export and import documentation irrelevant. But, because of VAT differences between countries and because the EU members still want to collect information and statistics for imports and exports, a document called the **single administrative document (SAD)** is still used for trade in the EU. In the UK, the SAD is known as **Customs 88**.

Paying for exports

Obtaining payment for goods has always been an uncertain process. Even in the UK domestic market, a great deal of trade goes unpaid for and producers often have to engage in lengthy and expensive court cases to recover their money. When sending goods abroad, the dangers of non-payment are even worse because it is much more difficult to 'chase' non-payers through foreign courts. Consequently, extreme care about payment is essential when sending goods overseas.

There are various ways of receiving payment and some are more reliable than others:

1. **An open account** can only be used where you know the buyers very well and trust them to pay. It involves you simply sending the goods, and then sending an invoice by post (in exactly the same way as with a UK customer). The buyer is then expected to pay after, say, one month. If they do not then it can be almost impossible to make them pay and will certainly cost a great deal of money – often more than the value of the shipment!
2. **Payment with order** is the way that all exporters would like to be paid. However, few buyers will send money for a product they have not yet seen, so it is not used for any but the smallest items.
3. **Draft** is the modern name for a **bill of exchange**. There are two basic types of draft: sight drafts and term drafts.

▶ with a **sight draft** the seller draws up a document saying that the buyer agrees to pay as soon as the goods are delivered and the documents handed over.
▶ with a **term draft** the buyer does not need to pay until 30, 60 or 90 days after the documents have been handed over.

4. A **letter of credit** is more modern than a draft. Letters of credit are arranged through a buyer's bank and the seller's bank and are normally made **irrevocable**, i.e. they cannot be cancelled once signed, and so the seller is guaranteed payment.

The effect of the EU

The European Union (EU) is a group of fifteen countries:

▶ United Kingdom	▶ France	▶ Spain	▶ Greece	▶ Austria
▶ Netherlands	▶ Luxembourg	▶ Italy	▶ Germany	▶ Finland
▶ Portugal	▶ Eire	▶ Belgium	▶ Denmark	▶ Sweden

The EU began life as the European Economic Community (EEC) in the early 1950s and had very similar aims to those of the EFTA countries (see below) – that is to help increase the prosperity of Europe by making trade easier. The idea of the original six countries – West Germany, France, Italy, Belgium, The Netherlands and Luxembourg – was to try to reduce 'tariff' barriers between themselves. They also decided to introduce a wide range of measures designed to help particular industries that were experiencing problems. Foremost among these were the agriculture, coal and steel industries, which formed the basis for the very first EEC policies in the 1950s: the European Coal and Steel Community (ECSC) and the Common Agricultural Policy (CAP). Both used subsidies and special support to help those industries survive and grow.

> ❝ All imports also have to be paid for. But because foreign businesses do not want £s (they cannot spend them in their own countries) we have to sell £s to *buy* foreign currencies. ❞

As the EEC became larger and became the European Community (EC), it also adopted a wider range of policies. Today, the EU, which replaced the EC in 1993, has a very wide range of policy areas in which it takes an interest. These include CAP, structural funds and competition.

1. The **Common Agricultural Policy (CAP)** still seeks to help farmers but is gradually taking up much less of the budget of the EU.
2. The **Structural Funds** are designed to help the countries and regions of the EU to adjust to change. These funds provide money and support for the regions where work is hardest to come by. They can support such things as new roads or railways being built in depressed regions, new schools and hospitals for the same regions, and provide a variety of help and support for jobs and training. The Structural Funds are becoming an increasingly important part of the EU's budget. See chapter 6, section 2.
3. The **Competition Policy** has been established to prevent unfair practices from making goods and services too expensive for European consumers. The European Commission may, for example, prevent a car company from charging different prices in different European countries or it may take an interest in the pricing of medicines or food.

Other policies range from fisheries and energy, to those on education and transport.

Another way in which the EU looks set to affect UK trade is through the possible introduction of a **single currency** for the whole of the EU. Although many people dislike this idea (usually because they have a strong sentimental attachment to their own pound, franc, mark or peseta) the business community welcomes the possibility. A single currency – probably called the *Euro* – will relieve business of all of the risks and problems associated with having to price their goods and services in different currencies and having to keep exchanging their francs for lire or their guilders for pounds. If you doubt how useful a single currency can be see the IMF example (page 121).

The European Free Trade Association (EFTA)

EFTA's main member, when it was set up in 1959, was the UK. The object of EFTA was to reduce tariffs to zero between the member countries, so that trade could increase. The members were: UK, Portugal, Switzerland, Austria, Sweden, Norway, Denmark, Ireland and (from 1970) Liechtenstein. Since several of these have joined the EU only Iceland, Norway, Switzerland and Liechtenstein remain as members.

B. IMPORTING

Barriers to trade

There are a number of ways in which countries seek to discourage imports.

1. **Tariffs** make trade between countries more difficult. Tariffs are taxes on goods coming into the country.
2. **Quotas** are a way of preventing too many imports from coming into any country. A quota on a product simply means that only a certain number can be imported in that year. In recent years, many EU countries have put quotas on the number of Japanese cars allowed to be imported, so as to protect their own car industries against the Japanese imports.
3. **Subsidies** are amounts of money given by governments to certain industries to help them to stay in business or to protect jobs. Because they make it easier for those companies to stay in business, the subsidies also make it easier for them to compete against imported products. In the last few years, American steel firms have complained that they find it difficult to export steel to Europe because of the subsidies given by European governments to their own steel firms.

Other barriers to trade

Firms which export have to face a great many additional barriers such as:

▶ the fact that they are usually exporting to a country with a different language and currency;
▶ possible exchange controls – limit on the amount of money which a firm can take out as profits;

> Note that, until 1987, it was difficult to export beer to Germany. The West German government had a very strict law which said that no beer sold in that country could contain any artificial additives or chemicals.

▶ import regulations – involving lots of complex forms;
▶ different technical standards for certain goods in foreign countries.

A good example of how standards can become barriers to trade occurred between Britain and France in the early 1980s. The French would not allow British lamb to be sold in France because, they argued, it had too many preservatives in it and did not, therefore, meet the French health regulations. Britain, on the other hand, refused to allow French UHT milk into the country on the grounds that it was not sterilised to a sufficiently high standard. More recently Germany health regulations have been used to ban the import of British beef to Germany.

Summary of barriers to trade:

▶ Tariffs
▶ Quotas
▶ Subsidies
▶ Language
▶ Exchange controls
▶ Money/currency
▶ Import regulations
▶ Standards

5 ORGANISATIONS IN INTERNATIONAL TRADE

There are a great many organisations involved in international trade today. Some come under the control of the **United Nations** (**UN**) in New York, while others have been set up by groups of countries. Among the organisations which come under the UN are:

▶ IMF (International Monetary Fund)
▶ UNCTAD (United Nations Conference on Trade and Development)
▶ GATT (General Agreement on Tariffs and Trade)

A. INTERNATIONAL MONETARY FUND (IMF)

The IMF was set up in 1947 to try to ensure that the world's currencies were kept at reasonably stable rates against each other. The IMF had a system of what were called **fixed exchange rates** so that, no matter how long the duration of a contract, a firm anywhere in the world would know exactly how much they would receive for selling their product. Unfortunately, this system broke down in the early 1970s and since then we have had a system of **floating exchange rates**. This means that the value of any currency can change at any time in terms of another currency.

IMF Example

If you sell a car to an American, he may well want to see the car when it arrives in the US before actually paying for it. You want £5,000 for the car, and the current exchange rate is $2=£1. A simple calculation tells you, therefore that you will have to charge the American $10,000 (5,000 x 2=10,000), and that is the agreed price. You then put the car on a ship and wait for it to arrive in the US. Two months later, the car arrives, and is examined by the American, who is very satisfied with it. He immediately sends you a cheque for $10,000.

Unfortunately, the exchange rate has changed during the period, and is now $2.50=£1. Another simple calculation, $10,000 ÷ 2.50 reveals that you will only receive £4,000 for the car, even though the American paid the full $10,000 as agreed. If you multiply this situation many times then you can see why business people worry about the way in which the exchange rate is moving.

Try the same example, but this time assume that the £/$ exchange rate weakens to $1.75=£1. How much will you then receive for your car?

B. THE UNITED NATIONS CONFERENCE ON TRADE AND DEVELOPMENT (UNCTAD)

Set up in the mid-1960s, UNCTAD has interests in many areas regarding international trade:

▶ **transport by sea** and the charges which shipping companies levy;
▶ the activities of **multinational companies** – those giant companies which have factories making products in many different countries, e.g. Ford, General Motors, IBM, British Petroleum;

▶ how **barriers to trade** work and, especially, how they work to the disadvantage of the poorer countries of the world;

▶ setting up systems to **protect the prices** of certain commodities (e.g. copper, tin, tea, sugar) which are particularly important to the economies of the world's poorer countries.

C. THE GENERAL AGREEMENT ON TARIFFS AND TRADE (GATT)

GATT was established after World War II with the object of reducing the average levels of tariffs on manufactured goods throughout the world. In this, it has been very successful. In 1945, it was not unusual to find tariffs of 80%, 100% or even 150% on certain types of goods. Today, the average level of tariffs on manufactured goods is just 7%. GATT operates through a series of discussions between member countries. These discussions can take many years to arrive at a conclusion and they are called 'rounds of negotiations'. The most recent 'rounds' were the 'Kennedy Round' (1961–63), the 'Tokyo Round' (1972–75), and the 'Uruguay Round' (1986–94).

The last mentioned round of negotiations was the most difficult in GATT history but resulted in agreement in 1994 to establish a new permanent body to replace GATT, called the **World Trade Organisation (WTO)**.

6 ▷ MARKETING ABROAD

British firms which decide to try to sell their products abroad can seek a great deal of help from various institutions:

▶ Overseas Trade Services
▶ trade organisations
▶ banks
▶ Export Credit Guarantee Department (ECGD)
▶ chambers of commerce
▶ commercial firms.

A. OVERSEAS TRADE SERVICES (OTS)

OTS is a Government agency whose main aim is to help British companies to sell their products and services overseas. OTS can give advice on all of the things which business people might be concerned about:

▶ What regulations apply in the countries they are exporting to?
▶ Who can they use to help market their product in that country (e.g. an agent or distributor)?
▶ How can they try to make sure that their overseas customer pays their bill?
▶ How might they guard against losing money because of currency movements?

OTS also offers British companies the chance to go on trade missions to other countries to see whether there is a market for their products.

B. TRADE ORGANISATIONS

Almost every type of business has its trade association, which gives its members help and advice on exporting matters.

C. BANKS

Banks will, of course, help exporters with loans to tide them over while they are waiting for payment for exported goods, but they also do much more. Many banks will give advice to small exporters about how they should set about the task of exporting. Bank managers will arrange finance and can suggest other experts who might be able to help.

D. THE EXPORT CREDITS GUARANTEE DEPARTMENT (ECGD)

The ECGD is an organisation whose job is to help British firms bear the risks of exporting. Just as with sales within the UK, bad debts might arise from overseas customers not paying for their goods. The ECGD offers a special 'insurance' scheme, known as the Export Credit Guarantee Scheme whereby, in return for a premium, the

Government will pay most of any bad debts which occur, subject to approval of the customer's status and any particular risks associated with certain countries.

E. CHAMBERS OF COMMERCE

Local Chambers of Commerce now offer a wide range of export and trade-related services to UK companies ranging from help with documentation to courses on Export Marketing Research offered by the Association of British Chambers of Commerce.

F. OTHER TRADE ASSISTANCE

In recent years, commercial firms have also set up schemes by which they help exporters; they now offer a wide range of services including:

► lending money to the exporter to cover the period while they are waiting to be paid
► helping to collect payment from the customer
► helping with the necessary sales documentation and record-keeping
► checking on customers' credit ratings, i.e. whether they will be able to pay their bills
► arranging credit insurance similar to that offered by the ECGD.

EXAMINATION QUESTIONS

QUESTION 1

Name a government organisation which offers insurance against many of the risks involved in exporting.

_____
_____
_____
_____
(ULEAC)

QUESTION 2

What is meant by

(i) visible trade?   (1 mark)
(ii) invisible trade?   (1 mark)

(NICCEA)

QUESTION 3

The information given is the trading figures for Rurilanda in 1995.

	£m
Visible exports	55,000
Invisible exports	50,000
Visible imports	70,000
Invisible imports	30,000

(a) Using the figures calculate
   (i) the Balance of Trade   (2 marks)
   (ii) the Balance of Payments on Current Account.   (2 marks)
(b) Name three items of invisible trade. (1 line provided)   (3 marks)
(c) Outline three ways in which British businesses benefit from international trade.
   (3 lines provided)   (6 marks)
(d) Why might the UK government urge the UK consumers to 'buy British'?
   (2 lines provided)   (2 marks)

TUTOR'S ANSWER TO Q.3

(a) (i) visible exports – visible imports = balance of trade
£55,000m – £70,000m = – £15,000m
(ii) balance of trade – invisible exports – invisible imports = balance of payments on current account
– £15,000m + £50,000m – £30,000m = £5,000m
(b) Insurance, banking and tourism.
(c) (i) The British business may obtain a number of its raw material requirements from abroad (visible imports).
(ii) The British business may sell a large proportion of its finished products abroad (visible exports).
(iii) The British business may wish to hire specialist services from abroad. One way in which it could achieve this is by a consultancy arrangement with a foreign firm (invisible import).
(d) The UK government may urge the UK consumer to 'buy British' because it wants to protect jobs in UK industries and improve the balance of payments on current account.

STUDENT'S ANSWER TO Q.3

'Trading figures for Rurilanda.'

(a) i) Balance of trade

Imports less Exports

70,000 – 55,000 = £15,000(m)

> **Imports and exports the wrong way round! Answer should be – £15,000(m).**

ii) Balance of payments on Current Account.

Visible Imports + Invisible Imports =

70,000

30,000

£100,000 (m)

> **Again, the wrong way round. The answer should be +£5,000(m). The usual method is to take the Balance of Trade and add that to the Invisible Balance.**

less

Visible Exports + Invisible exports =

55,000

50,000

£105,000 (m)

= –£5,000 (m) deficit

 Good. Should strictly say British Government expenditure on armed forces and embassies *overseas.*

(b) Three items of invisible trade are: the British Governments' expenditure on armed forces; the British Governments' expenditure on embassies; and British Tourists' expenditure overseas.

(c) Three ways in which British businesses benefit from International trade: what raw materials the UK is lacking from can be obtained from other countries – this is very important for home businesses; foodstuffs which Britain cannot supply must be imported e.g. cereals, sugar, tea, coffee. UK producers cannot meet the total home demand, so they have to import many finished goods to satisfy the demand.

Good, though language a bit clumsy.

(d) The UK Government may urge UK consumers to 'buy British' to boost the production of home companies and so reduce unemployment. Also to reduce the threat of unfair competition from other countries whose labour is very cheap and can steal our market with their cheaper products.

A good answer.

COURSEWORK

ASSIGNMENT – ADVERTISING TOURISM

Tourism is a growing contribution to Britain's trade and, wherever you live, you will undoubtedly be close to a tourist area.

► Obtain a copy of the local tourist guide book. Every area in the British Isles produces a booklet which tells visitors what attractions there are in the region.
► Make a list of the attractions which you think would be of most interest to American tourists in your region and make up an advertisement which might be placed in an American travel magazine and which would attract them to your area.
► What sort of businesses benefit from tourism in your region and why?
► Are there any parts of the region which you think tourists would *not* want to see? Is there any way that these 'unattractive' areas could be made more interesting and attractive?
► Make a list, with explanations, of the ways you would improve your region for tourists.

A Review Sheet for this chapter will be found on pp. 243-4.

CHAPTER

11

BUSINESS ACCOUNTS

CASH FLOW

BOOKKEEPING

DOUBLE-ENTRY

THE TRIAL BALANCE

PROFIT

THE BALANCE SHEET

ANALYSIS OF ACCOUNTS: BUSINESS RATIOS

GETTING STARTED

If you were to start your own business, you would probably begin in a relatively simple fashion; there would be products or services to make or provide, you would sell these to the public, and, with luck, there would be profits.

Let us imagine that Julie decides to start up in the clothing trade under the name of Julie's Fashions. She has an assistant (Sally) who is good at selling, while Julie is good at designing and making clothes. Julie's first task will be to design the clothes, after which she will make up a set for demonstration and try to sell these and further copies. The very first thing which needs to be done is to try to see what the demands of the business will be for cash.

ESSENTIAL PRINCIPLES

1 > CASH FLOW

All firms need to make payments for wages, rent, goods purchased, electricity, etc., but these payments are not all going to be made at the same rate throughout the year. Julie's first task therefore, is to calculate what payments will have to be made month by month and what cash will be coming in during these same months. The chart she might use would be similar to Table 11.1.

(£) MONTH	JAN	FEB	MAR	APR	MAY	JUN
Bank balance on 1st of month	0	3500	3400	2900	(600)	250
Sales	0	5000	6000	5000	8000	9000
Owner's capital	10000	–	–	–	–	–
Total receipts (A)	10000	8500	9400	7900	7400	9250
Outgoings:						
Purchases	5000	3000	5000	6000	4000	3000
Wages	1000	1000	1000	2000	2000	2000
Rent	500	500	500	500	500	500
Electricity	–	600	–	–	650	–
Total Payments (B)	6500	5100	6500	8500	7150	5500
Bank at month end (A–B)	3500	3400	2900	(600)	250	3750
( ) = overdrawn						

Table 11.1 Cash flow forecast

Table 11.1 shows a **cash flow forecast** for a business which has begun with £10,000 of capital from its owner. The owner has calculated how much cash is likely to come in over the first six months, from his **capital** plus cash from **sales**. It represents an estimate of what the firm will be 'earning' on a month by month basis. Beneath these are all the **outgoings** of the firm, including wages, purchases of materials, and electricity.

The chart looks complicated, but it is a very useful way of planning what the cash needs of a business will be. For example, the owner now knows that an overdraft of £600 will be needed in April.

2 > BOOKKEEPING

In the case of Julie's Fashions, we are assuming that Julie has not calculated her cash flow requirements but has merely begun business. This is a very common way for businesses to start, but it is inadvisable. Proper planning at the start can help to avoid many problems. Indeed, if the business is going to need to borrow money from the bank, the bank manager will insist on seeing a full cash-flow forecast before he or she will consider lending any money.

Assuming that Julie's Fashions has begun business, the minimum that Julie has to do is keep some financial records. Keeping accounts does not come easily to many business people, and few have had any formal training.

At the end of the first month of trading, let us assume that Julie's Fashions has had the following transactions:

DAY	DETAILS OF TRANSACTION	AMOUNT (£)
1	From Julie to start business	1000
2	Bought material	150
5	Bought new sewing machine	360
6	Paid Sally's wages	30
9	Sale for cash to 'Young Fashions'	400
11	Bought materials	600
17	Julie took for herself	100
20	Sale for cash to 'Jim's Market Stall'	300
23	Paid rent and electricity for new workroom and office	150
25	Sold on credit to 'Stephanie's Boutique'	50
28	Sold on credit to 'Maison Roger'	1000

Table 11.2

At the end of the month, Julie is likely to wonder whether her business has made a profit, and also whether she is running the business efficiently. To answer such questions, she needs to keep 'books'; it is not enough simply to keep lists of amounts spent and amounts received.

3 > DOUBLE-ENTRY

Bookkeeping methods have remained largely unchanged for hundreds of years, but nowadays, computers are likely to be used by many businesses to speed up the process. Double-entry bookkeeping sounds very difficult but it simply means that two separate records are made for each transaction. This sounds like double the work for accountants, but in fact it makes very good sense.

Every transaction of a firm has two effects; for example, when Julie bought the sewing machine, *two* things happened:

1. Julie had to take £360 out of the business's cash
2. she was able to bring in a new sewing machine as an **asset** for the business.

To record this in the books, she needs two entries:

1. taking £360 out of the Bank Account
2. adding a machine worth £360 to the Machinery Account.

We can take some of the other transactions and see how the double-entry works. For example, the **cash sale** of clothes to Young Fashions for £400 can be split into:

1. an addition to the Bank account of £400
2. an entry in the Sales account to show that £400 of goods (at selling prices) have left the business.

A second example could be when Stephanie's Boutiques bought some clothes on **credit**. This means that Julie has sold the goods but has not yet received the cash for them. The book entries would be:

1. £50 in the Sales account, this is shown on the *credit* side (right-hand side) of the account
2. an entry in a debtors account for Stephanie's Boutiques, entered on the *debit* side (left-hand side), showing the amount of money which Julie is owed by Stephanie's Boutiques.

No money has yet been received, so we cannot make an entry in the Bank account!

4 > THE TRIAL BALANCE

Before we are able to say whether the business made a profit or loss, a check must be made that all the bookkeeping entries are correct. We can check the arithmetic is correct by producing a **trial balance**, which is simply a list of all the accounts, showing whether they have a debit balance or a credit balance. Because all the transactions are entered in two accounts (a debit entry matched by a credit entry), the total of all the debits should equal all the credits. For Julie's Fashions, the trial balance at the end of the first month would look like this:

 Notice that the amount in the Bank Account of Julie's Fashions is a debit total not a credit one.

	DEBIT £	CREDIT £
Bank Account	310	
Capital Account		1000
Debtor (Stephanie's Boutique)	50	
Debtor (Maison Roger)	1000	
Drawings (i.e. cash for Julie)	100	
Materials purchased	750	
Machinery	360	
Wages	30	
Rent and electricity	150	
Sales		1750
	2750	2750

Table 11.3 Trial balance

As both totals are equal, we can be sure that the arithmetic is correct. Unfortunately, it is not a perfect check, as certain types of error (e.g. wages might be entered on both sides incorrectly as £300 instead of £30) will not be disclosed.

| **5** > | **PROFIT** |

One of the most important questions that business people will ask is: 'Am I making a profit?' **Profit** can mean various things:

▶ the reward to the owner for the risks taken in setting up and running the business
▶ the **surplus** which provides the money for future investment in the business or in other projects
▶ the difference between **income** and **expenses**.

Profit is calculated by setting out whatever sales have been made by the business (regardless of whether the customers have all paid the money for those sales), and taking away from this total the amount of the expenses of the business.

Depreciation

One expense is **depreciation**, which is the loss in value of the **fixed assets** (see p. 130) such as cars, computers, sewing machines, caused by these assets being used in the business. In Julie's Fashions, we could estimate that her sewing machine will last three years, and so the depreciation to be shown as an expense in her first month of trading will be:

$$£360 \div 36 \text{ months} = £10 \text{ per month}$$

Trading and Profit and Loss Account

To show the profit for the first month, we can draw up a simple **trading and profit and loss account**, as shown in Table 11.4.

JULIE'S FASHIONS TRADING AND PROFIT AND LOSS ACCOUNT FOR MONTH 1		
	£	£
Total sales (including those on credit)		1750
Less materials used for making the dresses		750
GROSS PROFIT		1000
Less expenses		
Wages	30	
Rent and electricity	150	
Depreciation of sewing machines	10	
		190
NET PROFIT		810

Table 11.4

Gross profit is calculated as the difference between the sales revenue and the cost of the products sold, *before* overheads such as rent have been deducted. **Net** profit is the gross profit less all the overheads.

Accounting concepts

In our simple example, we have followed a number of **accounting concepts**, including depreciation, accrual and realisation. The reason for depreciation has already been explained, but the reasons for the other two are as follows;

The accrual concept

The **accrual concept** simply means that the expense of the period should be matched with the period in which the relevant income occurs, regardless of when money is actually paid or received. For example, if Julie still had £300 of materials in stock at the end of the month, the 'materials used' total would have been only £450, and the gross profit increases to £1,300 as shown in Table 11.5.

	£	£
Total sales (including those on credit)		1750
Less materials used for making the dresses	750	
Less closing stock	300	450
GROSS PROFIT		1300
Less (total) expenses		190
NET PROFIT		1110

Table 11.5

The realisation concept

The **realisation concept** stops a business person 'counting chickens before they are hatched'. For example, if the boss of 'Maison Roger' had only said that he *might* make an order worth £1,000, then Julie would not have been able to include this in her sales total. It is only when the customer has committed himself to the order (e.g. by accepting the goods), that the sale becomes real.

Having found out what the profit has been in the first month of trading, it is now necessary to construct a balance sheet to show all **assets** and **liabilities** of the business on the last day of the month. For Julie's Fashions, the balance sheet is as shown in Table 11.6.

JULIE'S FASHIONS BALANCE SHEET AS AT END OF MONTH 1	£	£
FIXED ASSETS: Sewing machine at cost	360	
Less depreciation	10	350
CURRENT ASSETS: Stock and work-in-progress	–	
Debtors (Stephanie's and Roger)	1050	
Cash at Bank	310	
	1360	
Less CURRENT LIABILITIES: Creditors		
(amounts owing to suppliers)	–	1360
TOTAL ASSETS LESS LIABILITIES		1710
Represented by:		
Julie's Capital Account:		
Cash introduced by Julie	1000	
Add net profit	810	
	1810	
Less Julie's drawings	100	
TOTAL CAPITAL EMPLOYED		1710

Table 11.6

The meanings of the various headings in the balance sheet are now explained:

A. FIXED ASSETS

These are assets which the firm buys, which are of relatively high value and are going to be used for earning profits for several years. In most cases, they are subject to **depreciation**.

B. CURRENT ASSETS

These are the things which belong to the business, just like fixed assets, but they are not as permanent. They include stock, work-in-progress (i.e. partly finished goods), debtors (such as the money owed by Stephanie) and cash.

C. CURRENT LIABILITIES

These are amounts which the business owes to suppliers. Although Julie did not owe anything at the end of the month, if for example she had not yet paid the rent and electricity bill of £150, then this would have appeared under this heading. There would have been no change to profit, but the Cash at Bank would have been £150 greater. The middle section of the balance sheet would then be as shown in Table 11.7.

The difference between the current assets and current liabilities (£1,360) is known as the company's **working capital**.

Note that some businesses also have long-term liabilities, such as loans from banks which are repayable over a number of years.

	£	£
CURRENT ASSETS: Stock and work-in-progress	–	
Debtors (Stephanie's and Roger)	1050	
Cash at Bank	460	
	1510	
Less CURRENT LIABILITIES: Creditors		
(amounts owing to suppliers)	150	1360

Table 11.7

D. CAPITAL

This is the amount which the owner is owed by the business as a result of the money lent to the business by the owner and the profits which the business makes. In Julie's balance sheet, the capital owed to her is £1,710. Capital is always the same total as the assets less liabilities of the business.

In a small business like Julie's Fashions, there will be relatively few people who are interested in the accounts. These include Julie herself, her bank manager and the taxman. For larger businesses, particularly PLCs, there are many more interested parties: employees, trade unions, managers, shareholders and creditors. To tell them how the business is performing, **business ratios** might well be used to analyse the figures in three main areas:

1. profitability – how profitable the business is
2. liquidity – whether it has enough money to stay in business
3. asset usage – how efficiently it is being run.

A. PROFITABILITY

There are three profitability ratios:

1. gross profit margin
2. net profit margin
3. return on capital employed.

Gross profit margin shows the overall gross profit percentage on sales.

$$\frac{\text{gross profit}}{\text{sales}} \times \frac{100}{1}$$

For example, a company which makes £1,000 gross profit on sales of £10,000 has a gross profit margin of 10%.
Net profit margin shows the net profit as a percentage of sales.

$$\frac{\text{net profit}}{\text{sales}} \times \frac{100}{1}$$

Return on capital employed shows how profitable the business is in relation to the amount of money 'tied up' in the business.

$$\frac{\text{net profit}}{\text{capital employed}} \times \frac{100}{1}$$

B. LIQUIDITY RATIOS

There are two liquidity ratios.

1. working capital ratio, or current ratio
2. acid test ratio.

The **working capital ratio** or **current ratio** is:

current assets: current liabilities

This shows the proportion by which the current assets exceed the current liabilities. A variation on this is the **acid test ratio**:

current assets – stock: current liabilities

This shows how likely the business is to survive a crisis where most of the current liabilities have to be repaid quickly.

C. PERFORMANCE RATIOS

There are two performance ratios:

1. stock turnover
2. debtor turnover

Stock turnover is calculated as:

$$\frac{\text{turnover} \text{ (i.e. total sales)}}{\text{stock}}$$

This is not a ratio as such, but the number of times on average that the stock is sold each year. In theory, if the rate at which stock turns over can be increased, then the profit made by the business will increase.

Debtor turnover is calculated as:

$$\frac{\text{turnover}}{\text{debtors}} \times 12$$

This shows how many months the firm takes to collect its debts from those who owe it money.

EXAMINATION QUESTIONS

QUESTION 1

Study the balance sheet of XYZ Ltd and answer the questions printed below.

BALANCE SHEET as at 31 December 1995				
	£			£
Authorised Capital				
30,000 £1 Ordinary Shares	30000	Premises		22000
		Machinery		12000
Issued Capital		Stock		8000
25,000 £1 Ordinary Shares	25000	Debtors		5000
Reserves	8000	Cash		1000
Creditors	4000			
Overdraft	7000			
10% debentures	4000			
	48000			48000

Table 11.8

(a) Give one example of a fixed asset owned by XYZ.   (1 mark)
(b) Give one example of a current liability owed by the company.   (1 mark)
(c) How much does the company pay each half year to debenture holders? (1 mark)
(d) Calculate the working capital of XYZ   (2 marks)
(e) What indicators are there that XYZ is a private company?
     (4 lines for answer)   (2 marks)
(f) Why do you think that XYZ Ltd may wish to remain a private company?
     (6 lines for answer).   (3 marks)

(ULEAC)

QUESTION 2

The balance sheet of a business shows the value of the _____ (items owned) and the extent of the _____ (items owed).

(ULEAC)

QUESTION 3

Study the final accounts of AZTEC Ltd., a private company, and answer the questions which follow.

TRADING AND PROFIT AND LOSS ACCOUNT FOR THE YEAR ENDED 31 DECEMBER 1993			
	£		£
Stock at 1 January 1993	80000	Sales	500000
Purchases	320000		
	400000		
Stock at 31 December 1993	100000		
Cost of sales	300000		
Gross profit c/d	200000		
	500000		500000
Expenses	75000	Gross profit b/d	200000
Net profit	125000		
	200000		200000

Table 11.9

BALANCE SHEET AS AT 31 DECEMBER 1993			
	£	£	£
Ordinary share capital	1000000	Fixed assets	1150000
Reserves	200000	Current assets:	
		Stock	100000
Long-term loan	50000		
		Trade Debtors	120000
Current liabilities:		Bank	30000
Trade creditors	150000		250000
	1400000		1400000

Table 11.10

(a) Why are debtors and creditors of AZTEC Ltd shown in its Balance Sheet?
     (3 lines for answer)   (2 marks)

(b) (i)   AZTEC Ltd allows cash and trade discounts to its customers. Explain the
          difference between cash discount and trade discount.
          (6 lines for answer)   (4 marks)

     (ii) State TWO advantages to AZTEC Ltd of allowing cash discounts to its
          customers. (4 lines for answer)   (2 marks)

(c) (i)   Calculate AZTEC's 'acid test' ratio as at 31 December 1993.
          (4 lines for answer)   (4 marks)

     (ii) Explain the usefulness of this ratio in assessing a company's financial position
          (6 lines for answer)   (4 marks)

(d) For EACH of the following items place a tick in the appropriate box below to show
     whether it is either revenue expenditure or capital expenditure.

1. Office Manager's salary
2. Purchase of new delivery van
3. Maintenance repairs to factory roof
4. Legal fees paid in connection with factory extension   (4 marks)

	REVENUE	CAPITAL
1.		
2.		
3.		
4.		

(e) (i)   Explain what is meant by the Gross Profit AND Net Profit of a business.
          (8 lines for answer)   (4 marks)
    (ii) In 1992, AZTEC's trading results were:

	£
Sales	400 000
Cost of Sales	200 000
Expenses	120 000

Stock in hand at 1 January 1992 was £120 000.
Calculate for 1992 and 1993 the company's
1. Gross Profit as % of sales

2. Net Profit as % of sales

	1992	1993
1.		1.
2.		2.

(4 marks)

(iii) Using all of the information available, explain whether AZTEC Ltd.
      was more successful in 1993 than in 1992. (14 lines for answer)   (9 marks)
                                                                    (MEG 1994)
                                                           (ACCOUNTING OPTION)

TUTOR'S ANSWER TO Q.1

(a) Premises (or machinery)
(b) Creditors (or overdrafts)
(c) The company pays each half year to the debenture holders an amount of £200.
     This is obtained by taking 10% of £4000 which is £400 and halving this to take
     account of it being paid half yearly, i.e. the £200.
(d) The working capital of XYZ is £3000. This is obtained by taking the current assets
     minus the current liabilities.

CURRENT ASSETS	£	CURRENT LIABILITIES	£
Stock	8000	Creditors	4000
Debtors	5000	Overdraft	7000
Cash	1000		
	14000		11000

Table 11.11

So the working capital is £14,000 - 11,000 = £3,000.

(e) The indications that XYZ is a private company are the word 'limited' in the title of
     the company, i.e. XYZ Ltd, and the fact that the company has less than the £50,000
     issued capital necessary to become a PLC.
(f) XYZ Ltd may wish to remain a private company because as such it will be able to
     keep more control over its own affairs. It may be a family business which, if it went
     public, would be accountable to a greater number of shareholders.

COURSEWORK

**ASSIGNMENT 1
ANALYSIS OF
COMPANY ACCOUNTS**

For this project you need to write to at least three large PLCs in the same business, for example, all food companies, or all oil companies. Ask them if they could send you a copy of their latest Annual Report and Accounts. When you receive them, read through them carefully. Do not worry if you do not understand all the figures and the technical terms, but just see what the companies are doing, how they view the future, and how successful they are.

The Chairman's Report is perhaps the most interesting part of the document, as it gives a review of what has happened and a forecast of future developments. You could also apply some of the *ratios* which were explained in the text.

You should write a report to a potential investor in these companies which explains the companies' financial performance, the problems they have faced and the things which have affected their businesses. Advise whether the investment should be made.

**ASSIGNMENT 2
LOCAL ACCOUNTING
SYSTEM**

Most businesses are too small to employ their own accountant. Instead they use independent firms of accountants.

Look through the *Yellow Pages* for your area, and choose four accountancy firms. Find out what services they offer and an idea of the costs. Do they produce any informative brochures for their clients? Do they have any links with local banks or solicitors?

Write a report for the owner of a new business explaining how a firm of accountants might be able to help, the range of services available, and give an idea of the likely costs involved.

A Review Sheet for this chapter will be found on pp. 245–6.

BUSINESS DOCUMENTS

GETTING STARTED

All businesses must have formal documents. They need letterheadings – headed notepaper – to write to their customers, suppliers and staff. They also need lots of other documents to carry on business efficiently, so as to **record** all important events and transactions, and to provide **proof** if needed, perhaps to settle a legal dispute.

Documents are very important, and need to be kept safely. Some of the largest companies use **computers** to issue and store these documents; others use the older system of typing the documents, but then have them all **microfilmed** for easier storage.

NON-FINANCIAL DOCUMENTS

TRANSACTION DOCUMENTS

ESSENTIAL PRINCIPLES

There are two main types of document.
Non-financial documents include:

▶ Letterheads   ▶ Compliment slips   ▶ Business cards

Transaction documents, which record transactions of money, goods and services, include:

▶ Letters of Enquiry   ▶ Quotations   ▶ Order forms
▶ Invoices   ▶ Pro-forma invoices   ▶ Advice notes
▶ Delivery notes   ▶ Consignment notes   ▶ Credit notes
▶ Debit notes   ▶ Statements

We now look at all these documents in some detail.

The essential **non-financial documents** required by all businesses are letterheads, compliment slips and business cards.

A. LETTERHEADS

Letterheads are printed with the firm's name, address, telephone, e-mail and fax numbers, plus any legal information required for a limited company, such as the registered number, registered office and directors' names. People often gain their first impression of a business from the letterheading, so it is important that it should be well designed and printed.

B. COMPLIMENT SLIPS

These are small slips of paper, with the company's name and address and the words 'with compliments' on them. They are usually sent with brochures, price lists, and samples, so that the recipient knows which company sent them. They are also cheaper than using a full letterhead.

C. BUSINESS CARDS

These are small cards carried by senior personnel to give to business contacts. They contain their name, position, business name and address and telephone number.

There are many different transaction documents, used to record financial transactions, movement of goods and so on.

A. LETTER OF ENQUIRY

A **letter of enquiry** is a detailed letter, sent to a company, which asks for information on one or more of their products. It usually asks for **price** and **delivery** details and gives full information – called a **specification** – of what the buyer requires.

B. QUOTATION

In return, the seller will send a **quotation**. This sets out exactly what the **terms of sale** will be (including any **discounts** available), how much delivery and postage might cost, and the estimated completion or **delivery time**.

C. ORDER FORM

If customers wish to order goods after receiving the quotation (or after seeing the goods in a catalogue or price list), they will use an **order form**. It is often pre-numbered for ease of reference and contains details such as date, name and address of both supplier and customer, exact details of the goods being ordered and the agreed price and delivery date, if relevant. It will be signed by one of the buying firm's senior officials, usually one of their purchasing officers. If an order is made by telephone, it is usually confirmed in writing on an official order form immediately afterwards.

D. INVOICE

The **invoice** is the bill for the goods or services supplied. It is usually numbered and gives details of:

▶ the names and addresses of buyer and seller
▶ an order number, if any, and the date of the order
▶ details of the goods and services supplied
▶ cost of the goods and VAT details.

Details of any discounts will be noted at the foot of the invoice (e.g. $2\frac{1}{2}$% for payment within one month), together with the letters 'E & O.E.', which stands for 'errors and omissions excepted'. This protects the seller against any mistakes on the invoice and allows them to be corrected at a later date: see debit and credit notes below.

E. PRO-FORMA INVOICE

Although invoices are used in most cases to allow customers to pay after they have received the goods or services, on some occasions, the seller might not be prepared to use this system, particularly if the customer is new or the goods are very expensive. In such cases, a **pro-forma invoice** is used, which is sent and must be settled *before* the goods are despatched.

F. ADVICE NOTE

An **advice note** is a form sent either immediately before the goods are despatched, or sent with the goods. It gives details of the goods being sent, enabling the customer to check that the correct items have been delivered.

G. DELIVERY NOTE

The **delivery note** is sent with the goods. It is signed by the customer, and brought back by the delivery driver as proof that the customer has received the goods. Because this is a form of **receipt**, the person signing the delivery note must be authorised by the customer to do so.

H. CONSIGNMENT NOTE

If the firm is not using its own transport to deliver the goods, it will send them with a **consignment note** to the haulage firm which has been hired to make the delivery. It asks the haulage firm to accept the goods and gives them instructions as to where it should be delivered.

I. DEBIT AND CREDIT NOTES

Once an invoice has been drawn up it must not be changed. Crossing out and writing over invoices can cause confusion in the accounts department. If errors occur on the invoice, or if the customer cancels part of the order before delivery, the amendment is made by using either a debit note, or a credit note.

Debit Notes

Debit notes add amounts to invoices. For example, if the original invoice charged the customer £50 instead of £500, then a debit note will be made out for £450.

Credit Notes

Credit notes deduct amounts from invoices. For example, if the invoice charged the customer £340 when the correct total was £300, a credit note for £40 will be issued. Credit notes are also issued if goods are returned after delivery (if they are unsuitable or faulty for instance).

J. STATEMENT

A **statement** is a copy of the customer's ledger account in the seller's ledger, usually covering a period of one month. It shows the opening balance at the start of the month, the invoices sent to the customer, and any cheques received. The final balance will be the amount owed at the end of the month and which is due for payment.

EXAMINATION QUESTIONS

QUESTION 1

A document used to notify the buyer of the amount due is an

_____

(ULEAC)

QUESTION 2

HIT & MISS SPORT LTD				
Ellis Road Newbridge Carsmere CA2 2DF		Tele: 01227 2543 Invoice No: 2883 VAT Reg No: 232–2254–62 Date: 11 December 1995		
Godfrey Sportswear High Street, Broxford BR1 1PT			Order No: 1237.	
Quantity	**Description & Product Code**	**Price per unit £**	**Total £**	
100	Tennis racquets XJ5	30.00	3,000.00	
50	Rugby ball SPS7	10.00	500.00	
10	Snooker cues SQ15	15.00	150.00	
200	Squash balls SB20	1.50	300.00	
20	Footballs FB10	25.00	500.00	
	Discount 10%		4,450.00 445.00	
	+ VAT 17.5%		4,005.00 700.87	
		TOTAL DUE	4,705.87	
Terms: 2½% 14 days. **E&OE.**				

(a) What is meant by an invoice? (2 lines provided)   (2 marks)
(b) Why should Hit and Miss Sport Ltd offer Godfrey Sportswear a 10% discount?
     (2 lines provided)   (2 marks)
(c) On an invoice, 'Terms' and 'E & O.E.' will normally be found. What do these
     signify? (4 lines provided)   (4 marks)
(d) What do you view to be the advantages of using an invoice?
     (3 lines provided)   (2 marks)

TUTOR'S ANSWER TO Q.2

(a) An invoice is a bill sent by the supplier, here Hit & Miss Sport Ltd, to the customer, here Godfrey Sportswear. The invoice gives details of the goods, the price per unit, the total cost including VAT and the discount offered (if any).

(b) Godfrey Sportswear may purchase a large amount of its stock from Hit & Miss Sport Ltd and, because it buys in bulk, be allowed a discount of 10%. It is, perhaps, easier for Hit & Miss Sport Ltd to process bulk orders and so it is worth giving a discount for such orders.

(c) 'Terms': This signifies that if the account is settled within a particular period of time then the customer will be allowed a discount. In the above invoice the period in which Godfrey Sportswear has to pay, to obtain the discount of $2\frac{1}{2}$%, is 14 days. The reason for this is to encourage prompt payment.

'E & O.E.' means 'errors and omissions excepted' and protects the supplier against any errors or omissions on the invoice.

(d) The advantages of using an invoice are that it acts as a record or proof for the buyer and seller. It helps to avoid confusion, as it makes both parties fully aware of their dealings with each other.

A Review Sheet for this chapter will be found on p. 247.

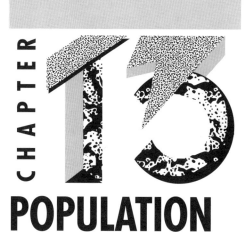

CHAPTER 13

POPULATION

GETTING STARTED

Population may seem a strange subject for a business studies book but it is less strange when you realise how vital people are to business: they are one of its most important *factors of production* – without people most goods could not be made; they are also the *customers* for all types of firms. Numbers and types of people, their income and wealth are, therefore, very important to business.

Almost all firms are interested in how many people there are in their market area, what age or sex they are, how much money they have, how much free time they have, how many children they might have, and so on. Each of these pieces of information can help a company to plan how many of its goods it is going to be able to sell.

For example, a firm producing disposable nappies may decide to build a new factory. How large should the new factory be and how many nappies should it produce a year? The answers are going to depend on approximately how many babies are going to be born in the next few years and how many of those babies will be using disposable nappies.

These may sound like impossible predictions to make but, using fertility rates and market surveys, the company can make a pretty accurate guess.

WORLD POPULATION

POPULATION OF THE UK

CHANGING STRUCTURE OF POPULATION

OCCUPATIONAL STRUCTURE OF THE UK

UNEMPLOYMENT

REGIONAL UNEMPLOYMENT

CHANGING SKILL REQUIREMENTS

LIFETIME LEARNING

ESSENTIAL PRINCIPLES

Before we go any further it might be useful to see how the population of the whole world has been growing recently. Table 13.1 shows how the population of the world has grown from just 2.5 thousand million people in 1950 to over 5 thousand million in 1994.

	£ (BILLIONS)
1950	2.5
1985	4.9
1992	5.5
2025	8.5

Table 13.1 World population (UN figures)

Note: 1 billion = 1000 million = 1,000,000,000
Source: Social Trends (24) 1994.

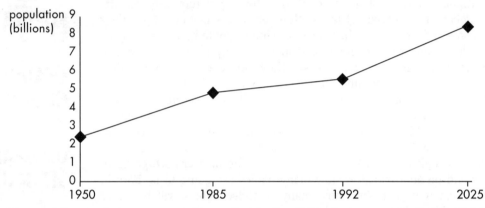

Figure 13.1 Growth in world population (billion people)

❝❝ The fertility rate shows the number of babies born to every thousand women of child-bearing age. ❞❞

The world's population was growing so fast in the 1960s that experts believed that it would reach over 10 billion by the year 2000. However, in the past ten years the rate of growth has slowed down and the prediction for total world population by that date is now just over 6 billion.

The experts at the UN now believe that the world's population may reach a state of balance (i.e. of very little growth) by the year 2100 (just 108 years from 1992).

Even so, it is surprising how fast the world's population has grown. In the year 1900, it was estimated at only 1.25 billion (and it had taken several million years to reach that figure). It then took 50 years for the figure to double to 2.5 billion and only another 37 years for it to double again. It is to be hoped that the really fast rate of growth is now over – for, in just 100 years the world's population will have grown by 5 times!

Like the world's population, the number of people in the UK has been growing, but much more slowly. The fastest rate of population growth for the UK was during the nineteenth century, just after the industrial revolution. Since 1900, the UK's population will have grown from about 38 million to 59 million by the year 2000 (see Table 13.2). In the nineteenth century, it was fairly common to find families with anything between 8 and 10 children, whereas today the most common size is 2, with even 4 children being regarded as a large family.

A. AGE STRUCTURE

Between 1900 and 1996, the number of children under 14 decreased but people in the 15–29-year-old category increased. Each of the over 30 age groups has increased in size since 1900, but the major growth has been in those over 60. In 1900, there were just 2.9 million people who were over 60 years of age. In 1996, that figure had reached 11.8 million. In other words, there are now almost four times as many elderly people as there were at the turn of the century. Important reasons for this are the improvement in medical care, and standards of living and conditions of work.

> The fastest population growth appears to occur *as countries change* from being mainly agricultural to being mainly industrialised. Then, as the standard of living further increases, the birth rate appears to slow down.

Table 13.2 Age structure of the UK population

YEAR	UNDER 16		16–39		40–64		65–79		OVER 80		TOTAL
	million	%	million	%	million	%	million	%	million	%	(m)
1901	12.4	*32.4*	15.8	*41.4*	8.2	*21.5*	1.6	*4.2*	0.2	*0.5*	38.2
1951	11.4	*22.6*	18.2	*36.1*	15.3	*30.4*	4.7	*9.3*	0.8	*1.6*	50.4
1961	13.1	*24.9*	16.6	*31.4*	16.9	*32.0*	5.2	*9.8*	1.0	*1.9*	52.8
1971	14.2	*25.5*	17.5	*31.3*	16.7	*29.9*	6.1	*10.9*	1.3	*2.3*	55.9
1981	12.6	*22.3*	19.6	*34.9*	15.7	*27.8*	6.9	*12.2*	1.6	*2.8*	56.4
1991	11.7	*20.3*	20.4	*35.3*	16.6	*28.6*	6.9	*12.0*	2.2	*3.7*	57.8
2001	12.5	*21.0*	19.6	*32.8*	18.2	*30.5*	6.8	*11.4*	2.5	*4.2*	59.7
2011	11.9	*19.5*	18.5	*30.3*	20.5	*33.7*	7.3	*11.9*	2.9	*4.7*	61.1

Source: Social Trends (24) 1994.

Note: The years listed above may seem a strange choice, in each case, being the first year of the decade (1981, 1991, etc.) instead of the last (1980, 1990). This is because the national census is always taken in the first year of each decade.

Although the rate of growth has slowed down quite a lot, the actual make-up of the population has been changing quite rapidly. Table 13.2 shows the way in which the **age structure** has been changing.

There are now (using 1991 data) approximately the same *number* of people aged under 16 in the UK population but, they represent only 20% of the population as compared to 32% at the beginning of the century.

The changes in population structure since 1901 are more visible if age groups are combined. For example, in 1901, over 70% of the UK population was aged under 40 (in 1991 the proportion was just under 50%). Similarly we now have over 15% of the population over retirement age (65) compared with less than 5% at the turn of the century.

Business can use the figures showing changes in the age structure of the population to predict demand for a wide variety of goods and products. The decrease in those under 40 and the corresponding increase in people over that age will lead to less demand for goods traditionally bought by the under-40s such as family cars, houses, household goods and insurance. Demand for goods and services bought by the over-40s — including holidays, smaller cars and health care — will probably increase.

Population can change in size and structure in a number of different ways:

► more people can die
► more people can be born
► people can leave the country (emigrate)
► people can enter the country (immigrate).

B. THE DEATH RATE

	AVERAGE CHANGE PER YEAR IN THOUSANDS			
YEAR	BIRTH	DEATHS	MIGRATION	ANNUAL CHANGE
1901–11	1091	624	–82	385
1931–51	785	598	+25	212
1961–71	963	639	–12	312
1971–81	736	666	–27	43
1981–91	757	655	+42	144
1991–93	779	637	+49	191
Projected:				
1994–2001	776	623	+50	203
2001–11	716	614	+44	146

Table 13.3 Population change

> Population can increase just as fast because the *death rate is dropping* as because the birth rate is increasing. In fact, decreasing death rates is one of the most important reasons for rapidly growing populations.

Source: Social Trends (25) 1995.

Table 13.3 shows how the UK population has changed since the year 1901. It is important to note that, although the numbers of deaths from 1901–11 were *less* than they were from 1991–3, the **death rate** was much *higher* from 1901–11. This is because it is wrong to compare the numbers of deaths when the total populations at the two periods were different (only around 38 million in 1901 and about 56 million in 1990). In 1901, about 16 people died every year **per thousand population** whereas the death rate had dropped to around 10.9 people per thousand population in 1992. Table 13.4 shows the death rates since 1961. Due to better living and working conditions and improved medical facilities, people are living longer.

	MALE	FEMALE
1961	12.6	11.4
1971	12.1	11.0
1981	12.0	11.4
1991	11.1	11.2
1993	11.1	11.5

Table 13.4 Death rates (per thousand population)

Source: Social Trends (25) 1995.

Death rates vary across the world; Table 13.5 shows some examples. How would you explain the rates for Africa and Japan?

(1990–5) COUNTRY/REGION	LIFE EXPECTANCY IN YEARS
UK	76
Europe	75
North America	76
Africa	53
Asia	65
Japan	79

Table 13.5 Expectation of life at birth (in years)

Source: Social Trends (25) 1995.

C. THE BIRTH RATE

Another influence on population change is the rate at which children are born. Table 13.6 shows how this is also falling. In 1901, there were roughly 29 births per thousand population. By 1990 this had fallen to 14. Part of this fall in the **birth rate** can be explained because families need to have less children to make sure that some will survive into adulthood: the death rate among children during the nineteenth century was very high. Children died of a great many diseases and of industrial and domestic accidents. Today, far fewer children die from these causes, so many parents feel that they need to have fewer children.

One interesting feature of Table 13.6 is that, while the birth rate continues to drop, the average age at which mothers have their first child dropped from 28.4 years in 1951 to just over 26 years in 1971 and has since been steadily rising again. Why do you think this has happened?

	CRUDE BIRTH RATE	MEAN* AGE OF MOTHERS (AT FIRST BIRTH)
1951	15.9	28.4
1961	17.9	27.7
1971	16.1	26.2
1981	13.0	26.8
1991	14.0	27.9
*Mean = average		

Table 13.6 Crude birth rate (total births per thousand population)

Source: Social Trends (24) 1994.

D. MIGRATION

Migration consists of people leaving the country (emigration) and people coming to live here (immigration). Net migration is the difference between the two.

The later years of the nineteenth century and the early years of this century were those of large scale **emigration** from the UK. People went mainly to the countries of the 'Old Commonwealth' — Canada, Australia and New Zealand — but also to the US and to South Africa. Part of this emigration is shown by the fact that an average of around 82,000 more people were leaving the UK than were coming in during the period 1901–11 (see Table 13.3). From the 1930s, however, that trend reversed to one of **immigration**, as more people began to enter the UK than to leave it.

There was another period of net emigration during the 1960s and 70s (possibly due to disillusionment with the state of the UK in those days) before immigration again exceeded emigration in the 1980s and 90s.

The countries to which Britain has a net emigration are Australia, Canada and US; while net immigration occurs from New Zealand, Africa and Asia. Interestingly enough, between 1988 and 1992 net immigration from Europe and New Zealand at 12,100 people was almost as much as that from India and Pakistan (at 14,900 people).

An even more interesting way of looking at migration is to examine the 'flows' i.e., the total numbers of people entering and leaving the UK in any one year (see Table 13.7).

AREA	NUMBERS (000)	% OF TOTAL MIGRATION FLOW
Europe	147.0	31.2
Australia	63.6	13.5
USA	59.6	12.7
Asia	28.5	6.0
Africa	19.3	4.1

Table 13.7 Migration flows for the UK (1992)

Source: OPCS, 1994.

4 **OCCUPATIONAL STRUCTURE OF THE UK**

There are three main ways to consider the **occupational structure** of the UK:

1. the balance of the working population as it is split between the various **sectors** – primary, secondary and tertiary
2. the **status** of employment – such as whether employee, self employed, or in the armed forces
3. the **sex** of the employed.

A. SECTOR OF EMPLOYMENT

There are three sectors: primary, secondary and tertiary.

▶ The **primary sector** is to do with the extraction of raw materials (coal, oil, tin, etc.) or with the production of food (agriculture). The primary sector accounts for only about 3% of the UK working population.

▶ The **secondary sector** includes industries involved in actually making things – manufacturing, construction, etc.

▶ The **tertiary sector** includes what are usually called the service industries, i.e. transport, communications, insurance, banking, education, tourism, etc. The tertiary sector now accounts for over 60% of the UK labour force.

	PRIMARY	SECONDARY	TERTIARY
1961	6.5	46.8	46.7
1971	3.7	43.8	46.7
1981	3.2	37.4	59.4
1987	3.0	35.5	61.5
1990	3.0	29.7	67.3
1993	2.9	24.0	73.1

Table 13.8 Annual abstract of statistics 1994, using SIC (80)

Source: Annual Abstract of Statistics, 1994 using SIC (80).

It is one of the trends of modern industrial society that, as western industrialised countries become richer, the numbers of people working in industry and manufacturing become a much smaller proportion of the total workforce. In the UK, the balance between the various sectors has changed a great deal even since 1961 (see Table 13.9).

B. STATUS OF EMPLOYMENT

The second way of looking at the occupational structure is to list the status of the people employed in the economy, such as whether they are employed by someone else, self-employed, or working in the armed forces.

CATEGORY	1993 (000)	
Employees in employment		
Males	10852	
Females	10475	
		21327
Self-employed		
Males	2226	
Females	752	
		2978
HM Forces		
Males	252	
Females	19	
		271
Unemployed		
Males	2238	
Females	674	
		2912
Work-related training programmes		
Males	204	
Females	117	
		321
UK workforce:		27809

Table 13.9 Disribution of the UK workforce (1993)

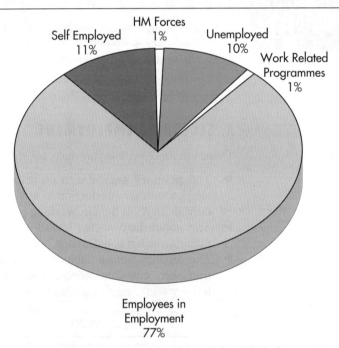

Table 13.9 lists the working population by this method. It is important to note that the term 'working population' includes those who are unemployed. This is because, officially, the unemployed are looking for work and are part of the total number of people who are able to work.

C. SEX AND EMPLOYMENT

Another trend which has to be noted is the growth of the female labour force and the decline in the employment of men (see Table 13.10).

	MALES	FEMALES
1970	14009	8470
1975	13536	9174
1980	13110	9401
1986	11890	9638
1990	12057	10807
1993	10852	10475

Table 13.10 Employees in employment (1993)

Source: Annual Abstract of Statistics, 1994.

The reasons behind this trend are extremely complex. However, the following four reasons are important.

1. The **decline of the older, heavier engineering industries** has tended to put men out of work rather than women.
2. The relative **growth of newer industries in the electronics sector** has favoured women because, on the whole, women tend to have better manipulative skills; their hands are smaller and they are able to perform the extremely delicate operations necessary when assembling electronic components.
3. The **growth of the service sector** – banks, shops, and insurance companies – has favoured women. All employ a large proportion of women in their labour force, partly because women have, traditionally, done the sorts of jobs required by these companies, e.g. counter work, secretarial duties and clerical work. Also, the service sector uses a large number of part-time workers and women tend to be more willing to accept part-time work due to their family obligations.
4. In 1951, only 21% of all women had jobs. Today that figure is well over 55% and is expected to reach well over 60% by the year 2000. The later years of the twentieth century have increased the opportunities for women to work, resulting in **increasing numbers of 'working wives'**.

▶ Smaller families mean that women are tied to the home for shorter periods.
▶ A change in social attitudes has given women greater status and equality with men.
▶ Most household chores, such as washing clothes, are now almost fully automated, and shopping – which took hours every day at the turn of this century – now takes only a few hours each week.
▶ A higher rate of marriage breakdown and of illegitimate births in recent years has meant that more women are the breadwinners in a single-parent family and have to go out to work to support their children.

5 ❯ UNEMPLOYMENT

Table 13.11 shows how the rate of unemployment has grown since the 1970s. In the 1950s and 1960s, the rate of UK unemployment (Fig. 13.3) was extremely low – varying around 2 or 3%. The rate has climbed since then until it reached a peak in 1982 of over 12%. Even in the 'boom' years of the late 1980s the rate never went below 6%.

During the 1970s, the **number** of unemployed began to grow, and had reached 1.3 million by 1980. Then came a period of explosive growth in the numbers of people unemployed. Between 1980 and 1983, unemployment climbed from 1.3 million to 3.1 million.

	UK UNEMPLOYMENT RATE %
1976	5.6
1980	9.8
1982	10.4
1984	10.6
1986	11.1
1988	8.0
1990	5.8
1992	9.7
1993	10.3
1994	9.4

Table 13.11 Unemployment rates 1976–94

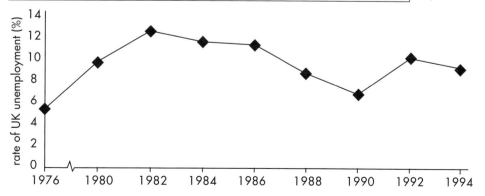

Figure 13.3 Unemployment since 1976

There are several reasons which may explain unemployment:

A. FRICTIONAL UNEMPLOYMENT

Frictional unemployment occurs when people change jobs and spend time looking for a new one; or when people lose their jobs and have difficulty – due, perhaps, to a lack of information – in finding a new one (even though there are new jobs to be had).

B. CASUAL UNEMPLOYMENT

Many people work in **casual** jobs, e.g. in catering, construction, printing, hotels, seaside resorts. Some unemployment results when these staff are laid off and have to find more work. It is really a slightly different form of frictional unemployment.

C. SEASONAL UNEMPLOYMENT

Seasonal unemployment occurs when people who work in '**seasonal**' occupations such as the tourist industry or farming, are laid off.

D. STRUCTURAL UNEMPLOYMENT

Structural unemployment happens when the demand for certain products falls – perhaps because they have gone out of fashion or been replaced by better products. It usually happens to whole industrial sectors at a time. In Britain, the shipbuilding, heavy engineering and textile industries have suffered massive decline during the period since 1945. The unemployment resulting from this decline is known as *structural* because it is caused by a change in the actual *industrial structure* of the country.

   In the UK, since the early 1970s, unemployment has been caused mainly by structural forces, i.e. by the adjustment of British industry to changes in the world economy. During the last twenty years, a great deal of the UK's manufacturing capacity has been lost and this has meant large numbers of people being made unemployed. A further structural factor, often forgotten, is the way in which information technology (computers, wordprocessors and electronic systems) has reduced the need for employment in the service sector.

E. CYCLICAL UNEMPLOYMENT

Cyclical unemployment is sometimes called **demand deficient unemployment** and is the result of a lack of demand throughout the *whole* economy for goods and services.

6 ▷ **REGIONAL UNEMPLOYMENT**

One of the most important problems about unemployment in Britain today is the way in which it seems to be concentrated in the North. Because the North of England was the centre of the first industrial revolution, its industries were the first to be affected by the structural decline of the older heavy industries, such as shipbuilding. Similarly, when the competition faced by industries of the second industrial revolution – manufacturers of cars, motor cycles, radios, etc. – increased from the rest of the world, the Midlands suffered structural decline.

   Today, unemployment rates in certain areas of the North can be as high as 25% of the labour force and in some towns and villages over 50% are unemployed. In the South, where the newer industries have grown up since 1945 (in electronics, light engineering, computers, etc.) unemployment rates are lower (averaging just 8%).

UK REGION	UNEMPLOYMENT RATE (1993)
North West	10.2
North of England	11.7
Yorkshire and Humberside	9.8
East Midlands	8.3
West Midlands	9.9
East Anglia	7.4
South East	9.6
South West	7.5
Wales	9.4
Scotland	9.9
Northern Ireland	11.5

Table 13.12 Regional unemployment in the UK

Source: Social Trends (25) 1995.

7 ▷ CHANGING SKILL REQUIREMENTS

The population of the late twentieth and early twenty-first century in the UK will have to be particularly flexible with regard to the skills which they are able to offer. In the nineteenth century, a young person would leave school, undertake an apprenticeship for a trade, and would then work in that trade for the rest of his working life. The speed of technological advance was slow and the person would probably not have needed to learn how to use many new machines. Besides, the differences between one machine and the next were usually so small that the operator could learn how to use the new machine in a morning.

Unfortunately for today's workforce, this is no longer so. The speed with which machines and techniques change means that workers have to be almost constantly retrained to use the next generation of machines.

Young girls who left school in the 1960s, after learning shorthand and typing, expected to be able to use the same skills throughout their working lives. The typewriters might change from manual to electric but the skills required would be exactly the same. Unfortunately for them the electronic revolution has changed their jobs almost out of recognition. Shorthand has largely given way to audio-typing (and, in the next generation of typewriters possibly to direct speech input) and typewriters have given way to wordprocessors. For the secretary, this revolution has meant continual retraining, as wordprocessors have become more and more powerful. Each new development which occurs often means a completely new wordprocessing system to learn.

In industry, the speed of change has been just as fast and has left many old skills high and dry. In the printing trade, the old skills of 'hot metal' composing (setting the newspaper stories in molten lead to print the paper) have given way to highly computerised wordprocessing systems which link up with photographic printing processes. In engineering, many of the older skills, such as turning (using a lathe), and fitting (making fine adjustments to a metal component after it has been produced), have been replaced by computer controlled machines.

8 ▷ LIFETIME LEARNING

Very few people who leave school in the last years of the twentieth century will be able to stay in one job for the whole of their working life. Most will not even be able to stay in the same *career*. Frequent change of job is already the norm while one or two changes of career during a working life may well become the norm.

The implication of this is that – whatever work one has – there will be a continual need to learn new techniques and skills. The days when you could learn a trade at 16 and rely on that knowledge for the rest of your working life are long gone.

The twenty-first century will require **lifetime learning**, i.e. regular updating of current skills and learning of new skills and knowledge. Modern training and educational systems, such as National Vocational Qualifications (NVQs), are designed to support lifetime learning.

EXAMINATION QUESTIONS

QUESTION 1

Give three reasons why less than half the total United Kingdom population is included in the working population.

(i) _____ (2 marks)

(ii) _____ (2 marks)

(iii) _____ (2 marks)

(NICCEA)

QUESTION 2

Study the following data and answer the questions printed overleaf.

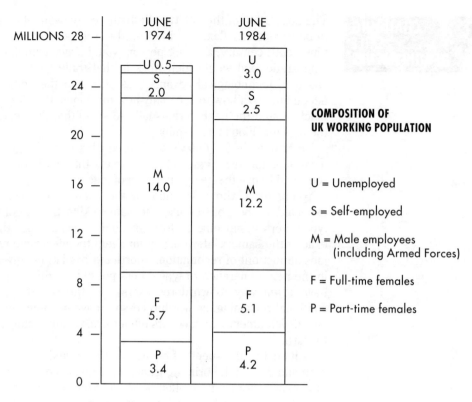

(a) By how much has the working population risen between 1974 and 1984? Label the categories in your calculations.   (4 marks)

(b) By how much has the employed population fallen between 1974 and 1984? Label the categories in your calculations.   (4 marks)

(c) Which section of the employed population has suffered most in the period between 1974 and 1984? Suggest reasons.   (6 marks)

(d) Suggest reasons why the number in the self-employed category hasrisen   (6 marks)

(e) Why do you think the number of female part-time workers has risen in the ten years under review?   (4 marks)

(f) Why do you think that Northern Ireland has the highest unemployment rate of any region in the United Kingdom?   (4 marks)

(NICCEA)

TUTOR'S ANSWER TO Q.2

(a)

1974	(millions)	1984
unemployed	0.5	3.0
self-employed	2.0	2.5
male employees	14.0	12.2
full-time female	5.7	5.1
part-time female	3.4	4.2
	25.6	27.0

The working population rose by (27.0 – 25.6) 1.4 million. When answering this type of question you must remember that the unemployed are *included* in the working population figure.

(b)

1974	(millions)	1984
self-employed	2.0	2.5
male employees	14.0	12.2
full-time female	5.7	5.1
part-time female	3.4	4.2
	25.1	24.0

The employed population fell by (25.1–24.0) 1.1 million between 1974 and 1984. The unemployed are *excluded* from the employed population.

(c) The section of the employed population which suffered the most is the male population with a fall from 14.0m to 12.2m which represents a fall of approximately 13%.

Reasons for this fall could have been the structural decline of basic industries such as the steel industry, coalmining, shipbuilding and traditional industries like engineering. Males had a higher proportion of employment in such industries than compared to, say, banking and education. This decline in the basic industries was the result of a number of reasons, the world-wide recession and overseas competition being important.

(d) One reason for the increase in the number of self-employed might have been the increase in unemployment. Some of those made redundant may have used their redundancy pay to start their own businesses instead of becoming employees of other firms. There have also been a range of measures by successive governments to encourage people to start their own businesses, e.g. grants, reducing 'red tape'.

(e) The number of female part-time workers may have risen partly because of the increase in the number of male unemployed; it became even more important for the female members of the household to bring some income into the home. Also the period 1974 to 1984 saw a rapid growth in the service sector of the economy. Many of these jobs were usually taken by females and many were part-time.

(f) Northern Ireland had the highest rate of unemployment of any region in the UK for a number of reasons. Northern Ireland suffered from being some distance from the main areas of growth in the UK such as the South-East. Being at a distance from the large markets within the UK meanS higher costs for transporting finished products to these markets. Northern Ireland also lacks natural resources and found it harder to attract businesses because of the political unrest during that period.

COURSEWORK

ASSIGNMENT 1 – A CASE STUDY OF INDUSTRIAL AND POPULATION CHANGE

Produce an illustrated report on the way in which your town or area has changed in recent years. Do not make the period too long because you will find it more difficult to obtain information. The period since 1970 would be the most interesting for most areas of the country.

1. Go to the local central library and ask for information on the town or area. You will find that they will have an entire section of books and reports on your area and will be able to recommend reports you should look at.
2. Collect information:

▶ In which way has the population changed? How has it grown? In what areas of the town has it grown?

▶ What new facilities, if any, have been needed to cope with the new population – new schools, housing estates, roads, hospitals?

▶ What new industries have come to the area? Which old ones have disappeared? Your parents, family, friends, and teachers may be able to help you best here.

3. When you write up the report pay particular attention to the growth of population and how it is related to the changes in the area's industry and commerce.
4. Include a section on what you believe the future holds for the area.

ASSIGNMENT 2 – A HISTORICAL STUDY OF POPULATION CHANGES

How has your town or area developed over the past hundred years or so? Has it grown, shrunk, or are roughly the same number of people living in it? What jobs did people in the area do a hundred years ago? How did they live and what were their working conditions like?

1. Use the local central library as your main source of information. You will find that they have a great deal of information about local history and may well be able to put you in touch with Local History groups who have already looked at this area of study.

2. You should look for the following information:

    ▶ What was the population of the area? How it has grown? Use local history books and the census information (the librarians will show you where to look for this).

    ▶ How did they live. What were their houses like? Where did they get food? What did they do for entertainment?

    ▶ Where did they work? Did they work on the land or in factories? What hours did they work and what were they paid? Was the work dangerous? What were the names of the main companies and what did they make?

    ▶ What were the transport facilities like? When did the railways come to the area? When did stagecoach services stop operating?

3. Try to find old pictures (usually available in the older books or reproduced in newer, local history books) which show what the town was like, what the factories or farms looked like and what people's homes looked like. Include photocopies of these in your study.

A Review Sheet for this chapter will be found on p. 248.

CHAPTER 14

RECRUITMENT, SELECTION AND TRAINING

GETTING STARTED

All businesses, whatever their size, may need to take on extra staff. This could be because the **business is growing** and there is a need for new posts to be created, or because **existing posts become vacant** as:

- ▶ the employee may have obtained a job elsewhere
- ▶ the employee may have obtained promotion within the company
- ▶ the employee may be retiring
- ▶ the employee may have been dismissed.

Recruitment is the first stage of filling a vacancy in the business. The recruitment process will involve a careful study of the vacancy, so that the activities expected of the new employee can be clearly defined in a **job description**. A decision must then be made on how to **advertise** the vacancy (what to say, and which newspapers and job agencies to use), and what questions should appear on the **application form**. Once the recruitment process has been undertaken, there then needs to be careful **selection**, first of the candidates to be interviewed, and then of which candidate to offer the job to.

The firm's responsibility does not end there. Once a person is employed, the firm has an interest in ensuring that its new member of staff is fully equipped to perform present and future activities. This brings us on to training. **Training** involves the sharpening of *existing skills* and the development of *new skills* and knowledge, so that best use can be made of the staff employed.

This chapter will deal with the recruitment, selection and training of a Junior Clerk/Receptionist, although the GCSE examination could ask about any kind of job. There is also a brief section on Redundancy, Retirement and Dismissal.

RECRUITMENT

SELECTION

CONTRACT OF EMPLOYMENT

INDUCTION

TRAINING

GOVERNMENT TRAINING

REDUNDANCY, RETIREMENT AND DISMISSAL

ESSENTIAL PRINCIPLES

❝❝ You may be called upon to plan out a job description in the exam. It will help if you practice writing out job descriptions for different jobs you see advertised in the newspaper. ❞❞

A. JOB DESCRIPTION

The **job description** sets out, in broad terms, the duties and responsibilities of a particular job. It gives information such as:

▶ job title
▶ the job location
▶ what the job entails
▶ who the employee will be responsible to
▶ whether the employee is responsible for the work of any other members of staff. It is the responsibility of the personnel department to produce job descriptions and this can be undertaken in a number of ways:

1. The present job holder can be asked to write their own job description.
2. The job holder can be interviewed in order to find out what the job entails.
3. The job holder can be observed actually doing the job.

A job description for the post of **Junior Clerk/Receptionist** would include the following information:

Job title:	Junior Clerk/Receptionist
Job location:	Personnel Department
Duties:	Answering the telephone
	Office filing
	Typing
	Welcoming customers
	General office duties
Reports to:	Assistant Personnel Manager

The job description would also include a more detailed description of the day-to-day duties of the Junior Clerk/Receptionist.

B. PREPARING A JOB ADVERTISEMENT

Figure 14.1 shows a typical **job advertisement** which might appear in a local newspaper. It advertises the post of Junior Clerk/Receptionist and invites candidates to apply within a certain time.

A great deal of time and effort is taken in designing **job advertisements** because it is important that the right candidates apply for the post. The advertisement has included the following information:

▶ job title
▶ the type of work involved
▶ where the office/factory is located
▶ qualifications/experience required (if any)
▶ salary/working conditions
▶ training given (if any)
▶ age of candidate required
▶ how the candidate should apply, e.g. application form, CV or by telephone.

As the job advertisement is being prepared, the Personnel Department at Edwards Foods Ltd will need to bear in mind its cost and destination. If a **budget** has been placed on the amount spent on the job advertisement, it may be necessary to reduce its size. If this is the case, then some of the less important information may have to be omitted. The **destination** of the advertisement may determine the way in which it is written. For example, the wording may be different if it is to be placed in a Job Centre, a newspaper or a school careers department. The personnel department will also need to take account of the law relating to recruitment when planning the job advertisement. Relevant Acts are:

► The Disabled Persons (Employment) Acts (1944, 1958)
► The Childrens and Young Persons Act (1933, 1969)
► The Sex Discrimination Acts (1975, 1987)
► The Race Relations Act (1976).

Further information on the law relating to employment can be found in ch. 18.

JUNIOR CLERK/RECEPTIONIST

EDWARDS FOODS LTD, a leading food manufacturer requires a Junior Clerk/ Receptionist at their new offices in Cambridge.

Applicants, ideally school leavers, should have a minimum of four GCSEs including Mathematics and English, an outgoing personality and be able to communicate with customers both on the telephone and in person.

This is an interesting and varied job requiring enthusiasm and commitment for which full training will be given.

Salary will be in the range £7,500 to £8,500 per annum, 25 days holiday a year and a subsidised canteen is available.

The closing date for application forms is 8th December.

For an application form and further details write to:

Mrs P Parke
Personnel Department
Edwards Foods Ltd
East Road Cambridge CB1 6GT

Figure 14.1 Typical job advertisement

C. ADVERTISING THE POST

Internal

The post may be advertised **internally** in the staff magazine or on the staff noticeboard and be filled by a member of the **existing** staff. The advantages of this are that the company will be aware of the employee's capabilities and it will be a cheaper and quicker method of recruitment. If, however, there is no suitable internal candidate, then there will be a need to advertise the post **externally**.

External

There are various places which could be used to advertise the post:

► the Job Centre
► private agency
► factory gate
► newspapers: local and national

Job Centre

You will find a **job centre** in your local town or city; they are self-service centres. Jobs are displayed on boards and are mainly for manual, clerical and unskilled work. In larger cities, Professional and Executive Recruitment centres can also be found which cater for professional people who are looking for employment. Both the Job Centre and Professional and Executive Recruitment are organised by the Department of Employment.

Private agency

There are a number of nationally organised **private agencies** such as Blue Arrow Personnel Services who deal with secretarial, office and retailing vacancies. The agencies advertise in newspapers and in their shop windows. If the agency fills a vacancy, the employer usually pays a fee calculated as a percentage of the starting salary.

Factory gate

Certain jobs may be advertised on noticeboards near to the **factory gate**. Now, of course, the term 'factory-gate advertising' is more likely to refer to noticeboards near to an office or administrative centre.

Newspapers

Many jobs are advertised in local and national newspapers. **Local newspapers** are normally used for *clerical* and for *manual* (skilled and unskilled) employment. They are often used to recruit school-leavers such as the advertisement in Fig. 14.1. Have a look in your local newspaper. The job vacancies will normally be advertised on a particular night each week. **National newspapers** are normally used for *professional* employment opportunities to attract applicants from different areas of the country, many of whom would have a degree or professional qualification.

Method of advertising

The appropriate **method of advertising** depends upon several factors:

1. The **type of post** is important. If it is to be filled by a school-leaver, then local newspapers may be the most effective form of advertising. If the vacant post is for a secretary, then the more successful way of advertising could be to register the vacancy with a private employment agency.
2. The **time scale** is important because to fill the post quickly, the solution may be to advertise the post internally. External advertising takes more time.
3. The **budget** limits the amount of money that can be spent on advertising and this may rule out national newspapers which are very expensive. National newspapers may only be used for vacancies which the company believes require skills or qualifications which are in short supply locally. The cheapest way would be to advertise in Job Centres and at the factory gate.
4. The **type of person** you want to apply for the vacant post must be considered. If you want to attract specialist staff then you may advertise with a specialist employment agency such as Professional and Executive Recruitment or a specialist journal such as *The Economist*. For this type of appointment, you may also advertise in a national newspaper.

2 SELECTION

A. DESIGNING A JOB APPLICATION FORM

When a post is advertised, the advertisement will normally state that the person interested should send for further details and an application form. The personnel department will then send out a standard printed form as in Fig. 14.2. The candidates fill this in, giving information to support their application for the post in question. The application form shown here refers to the post of Junior Clerk/Receptionist.

The advantages to the business of using an application form are that:

▶ it gives a precise picture of the individual applying for the post
▶ it outlines the candidate's suitability for the post
▶ will also serve as a personnel record and be of legal importance in the employment contract.

Businesses lay out their application forms in different ways but the information they require will, in most cases, be the same as in Fig. 14.2. The information given on the form will be helpful in assessing the candidate's suitability for the post, in comparing that candidate with other applicants and, therefore, in selecting certain candidates for interview. Beside Fig. 14.2, information is given as to why the firm is asking certain questions.

From the candidate's point of view, the application form is the first impression the firm will obtain of him or her and will form the basis of the firm's short list for interview. It is, therefore, important that the candidate completes the form clearly and carefully.

> The address to which all correspondence should be sent, is it local?

> Is the applicant old enough/ too old for the post?

> Has the applicant obtained the relevant qualifications?

> Has the applicant undertaken any work which may be useful for the post? Is it relevant experience?

> Has the applicant been given any positions of trust?

> References are asked so that further information can be obtained as to the applicant's suitability for the post.

EDWARDS FOODS LTD
Application form for the post of: JUNIOR CLERK/RECEPTIONIST

Please fill in the application form and return it to us as soon as possible.

1) FULL NAME:
2) FULL ADDRESS:

3) TELEPHONE NUMBER (IF ANY):
4) DATE OF BIRTH:
5) MARRIED OR SINGLE:

6) EDUCATION: Secondary School(s), Address(es)	DATE	
	From	To

7) QUALIFICATIONS	DATE TAKEN & GRADES

8) WORK EXPERIENCE	DATE	
	From	To

9) POSITIONS OF RESPONSIBILITY

10) LEISURE ACTIVITIES

11) NAME AND ADDRESS OF TWO REFEREES

12) I certify that to the best of my knowledge all the entries on this form are correct.

Signed.. Date................................

Figure 14.2 Job application form

B. PROVIDING A CURRICULUM VITAE (CV)

The advertisement for the post of Junior Clerk/Receptionist asked that anyone interested should send for an application form and further details. Instead of this, the firm could have asked the applicant to send a **CV**. The CV should contain brief, relevant information on the applicant such as schools attended, qualifications, interests and activities and the name and address of two referees; see Fig. 14.3.

C. REFERENCES

Many application forms will require the name and address of at least two individuals who can act as referees (i.e. provide references). The referees may be contacted and asked whether or not they consider the applicant to be suitable for the post. Normally,

CURRICULUM VITAE

Name:	Susanna J. Hattrick
Home address:	1 The Lane Manchester M16 2PT
Date of Birth:	22.3.79
Place of Birth:	Manchester
Nationality:	British
Education:	Stonebroom Comprehensive School West Park Manchester Sept. 1990 –July 1995
Qualifications:	July 1995 GCSE Mathematics (B) English (C) Business Studies (A) French (C) Art & Design (D)
Interests & activities:	Swimming Reading Horse riding
Work experience:	Work on a market stall on Saturday
Referees:	Mr Mills The Headmaster Stonebroom Comprehensive School West Park Manchester
	Rev. G. Cray St. Michael le Belfrey Church Street Urmstow Manchester

Figure 14.3 Curriculum vitae

the firm will ask for the names of present and former employers or supervisors. In the case of the Junior Clerk/Receptionist, where the applicants are likely to be school-leavers, then the name and address of the Head teacher at the school attended are more likely to be requested. The candidate may also have to name one other person to act as referee, such as a vicar, a doctor, an old family friend or an employer who has employed them for part-time work.

D. CHOOSING SUITABLE CANDIDATES FOR INTERVIEW

❝❝ It would be useful for you to produce your own CV. ❞❞

Once the company has obtained all the completed application forms, the next step is to compare them. This can be a lengthy process, trying to match the attributes of the applicants to the needs of the post. Some application forms will be discounted straight away because, for example:

▶ they are badly written (perhaps they have poor spelling and are untidy)
▶ the applicant's qualifications may be inadequate for the post
▶ the applicant may be too old.

These applicants will be sent a letter informing them that they were unsuccessful in their application. In choosing applicants for interview the company needs to observe the Sex Discrimination Acts (1975, 1987) and the Race Relations Act (1976), which make it illegal to discriminate on the grounds of sex and race (see ch. 18). Of the application forms remaining, a 'short list' will be drawn up. This is a list of the applicants seen as best suited for the post. A letter will be sent to those listed, inviting them for interview on a certain date. At the same time, the company will usually send for references (as dealt with in the previous section).

E. THE INTERVIEW

This is the major way companies assess whether a candidate is suitable for a particular post. It allows the company to make a judgement on:

▶ the candidate's personality (will they fit into the company and be able to mix with the other staff?)
▶ the ability of the candidate to communicate
▶ whether the information on the application form is correct.

It also gives the candidate the chance to find out more about the company, such as the working conditions, hours of work, pay and training. It is important that the interview is planned carefully. With this in mind, the *interviewer* should make sure that:

1. there are no interruptions while the interview is taking place;
2. the application form has been read carefully, and that the interviewer has decided which are the relevant questions to ask;
3. the interview does not have to be rushed because of a lack of time;
4. the interviewee is put at ease, perhaps by being asked a few simple questions at the beginning such as how they travelled to the interview;
5. the questions are phrased in such a way that they encourage the candidate to talk and to give his or her own views and opinions – questions should be avoided which call for one word answers such as 'I can see you are interested in horseriding';
6. the questions are phrased so that the candidate can understand them. The wording and type of question the interviewer would ask a candidate for a management post would differ from those asked of an applicant for the post of Junior Clerk/Receptionist.

F. MAKING A SELECTION

Once all the candidates have been interviewed then the interviewer must compare the information obtained from each candidate and decide on the most suitable person for the post. The candidate may have been interviewed by more than one person, perhaps someone from the personnel department and a staff member from whichever department the post was advertised for. The two interviewers would then compare notes before deciding which candidate to appoint.

The candidates may have been given a test, in which the candidates' *potential* to perform the necessary activities is measured. An **aptitude test** will cover areas such as:

▶ **mental** *abilities*, e.g. powers of reasoning
▶ **physical** *qualities*, e.g. co-ordination
▶ **arithmetical** *abilities*, e.g. addition and multiplication.

An **intelligence test** may be used to find out the candidate's *general* powers of reasoning. The test will normally be a written one, made up of numerical, diagrammatical and verbal questions, such as identifying one or more shapes which have common features, writing down the next number in a series, or comparing a series of words to see which have similar meanings. Once the test is completed, it is marked and a score obtained.

The company may also insist on a **medical examination** before the job offer is confirmed. This will give a clear indication as to whether the applicant is physically suitable for the post. For example, if the applicant for the Junior Clerk/Receptionist post is hard of hearing, then answering the telephone may be a problem. The firm will also be interested in knowing whether there is likely to be a high degree of absenteeism through sickness.

3 > CONTRACT OF EMPLOYMENT

Once an applicant has accepted a post, a letter is sent, confirming the appointment. In the same letter, the **conditions of service** will often be included. This sets out the employee's statutory legal rights and obligations as covered by the Employment Protection (Consolidation) Act (1978). The *terms and conditions* will cover areas such as:

▶ name and address of the employer and employee
▶ date employment begins
▶ job title and job description
▶ level of pay and whether it will be received weekly or monthly
▶ holiday entitlement
▶ hours of work
▶ conditions relating to sickness pay
▶ conditions relating to the pension scheme
▶ amount of notice the employee has to give the firm if he/she is leaving
▶ notice of any grievance or disciplinary procedure used by the company.

4 > INDUCTION

Any new employee needs to be introduced to his or her new working environment, in much the same way that first-year students are taken round the school at the beginning of term, so that they can become familiar with their new surroundings. New employees may be:

▶ introduced to their new colleagues
▶ told how the firm is organised (see ch.5)
▶ given talks by relevant departmental managers
▶ taken on a tour of the office/factory to see where fire exits, lavatories, canteens etc., are located.

This **induction programme** may last for a day or a week depending on the level of the post, and often takes place *before* the job actually starts.

5 > TRAINING

Once appointed, staff may need **training** in their particular post. Such training can be either **internal** (within the company) or **external** (taking place outside the place of work). The aim is to improve the employee's ability to do the job.

A. INTERNAL TRAINING

There are two forms of internal training:

1. **On-the-job training** may be provided, i.e. the employee learns to do the job during the normal working day. In the case of the Junior Clerk/Receptionist post, this could involve being taught to use the telephone switchboard. The advantages of internal training are that it is usually less costly to the company, and that it is undertaken in the environment in which the employee will actually be working.
2. The company may organise short courses which the employees attend on the company's premises. Organised by the training department, they are an important form of **off-the-job training**.

B. EXTERNAL TRAINING

There are two forms of external training:

1. Off-the-job training could involve **'day-release' courses** at local colleges which are an important type of external training. For example, the banking profession sends staff on day release to undertake Chartered Institute of Bankers (CIB) courses.
2. It is possible that courses, like the one above, could be undertaken by **correspondence course**. The employee would enrol with a correspondence college, which would send study-books and exercises for the employee to work through. The exercises would then be sent to the college for marking and comment. The advantage to the company of correspondence courses is that the staff do not require time off work.

6 ▷ GOVERNMENT TRAINING

In 1991, a network of **Training and Enterprise Councils (TECs)** was introduced in England and Wales and Local Enterprise Companies in Scotland. Their responsibility is to plan and deliver training and vocational education locally for young people and unemployed adults. The Government's Employment Department contracts a number of provisions to the TECs, including youth training (YT), training credits, training for work (TfW) and vocational and educational training.

A. YOUTH TRAINING (YT)

The aim of YT is to provide young people with, in the words of the Employment Department, 'the broad based skills necessary for a flexible and self-reliant workforce' and 'with training leading to National Vocational Qualifications'. YT is guaranteed to all those between the age of 16 and 17 years who are not in full-time education or training and who do not have a job. It is the responsibility of TECs to choose the YT providers and to ensure that all the trainees on YT receive at least the minimum weekly allowance. Summer school leavers are generally entitled to up to two offers of suitable training.

B. TRAINING CREDITS

Training credits are offered by a number of TECs; they allow young people to choose and buy training to meet their requirements. It is the responsibility of each TEC to develop their own approach to training credits in terms of, among other things, giving guidance to young people as to how to use their credits, guaranteeing suitable training places and making sure that credits are aimed at NVQ Level 2 and above.

C. TRAINING FOR WORK (TfW)

TfW started in April 1993 with the aim of aiding the long-term unemployed, i.e. those who have been out of work for six months, the unemployed with disabilities, those with literacy problems and those leaving the Armed Forces or prison. Those embarking on TfW will be set a programme of activities including training leading to vocational qualifications, training in specific jobs and preparation for work.

D. VOCATIONAL EDUCATIONAL AND TRAINING

The late 1980s saw the beginning of a revolution in education and training which is still taking place. The National Curriculum has sought to make education from 5 to 16 more relevant to the knowledge and skill that people will need when they leave school, while new General National Vocational Qualifications (GNVQs) have brought work-related study and practice to the last few years of schooling.

Young people, on leaving school, now have a much wider range of options open to them than were possible during the 1970s and 1980s. National Vocational Qualifications (NVQs) now cover most occupations at Levels 1 to 5 and have been specially designed to be available to people throughout their working lives.

In effect, NVQs set standards for the level of competence you should have for any job and at any point in your working life. The concept of 'lifetime learning' is here to stay.

Tables 14.1 and 14.2 offer examples of lifetime learning. Table 14.1 records Susan Richards proposed learning programme – she wants to go into mechanical engineering services.

Table 14.2 shows the plan for John Richards who wants to go into sales and marketing.

AGE	ACADEMIC QUALIFICATIONS	VOCATIONAL QUALIFICATIONS	PROFESSIONAL QUALIFICATIONS	JOB ROLE
15	GCSEs	—	—	—
16	GCSEs	GNVQ (Built Environment)	—	—
17	—	NVQ L2 Plumbing	—	Apprentice Plumber
19	—	NVQ L3 Plumbing	Advanced Plumber	Supervisor
24	HND Building	NVQ L3 Supervision	Technical Plumber	Quantity Surveyor
30	—	NVQ L4 Management	—	
35	—	—	—	Contracts Manager
40	Degree	NVQ L5 Management	Chartered Institute of Building Services	Director Engineering

Table 14.1 A training route into mechanical engineering services

AGE	ACADEMIC QUALIFICATIONS	VOCATIONAL QUALIFICATIONS	PROFESSIONAL QUALIFICATIONS	JOB ROLE
15	GCSEs	—	—	—
18	A Levels	GNVQ		
21	Degree	—	—	—
22	—	NVQ 2 Selling	—	Sales person
23	—	NVQ 3 Selling	—	Sales person
25	—	NVQ 4 Management	Chartered Institute of Marketing	Sales Manager
30	MBA	NVQ 4 Marketing	Chartered Institute of Marketing	Marketing Manager
35		NVQ 5 Management	Institute of Sales & Marketing Management	Regional Director or Sales & Marketing
40	PRD in International Marketing	NVQ 3 French NVQ 3 German	Institute of Sales & Marketing Management	Marketing Director (Europe)

Table 14.2 A training route into sales and marketing

7 REDUNDANCY, RETIREMENT AND DISMISSAL

A. REDUNDANCY

An employee may be made redundant if his or her job is no longer required by the firm. It may be that the firm is closing down or is reorganising its operations. The employee may be eligible for redundancy pay and this will be calculated on the basis of how long the employee has worked for the company, also on age and salary.

B. RETIREMENT

Retirement is at 65 for men and women. The employee may have paid into the employer's pension scheme and this will mean that the individual will obtain a pension on retirement based on the number of years of service.

C. DISMISSAL

On page 160 we dealt with the contract of employment. This can be terminated by employers if they are dissatisfied with the work or conduct of the employee. Normally, notice of dismissal will be given to the employee. This could be for failure to obey an instruction, stealing from work, violence towards other staff, or excessive absence. Notice of dismissal usually follows a number of verbal and written warnings. Dismissed employees may feel they have been unfairly dismissed. If so, they have certain rights, as granted by the Employment Protection (Consolidation) Act (1978). This allows the employee to take his or her grievance to an industrial tribunal which will review the case of unfair dismissal.

EXAMINATION QUESTIONS

QUESTION 1

A _____ is an agreement under which an employee offers service in return for wages.

(ULEAC)

QUESTION 2

The _____ department of a business is responsible for the recruitment of employees.

(ULEAC)

QUESTION 3

Read the information below which has been taken from a local newspaper and then answer the questions which follow.

Due to the impending launch of a new Peugeot outlet at York Street, Belfast, The Phillips Motor Group urgently require the following staff:

SALES PERSONNEL

Experience in all aspects of New and Used Car Sales is essential. The successful candidates must have the enthusiasm and determination to make substantial contributions to the success of this new outlet.

AFTERSALES SUPERVISORS

Vacancies exist for both Parts and Service Supervisors. Experience of Peugeot procedures preferred, but not essential.

SERVICE PERSONNEL

Experienced Mechanics plus Third and Fourth Year Apprentices required.

The above posts offer an exceptional opportunity to participate in the success of this new outlet from inception. The rewards for suitable applicants will be attractive and will include the numerous benefits associated with a large expanding company.

Applications in writing only to:

F. S. A. HEWITT

The Phillips Motor Group
226 YORK STREET, BELFAST

(a) Why is the firm advertising for staff? (1 mark)
(b) In which of the jobs is experience essential? (1 mark)
(c) Give two benefits, apart from salary, which successful applicants might receive. (2 marks)
(d) What other information would you want to know before applying for any of the jobs? (2 marks)
(e) Put yourself in the place of the Personnel Officer of Phillips Motor Group and design a job application form suitable for the jobs advertised. (10 marks)

(NICCEA)

QUESTION 4

Marion and Peter need to employ ten assembly workers. Each worker will be required to do a variety of jobs including welding and joinery. They are prepared to give training to some workers if needed. Marion and Peter had already appointed nine workers when they received two more applications. The curriculum vitae of each candidate is shown below.

Curriculum Vitae	
MOHAMMED SINGH	
Address:	14 Hope Street
	Manswood
Date of Birth:	18 May 1938
Education:	Althorp School
	Manswood
	1950–1955
	No qualifications
Career:	Apprentice Welder
	Wengen Metals
	1955–1959
	Welder
	Wengen Metals
	1959–1974
	Foreman
	Wengen Metals
	1974–1992
	Redundant 1992

Curriculum Vitae		
DAMIAN McNULTY		
Address:	14 Riverside	
	Meltham	
Date of Birth:	23 June 1977	
Education:	All Saints School	
	Meltham	
	1988–1993	
GCSEs:	Subject	Grade
	English Lang	D
	English Lit	D
	Mathematics	B
	CDT	A
	Art	B
	History	F
Work Experience:	Two weeks at Dench	
	Steel Works, Meltham	

(a) (i) Using the information provided above, which of the two applicants would you advise the firm to employ? Give reasons for your choice.
(12 lines provided)   (9 marks)

    (ii) State *three* sources of information about the applicants, other than the curriculum vitae, which would help Marion and Peter to choose between them. (5 lines provided)   (3 marks)

The Contract of Employment Act (1972) requires employers to give a Contract of Employment to employees.

(b) (i) State *four* things that you would expect to be included in a Contract of Employment. (6 lines provided)   (4 marks)

    (ii) What are the benefits of a Contract of Employment to the worker?
(7 lines provided)   (4 marks)

Most of the employees at Marpete Trailer Tents are members of a trade union.

(c) What are the advantages to the employee of being a member of a trade union? (8 lines provided)   (5 marks)

Marpete Trailer Tents has agreed a no-strike deal with the unions. This agreement has the following features:
► Only one union will be able to negotiate pay and conditions on behalf of all workers.
► Labour can be used flexibly.
► Arbitration is binding on both management and the union.
► All employees have the same status.

(d) Give reasons why both the employees and management have accepted the deal. (9 lines provided) (8 marks)

(MEG)

(Sections (c) and (d) will be dealt with in Chapter 17.)

TUTOR'S ANSWER TO Q.3

(a) The firm is advertising for staff because it is launching a new outlet.
(b) Experience is essential in the Sales and Service Personnel jobs.
(c) The two benefits which successful applicants might receive could be a subsidised canteen and membership of a private medical insurance scheme.
(d) Before applying for the jobs you may wish to obtain information on (1) salary (2) number of weeks holiday per year (3) pension scheme (4) the length of the working week (i.e. hours worked per week).
(e)

THE PHILLIPS MOTOR GROUP

Application for the post of _____

Full name _____

Address _____

_____

_____

Date of Birth _____

Education: Schools and colleges attended plus dates

_____

_____

_____

Qualifications: Grades, plus dates taken

_____

_____

_____

Work experience: with dates

_____

Other information

_____

Name and addresses of TWO referees

_____

Signature _____ Date _____

STUDENT'S ANSWER TO Q.3

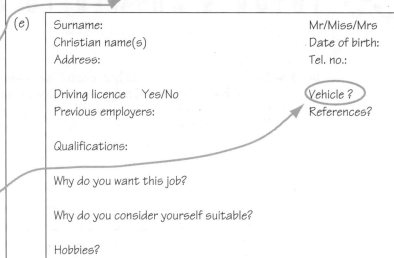

> Do read the question carefully. The firm is launching a new outlet, *not* a new car.

> Experience is 'required'; *essential* is a stronger term.

> It doesn't actually say that the company is a PLC.

> Fine. You may also want to know the number of weeks of holiday per year.

> At the top of the application form you might put: Application for the post of...

> Is this necessary?

> Quite a good application form. Perhaps a bit 'squashed'! Also, it needs space for signature and date at the bottom.

(a)   The firm is launching a new Peugeot.

(b)   Experience is essential with a sales personnel and a service personnel.

(c)   (i)   Share's in the company
      (ii) Company car

(d)   Before applying for any of the jobs I would want to know the salary/wages, work hours, age and sex of the person required.

(e)

Surname:	Mr/Miss/Mrs
Christian name(s)	Date of birth:
Address:	Tel. no.:
Driving licence Yes/No	Vehicle ?
Previous employers:	References?
Qualifications:	

Why do you want this job?

Why do you consider yourself suitable?

Hobbies?

COURSEWORK

ASSIGNMENT – JOB ADVERTISEMENTS AND APPLICATION FORMS

1. Choose the type of job you would like to do on leaving school.
2. Choose *three* ways in which the job is likely to be advertised. It may be in (a) the local job centre, (b) the local newspaper (c) the school careers office.
3. Obtain information on the chosen job from all three sources. You will have to visit the local Job Centre and, perhaps, buy the local evening newspaper several times before the type of job you want appears.
4. Compare the three ways of advertising a job vacancy. Do they differ? Is there any important information they have omitted? Could you suggest ways in which the advertisements could be improved? Once you have obtained the information and made your decisions, write up your findings in a presentable form.
5. Send for the application forms and further details (if they are sending out printed forms). Compare the forms. What are the differences, if any? Have you the right experience/qualifications for the job? Could you suggest ways in which the forms could be improved? Again write up your findings in a presentable form.
6. Having obtained the advertisement and application forms and presented your findings, did you find:
    (a) that the advertisements were misleading?
    (b) the application forms were difficult to understand and complete? (If so, why?)
    (c) that you would stand a good chance of obtaining one of the jobs you chose? (If not, why not?)

(Item 6 could also be written up as part of the assignment.)

A Review Sheet for the Chapter will be found on p. 249

MOTIVATION

GETTING STARTED

Throughout the UK there are a great number of different occupations, in which individuals contribute to the production of goods and services. There are three broad categories of productive activity (often called stages or sectors) in which the working population is involved:

1. **primary**, 'extractive' stage workers, e.g. farmers and miners
2. **secondary**, 'manufacturing' stage workers, e.g. steel workers and car workers on a production line
3. **tertiary**, 'service' stage workers, e.g. bankers and advertisers.

The various stages are part of the 'chain of production' and are dealt with in more detail in ch. 3. You can perhaps think of many reasons why people go to work, but I am sure without too much thought you would put 'to obtain an income' at the top of your list.

Motivation means the reason why people act or behave in a particular manner. Two extremes of motivation, low and high, can be seen if one compares a student's willingness to get up for school on a Monday morning with the willingness to get up to go out with friends on a Saturday morning. Motivation is an important area for any company because if the workforce is not motivated then the company will not be achieving its full potential.

There are a number of factors which could influence a worker's motivation:

1. wage level
2. attractive working environment
3. fringe benefits
4. effective management team
5. satisfaction in the work.

It may be possible for you to memorise the above factors by the mnemonic WAFES (W = wage level, A = attractive working environment, F = fringe benefits, E = effective management team, S = satisfaction in the work).

Many managers would go along with the 'carrot and stick' theory of motivation: the 'carrot' being the reward you offer an employee, usually money, so that he or she will work harder; the 'stick' being that if they do *not* work harder they will lose money or even their job. This chapter deals with the factors which influence motivation, concentrating mainly on the financial incentives.

WAGES

SALARIES

EARNINGS

WAGE DIFFERENTIALS

TYPES OF PAYMENT

THE WAGE SLIP

GROSS AND NET PAY

DEDUCTIONS FROM PAY

ALLOWANCES AND OUTGOINGS

TAX CODES

FRINGE BENEFITS

JOB SATISFACTION

MANAGEMENT AND JOB SATISFACTION

ESSENTIAL PRINCIPLES

1 ▷ WAGES

Wages is money which is paid weekly, often in the form of a pay packet including notes and coins. Many companies, however, are now insisting that their employees are paid in the form of a direct transfer into their bank account. This involves less administration for the company and is therefore less costly. As it avoids the need to transport large amounts of cash, it is also more secure.

The wage is, in most cases, expressed as a **rate per hour** and the employee is paid extra for any **overtime** worked, beyond their basic working week. This overtime is usually paid at 'time' (i.e. the basic rate per hour) plus a 'quarter' or 'time plus a half'. Overtime beyond a certain number of hours or at an unsocial time is usually paid at 'double time'.

Waged employees are usually **manual workers**.

2 ▷ SALARIES

Salaries are paid monthly, normally directly into a bank account.

The salary will in most cases be expressed as an **annual amount** which will not normally be based on hours worked. Salaried staff are *not* usually paid overtime.

Salaried staff are usually **'white collar' workers** and are given greater notice of dismissal than waged employees. Weekly paid workers are normally on one week's notice while salaried staff are usually given, and have to give, a month's notice.

3 ▷ EARNINGS

The wage rate can be seen as the 'basic rate', which is the wage an individual would receive for working a normal working week. **Earnings** include the wage rate *and* payments for such things as overtime and bonuses (which may be for increased productivity). Earnings will therefore tend to be much greater than the wage rate might suggest.

4 ▷ WAGE DIFFERENTIALS

Wage differentials are the differences in wages earned by employees in different jobs. Workers will view their level of pay as being very important since it determines their standard of living and may also determine their status within the firm and, perhaps, also within society at large. For these reasons, they will be interested in how their pay compares to other groups of workers.

Wage differentials may affect individual or group motivation at work. They can lead to industrial disputes, as one group of workers may feel their differentials are inadequate compared to another group.

5 ▷ TYPES OF PAYMENT

There are a number of ways that the employer can calculate the employee's wage: time rate, piece rate, standard rate, by profit sharing or bonus systems.

❝ Make sure you understand the differences between time rate, piece rate and standard rate. ❞

A. TIME RATE

With a **time rate** of payment all employees doing a similar job (maybe working on a production line) are paid a certain amount per hour. For example they may be paid £3.00 per hour (the basic rate) for a normal 40-hour week thus giving them a **gross weekly wage** of £120. Any hours worked over 40 hours may be paid at an overtime rate, perhaps one and a quarter times the basic rate (i.e. £3.75 per hour). The basic rate will, of course, vary from firm to firm.

The **advantages** of a time rate system of payment are:

▶ it is easy for the firm to calculate wages
▶ the worker knows exactly what he is to receive for spending a certain period of time at work.

The **disadvantages** are:

▶ good and bad workers are paid the same rate per hour
▶ there has to be a 'clocking in' system to determine the hours worked
▶ there needs to be supervision to make sure that the quantity and quality of the work produced is maintained.

B. PIECE RATE

With a **piece rate** system, employees are paid on the basis of the quantity of work produced. This type of payment is usually used when quality is not very important. The employees will normally receive a basic rate to which is added an extra payment based on the amount produced.

The **advantages** of a piece rate system are:

▶ the workers who are quicker are rewarded for their effort
▶ it provides an incentive to work harder
▶ the workforce will need less supervision, at least as regards the quantity of work produced.

The **disadvantages** are:

▶ the work may be rushed, which means that quality may suffer
▶ careful employees will earn less
▶ the employees may be tempted to work too quickly, which may result in accidents
▶ it can be difficult to fix a piece rate.

Instead of being paid entirely on a piece rate system, workers can be paid partly on a time rate basis and partly on a piece rate basis, through a bonus scheme linked to results.

C. STANDARD RATE

Standard rate is also called a '**flat rate**' and is the same payment to all workers engaged in similar work. This normally applies to salaried staff, who are paid the same annual amount if they are on the same grade as other workers in that occupation.

The **advantage** is that it is easy for employers to calculate. The **disadvantage** is that employees may lack the incentive to work extra hours or to provide a better quality product or service.

D. PROFIT SHARING

The company may distribute a part of the profits in the form of cash, or shares in the company, on a yearly basis to the employees. This is called a **profit sharing scheme** and one well-known company involved in this type of scheme is the John Lewis Partnership.

The **benefit to the employees** is that they obtain a share of the wealth they helped to create and may, therefore, feel greater commitment to the company. The **benefit to the company** is that, hopefully, it will persuade the employees to work harder.

E. BONUS SYSTEMS

The company may make cash payments to their employees at particular times of the year. This could be at Christmas or just before the summer-holiday period. Such **bonus** payments may be linked to a particular standard, such as the length of service, in order to encourage loyalty and to improve motivation. Alternatively, the bonus may be linked to merit (i.e. a merit bonus) perhaps for salesmen who have exceeded a certain sales target.

Figure 15.1 shows a typical wage/payslip for an individual, Mrs S. Jones, who works for Zavros Office Supplies plc, as a personnel assistant.

You will note from the pay slip that Mrs Jones' gross pay for May 1995 was £599.15. The **gross pay** is the amount earned for May before any deductions have been made. The **net pay** or take-home pay is the amount the employee actually obtains after the various deductions have been taken into account. This will be the £417.17 noted in Fig. 15.1, after deducting pension contributions, tax and national insurance contributions. The net pay will be paid straight into the bank account of Mrs Jones at Northwich Bank plc, York. On the other hand, the net pay could be paid in the form of a pay packet, containing cash or a cheque, at the end of each week.

The wage slip can be quite complicated to understand, so read this section carefully.

PAY ADVICE

ZAVROS OFFICE
SUPPLIES PLC

Reference		Account		Date
1 232 710 1995		113627566		MAY 95

Gross Pay to Date	Tax Code
6518.00	352 L

Bank, Branch and Code

15 30 80

NORTHWICH BANK PLC

YORK

Pensionable Eligible Earnings	Net Taxable Pay to Date
389.50	6272.13

Tax to Date	Net Taxable Pay this Mth.
1197.12	585.13

N I NO. YY703613/A

DEDUCTIONS   PAYMENTS

Pension Contribution	Salary
23.37	599.15

Additional Vol. Pension Cont.	Statutory Sick Pay
0.00	0.00

Tax this Month	Other Emoluments
113.39	0.00

National Insurance Cont.	O/Emol. not Rank'd for Pen.
45.22	0.00

Other Salary Reductions	Non Taxable Emoluments
0.00	0.00

DSS Benefit Received	**Net Pay**
0.00	417.17

Total Non Stat'y Ded'n.	THE NET PAY ABOVE IS CREDITED TO YOUR ACCOUNT
0.00	

MRS S JONES

ZAVROS OFFICE SUPPLIES PLC
HUNTINGTON ROAD
YORK
YO2 4JG

ITEMISED NON-STATUTORY DEDUCTIONS

Figure 15.1 The pay slip

GROSS PAY – DEDUCTIONS = NET PAY

As can be seen from the pay slip in Fig. 15.1, there is a running total of gross pay (£6518.00) and of tax deductions so far (£1197.12) for the tax year, which starts on April 6th and ends on April 5th the following year. This is so that the company and the Inland Revenue can keep a check on whether the correct tax has been paid throughout the year.

8 ▷ DEDUCTIONS FROM PAY

There are both compulsory and voluntary deductions from pay. **Compulsory deductions** are enforced by law and include:

▶ income tax
▶ national insurance contributions.

Voluntary deductions are not enforced by law. These include:

▶ union membership subscriptions
▶ contractual saving schemes
▶ company pension.

A. INCOME TAX

Income tax is almost always deducted from gross pay before the employee actually receives any payment. It is organised automatically under a system known as **Pay As You Earn (PAYE)**. In Fig. 15.1, the income tax is £113.39, almost 20% of the gross salary. The income tax goes to the Inland Revenue and forms part of the Government's finances to provide goods and services. There are certain tax allowances to which employees are entitled and these can be found in the section entitled 'Allowances' (see p. 171). Deducting tax allowances from gross pay gives **net taxable pay**. In Fig. 15.1, this was £585.13 for the month in question.

B. NATIONAL INSURANCE CONTRIBUTIONS (NI)

The National Insurance contributions go mainly towards providing the state pension when we retire, and the sickness benefits to which we are entitled during our working lives. In Fig. 15.1 the NI is £45.22 per month, approximately 8% of the gross salary. As can be seen from Fig. 15.1, the pay slip includes a National Insurance Number, Mrs Jones has the Number YY703613/A, and everyone will be given a number if they are paying National Insurance Contributions. The number is given so that a record can be kept of who has paid and exactly how much. A school leaver will normally receive a National Insurance number on starting work and this number will remain with the employee throughout his or her life.

C. UNION MEMBERSHIP SUBSCRIPTIONS

You may be a member of a union and rather than pay your membership subscription on a yearly basis you may decide to pay it monthly. So, for example, if your union membership subscription is £96 per year you may make twelve monthly payments of £8. Your employer may pay this directly to the union and deduct the amount from your gross pay.

D. CONTRACTUAL SAVING SCHEME

Save as you earn (SAYE) has been set up by the Government as a way of regular saving. You contract to save so much per month for a period of five years, on which you receive a rate of interest. It is linked to the rate of inflation (which means that your money still keeps its purchasing power) and is tax free. You can pay into the state scheme by having your employer transfer part of your income directly into the scheme.

E. COMPANY PENSION

You may obtain a company (occupational) pension, in addition to a state pension, if you make contributions on a yearly basis (out of your gross pay) into a pension fund. The money in the pension fund is then invested and goes towards providing pensions for those who have contributed to the fund. Your contributions to the pension fund can be taken out of your pay before you receive it. It is a voluntary deduction and in Fig. 15.1 is shown as £23.37. Pension contributions are made free of tax.

Tax is calculated on your gross pay – after certain allowances and outgoings.

A. ALLOWANCES

You are entitled to earn a certain amount of money before you pay taxes. These are called tax free (or **personal**) **allowances**. The personal allowances for the 1995–96 tax year were:

► **Personal allowance**:
Basic amount	£3525
Age 65–74	£4630
Age 75 and over	£4800

► **Married couple's allowance**:
Basic amount	£1720
Age 65–74	£2995
Age 75 and over	£3035

There are other allowances, such as the blind person's allowance. All these allowances are deducted from the gross pay before the tax is calculated.

B. OUTGOINGS

These are **expenditures** which the Inland Revenue will accept as being valid for tax relief. They can, therefore, be deducted from gross pay (as well as personal allowances) before calculating taxable pay. For example, for certain jobs it is necessary to be a member of a trade union or a professional body, as with accountants and solicitors. You can obtain tax relief on the subscription, provided the trade union or the professional bodies are recognised by the Inland Revenue and are seen as being relevant to the job.

C. ALLOWABLE BUSINESS EXPENSES

These also qualify for tax relief. If **business expenses** are seen as an important part of the job then they can be allowed for in the tax calculation. Business expenses normally relate to those who are self-employed and could cover such things as advertising and rent. A written record of all expenses will be needed, which means that receipts must be kept.

The Inland Revenue can keep a check on an invidual's earnings through the returns made by his employer and through the annual Tax Return filled out by the individual. For most people, those earnings come from a single job and they will only be asked to fill in a tax return very infrequently. Others with earnings from several sources will be asked to fill one in every year. Individuals are sent tax forms in April each year. The forms require details of their income, allowances and outgoings. The allowances and outgoings are then set against gross income to give net taxable income for the year. When this has been calculated, a tax code is issued by the Inland Revenue. This makes sure that the employer deducts the correct amount of tax each month.

The tax code in Fig. 15.1 is 352L. The letter L means that the individual is taxed as a single person. As stated, the personal allowance is £3525 and 352 in the tax code represents the first three numbers of the allowance. For Mrs Jones, there are no other allowances or outgoings; if there were, the code would be higher than 352. A tax code of 524H would mean that the individual receives not only the personal allowance but also the married couple's allowance (total £5245) and 524 in the tax code represents the first three numbers of the allowance. H represents the code for a married person.

Any other allowances, as stated in the last section, will also be added on to the personal allowance and will be included in the code. So if a married man pays union fees of £100 per annum, and these have been agreed by the Inland Revenue, then his code will be 534H.

11 ⟩   FRINGE BENEFITS

An employee can obtain benefits from the company which are extra to the wage or salary. Mrs Jones works for Zavros Office Supplies and she may be able to receive a number of **fringe benefits**.

A. SUBSIDISED CANTEEN

Zavros Office Supplies may be large enough to provide meals either at a reduced rate or free of charge to their employees.

B. COMPANY CARS

A company car may be provided with the job. This could be to employees at a senior level in the company and is a major fringe benefit. All benefits are, however, subject to income tax. Mrs Jones works as a personnel assistant and she may not be senior enough to be allocated a company car.

C. LOWER PRICES PAID FOR COMPANY GOODS

In many manufacturing companies, the employees are allowed to purchase the company products at a discount. This is also true for many stores which allow discounts to their staff on the products they sell. Companies which provide a service may also allow discounts to employees.

D. REDUCED INTEREST ON LOANS

Financial institutions may allow their employees to obtain loans at reduced rates of interest. Many banks and building societies offer their staff reduced rates on mortgages and personal loans.

E. CHILDREN'S EDUCATION

An employee may have to work abroad for a certain period of time and while abroad the company may provide for their employee's children to attend private schools in the UK.

F. REMOVAL EXPENSES AND LEGAL FEES

If an employee moves within the country, for example with promotion, then the company will normally help with the removal expenses and the legal costs of buying and selling property.

G. HEALTH BENEFITS

The company may provide membership of a private medical insurance scheme free or at a reduced rate. This will allow the employee and perhaps his or her family to receive private medical care.

Individuals will have different ideas as to what makes a job satisfying:

A. PAY

Pay is of key significance to job satisfaction and is covered in detail in this chapter.

B. PROMOTION PROSPECTS

Good promotion prospects are likely to increase job satisfaction. Mrs Jones is undertaking the Institute of Personnel Management course on a day-release basis at the local college. If she passes the examinations then there is a strong possibility she will be promoted to be a personnel manager.

❝❝ Note that job satisfaction is about much more than pay. ❞❞

C. ENVIRONMENT

The environment in which the employees have to work can affect their job satisfaction. The levels of noise, heating, ventilation and dirt and the presence or absence of facilities such as changing rooms and canteens, are all seen as important. Here Mrs Jones is fortunate because her offices have only recently been built and offer an ideal working environment, being quiet, centrally heated, well-ventilated and clean.

D. COLLEAGUES

If you find your colleagues are difficult to work with, then this will obviously affect your job satisfaction. Mrs Jones works closely with eight people in the personnel department and, although she works well with most of them, there is one she finds very difficult to work with. This personality clash tends to upset her from time to time, and reduces her effectiveness at work.

E. FRINGE BENEFITS

The job may provide 'perks' (perquisites) which are extra to pay and can take a number of different forms. (See earlier.)

F. MANAGEMENT STYLE

Management style, whether autocratic or democratic, may influence a person's satisfaction at work. Management style is dealt with in more detail in ch. 5.

G. WORKING HOURS

'Working hours' refers not only to the hours the employee actually works but also the times of day or night the hours are worked. Many people work a fixed day, say from 9.00 a.m to 5.00 p.m., but others work shifts or flexitime.

Shift work is used extensively in manufacturing industries, because it is less expensive to keep machinery going through the night. So, as one group of workers (a shift) finishes then another shift starts. Many individuals do not enjoy working on the night shift and this may affect job satisfaction. Hours worked outside a period from 8 a.m. to 5 p.m. are called **unsocial hours** and are paid at a higher rate.

Flexitime is a flexible working hours scheme which may increase job satisfaction because it allows employees to vary their hours of work, within limits. Flexitime normally operates on the basis that employees have to be at work between 10.00 a.m. and 12 noon and 2.00 p.m. and 4.00 p.m. (known as the **core time**) but that they can arrive at work early (usually not before 8.00 a.m.) and leave late (usually up to 6.30 p.m). Employees will have to work a certain number of hours per week but have flexibility in deciding how those hours are made up. Zavros Office Supplies operates flexitime, which pleases Mrs Jones as it allows her to build up extra hours which she can use to take a half-day holiday every so often.

H. JOB CONTENT

There is no substitute for an interesting job. If you work in a factory on a mass-production line, putting chocolates into boxes for example, then you may find it boring and frustrating. Here the lack of job satisfaction may in some way be compensated by higher pay. Attempts to give varied experience to employees may increase job satisfaction.

I. RECOGNITION

Employees may feel a greater degree of satisfaction in their job if recognition is shown of the work they have undertaken. This again refers to the style of management and how those in managerial positions relate to their work force. (See ch. 5.)

J. LEVEL OF RESPONSIBILITY

The greater the level of responsibility given to the employee the greater may be his or her feeling of worth and, as a result, the greater the job satisfaction.

Management can attempt to deal with the problem of a lack of job satisfaction and motivation by:

▶ job enlargement
▶ job enrichment
▶ job rotation.

A job may be **enlarged** to allow the employee to undertake a wider range of different tasks but all with the same level of difficulty and responsibility. This may reduce the level of boredom and frustration.

A job may be **enriched** by giving the employee a greater range of tasks to do, with variations in the level of difficulty and responsibility. This will obviously demand more of the employee and, hopefully, increase job satisfaction.

With **job rotation** the employees all learn a number of basic skills and exchange jobs at regular intervals, perhaps working as a team. Job rotation reduces boredom and can help increase job satisfaction.

EXAMINATION QUESTIONS

QUESTION 1

A firm pays its employees by piece-rates.

(a) State ONE advantage to the firm. (3 lines for answer)
(b) State ONE advantage to the employees. (3 lines for answer)

(ULEAC)

QUESTION 2

The monthly pay slip of John Brown, an office worker, is shown in Fig. 15.2
Unfortunately the computer has left out the figure for net pay.

PAY SLIP

	Location	Pay No.	Name	Month	N.I. Number
	247	9090021	J BROWN	SEP 1992	ZT128578C

Pay to Date (excl. Supn.)	Pay with other Employment	Tax to Date	Tax with other Employment	Supn. to Date	N.I. to Date	Tax Code
3668.09		804.90		234.16	124.86	156L

Gross Pay	Overtime etc.	Sick Benefit Adjustment	Sup'n Addit Pay	Gross Pay After Adjustment	Superann.	Income Tax	Nat. Ins
671.00				671.00	40.26	150.00	21.47

Advances	Other Deductions	Round up last month	Non Taxable Allowances	Net Pay	Round up this month
	20.00				

Figure 15.2

(a) What is John Brown's Pay Number? (1 mark)
(b) What do the initials N.I. on the pay slip stand for? (1 mark)
(c) State how much John Brown paid in September towards his pension scheme. (1 mark)
(d) How much tax had John Brown paid BEFORE receiving his September pay slip? (1 mark)
(e) Calculate John Brown's net pay for September. (2 mark)
(f) State:
  (i) John Brown's tax code number. (1 mark)
  (ii) How this number is arrived at. (3 lines for answer) (2 mark)
  (iii) How John Brown is informed each year of his tax code. (2 lines for answer) (1 mark)

(ULEAC)

TUTOR'S ANSWER TO Q.2

(a) 9090021
(b) N.I. stands for National Insurance.
(c) £40.26 superannuation. (Take your time over these questions because it is very easy to write down the wrong figure.)
(d) £804.90
(e) (Again, you need to be careful when working out these calculation questions.)

Gross pay	=	£671.00
Income tax:		£150.00
National Insurance:		£21.47
Pension:		£40.26
Other deductions:		20.00
Total deductions	=	£231.73
Gross pay – deductions	=	net pay
£671.00 – £231.73	=	£439.27

Net pay is £439.27

(f) (ii) 156L.
  (ii) The tax code is arrived at by taking into account his personal allowances. He will be able to earn a certain amount before he is taxed; because he is single (denoted by the letter L in the code) then he is eligible for the single person's allowance. He may also be entitled to other allowances.
  (iii) The Inland Revenue will inform John Brown of his tax code.

STUDENT'S ANSWER TO Q.1

‪❝❞‬ Good. You can also mention that the firm will benefit from having less need to supervise its workforce. ‪❞‬

‪❝❞‬ Good. This answer puts across the idea that wages are directly linked to the amount produced. ‪❞‬

‪❝❞‬ A good answer overall, showing that the student understands what is meant by piece rates. Make sure that you can distinguish between piece rates and a standard rate. ‪❞‬

(a)   One advantage to the firm:

The firm can see the amount of work individual staff are producing, and can compare the efficiency between members of staff:

(b)   One advantage to the employees:

Gives them an incentive to work faster and more efficiently. The more they produce, the larger wage packet they will receive at the end of the day.

COURSEWORK

ASSIGNMENT – WORKING FOR A LIVING

In this assignment you should describe how a selection of your family and/or friends are motivated in their work. (Be sure to tell them that any information will be treated as confidential and that their names will not be revealed in the assignment.)

You might divide your questions into: pay, conditions at work, job satisfaction and fringe benefits. The following questions will give you a start to the assignment but there may be others you can think of.

1. Find out the method by which they are paid:
    (a) time rate
    (b) piece rate
    (c) standard rate.

2. What do they see as the advantages and disadvantages of their method of pay? Do these match the advantages and disadvantages given in this chapter?

3. Are they members of any profit-sharing or bonus scheme? If so, what do they see as the advantages or disadvantages of such schemes?

4. In this chapter (p. 173–4), we listed the factors which influence job satisfaction. Ask your chosen friends/family to give a list of factors which *they* feel affect their job satisfaction. Do they agree or disagree with the list?

Are there any other influences on job satisfaction (for example, closeness to home) which are not on the list?

5. Are there any fringe benefits obtained with their jobs? If so, what are they? Are they a major factor in job satisfaction and motivation?

Use any illustrations and examples that you feel are relevant.

A Review Sheet for this chapter will be found on p. 250.

GETTING STARTED

Communications are becoming increasingly important for today's businesses. Modern firms need to communicate with a large number of different groups of people (Fig. 16.1). All these groups communicate with business in different ways. At one end of the scale, there is the humble letter; at the other, there are all the very high-speed links between modern computers, which pass millions of bits of information every minute.

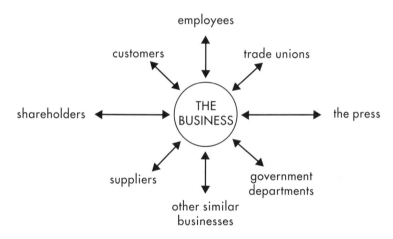

Figure 16.1 Communication lines for business

There are **written** forms of communication (like letters and reports), **visual** forms (such as charts, diagrams and television programmes), **oral** forms (such as speeches, interviews and telephone conversations) and **electronic** forms (like telex, fax and computers). A further type of communication is usually ignored or forgotten: human communication on a **non-verbal** basis. This type of communication is normally called **body language** but it really uses our faces more than our bodies.

Remember the different **types of communication**, by the acronym WOVEN:

▶ **Written**
▶ **Oral**
▶ **Visual**
▶ **Electronic**
▶ **Non-verbal**

To simplify the extremely complex subject of communications, it is best to divide it into those forms of communication which take place *within* the business and those which take place *between* the business and the outside world: **internal** and **external** communication.

INTERNAL COMMUNICATIONS

EXTERNAL COMMUNICATIONS

EFFECTIVE COMMUNICATIONS

ESSENTIAL PRINCIPLES

A. WRITTEN COMMUNICATIONS

Written internal communications include: letters, memos, reports, agendas, minutes, in-house journals or magazines, and electronic mail (e-mail).

Letters

The letter is a form of written communication which is rarely used *within* companies except in special circumstances:

(a) between separate parts of the same company which happen to be situated in different parts of the country or in different parts of the world;

(b) between managers and employees in a formal matter, such as employment (the letter of appointment), changes in conditions of service (e.g. promotion or an increase in holiday entitlement) or dismissal.

The letter is treated in greater detail under *external communications* below.

Memos

Almost all of the written communication within businesses is in the form of *memorandums*, **memos** for short. A memo is an informal type of letter which, because it is only sent to people in the same company, does not need to be fully addressed. (Compare Figs 16.2 and 16.3 which demonstrate the headings of both letters and memos.) Memos are not usually signed and they are relatively informal but this does not mean that they do not matter. Memos are part of the official communications of the business and must be treated seriously – in court actions, the memos between members of staff in a business can be used as evidence.

THE SICK PARROT RECORD COMPANY LTD

15 High Street
Hollywoodville
HD15 9FN

14 February 1995
Mr L. J. Silver
The Ship Inn   Our ref: AB87/D
Treasure Island   Your reference: SP/LJS
TI5 8PE

Dear Mr Silver

RECORDING PROPOSAL

Thank you for your letter of 24 January and for the demonstration tape
enclosed with it.

I am afraid that our record company does not normally publish sea-shanties
and, even if we were to change our policy, we do not think that "Yo, Ho, Ho,
and a bottle of rum" is a suitable lyric for the younger audience today.

I am returning your tape with this letter and wish you luck in finding a
publisher.

Yours sincerely,

Brian Opstein
Managing Director

Figure 16.2 A business letter

MEMORANDUM

To: Post Clerk,   Date: 14 February 1995

From: B. Opstein

Subject: Letters from Mr L.J. Silver

Please note that I have received yet another demo tape from this character. That makes 372 to date!

I am thoroughly tired of sea-shanties and promises of maps of buried treasure and chests full of pieces of eight. In future, please intercept these letters (you will recognise them by the parrot beak marks on the envelope) and return them, unopened, to the sender.

Figure 16.3 A business memo

Reports

Reports are used where a much longer piece of work has to be communicated within the company or by outsiders who are working for the business on a temporary basis. A report is generally a detailed written statement on a particular subject. It can be compiled by an individual or by a group, and usually contains specific elements, although the shape and order of these elements can differ between companies:

▶ a section stating the **objectives** of the report usually in the form of **terms of reference** (the limits which are placed on the investigation needed to compile the report);

▶ a section detailing the **findings** of the report, i.e. the results of the investigations which were carried out;

▶ a **conclusion** which will usually also contain **recommendations** about the subject of the report.

Agendas

Meetings are a form of oral communication but they need to have some written elements so that people can know what the meeting is supposed to cover and, after it has happened, what the meeting decided. *Before* every meeting, therefore, the secretary of the committee will send out an **agenda** – a list of headings under which points will be discussed. They are usually given in a set order:

▶ **Apologies for absence** – from anyone who cannot attend.

▶ **Matters arising** – any matter which a member might want to bring up concerning anything which happened at the last meeting.

▶ **Main points for discussion.**

▶ **Any other business** – any relevant subject which may not have been announced on the agenda.

▶ **Date of the next meeting** – date, place and time.

Minutes

Following a meeting, the secretary of the committee, or someone who is nominated, will draw up and issue a record of what was decided by the meeting. This record is called the **Minutes of the Meeting**.

The minutes are *not* a word-by-word account of exactly what was said (which would be called a **transcript**); instead, they are an account of the main matters which were covered, together with the decisions which were taken and a list of who is responsible for carrying out those decisions (see Fig. 16.4).

In-House Journals or Magazines

Many companies communicate with their staff through regular newsletters or newspapers which are usually called *in-house magazines.*

They are magazines produced by the firm itself, circulated purely within the company and will contain news about new products, new employees, special trips being organised, and so on. The magazines are intended to help make staff feel more a part of the organisation and make sure that they know more about what is happening.

There will, of course, be many other forms of written communication within a company, including rule books for the pension fund and sickness scheme, and brochures explaining any discount schemes which may be available. Most large companies also produce an *Annual Report* for their employees which tells them, often in a very colourful and graphic way, how the company is progressing and what its plans for the future are.

MINUTES OF A MEETING OF THE BOARD OF DIRECTORS OF THE SICK PARROT RECORD COMPANY LTD. HELD AT 15, HIGH STREET, HOLLYWOODVILLE ON 30 MARCH 1995.

ACTION

Present: Lord Carrott of Cockleton, Chairman.
B. Opstein, Managing Director
Lady Carrott,
P. McCourtney
M. Jogger

Apologies for absence: were received from Sir Eric Whipsnade.

Minutes: The minutes of the last meeting were agreed.

Matters Arising: Lady Carrott reminded the Board that the gold record for Mr Elton Frank had still not been delivered to his mansion in Chelsea.

Mr L.J. Silver: Mr Opstein brought the Board up to date on the matter of the large quantities of demo tapes submitted by Mr Silver, and asked the Board for advice as to how to discourage future supplies of sea-shanties.
It was decided, following a suggestion by Lady Carrott, that
Mr P. McCourtney would ask Mr Silver to join him for a re-recording of the   P.M.
old favourite 'The Skye Boat Song'.

Any Other Business: Mr Jogger asked the Board why the company had not yet re-released his hit-album, 'This is the Perambulating Boulders No 37'. It   B.O.
was agreed that Mr Opstein would look into the matter.

Next Meeting: It was agreed that the next meeting would be held at the Board's premises on 4 April 1995.

Figure 16.4 Minutes of a board meeting

Electronic Mail

As businesses become more and more computerised, many larger organisations are switching to **e-mail** for internal communications. Many such organisations now provide a networked computer terminal for almost every member of staff (the 'one per desk' policy). This makes it a relatively simple step to allow all internal memos and reports to be sent electronically. Not only is this quicker and more reliable than the old 'internal mail' systems but it is also cheaper: the organisation saves on paper and envelopes as well as on the much more expensive need for one or more people to operate the internal mail system.

First you type the message, memo or report, then fill in the electronic 'address' of the person or persons to whom you want to send it, and finally press a key. The material is sent instantaneously to the addressee and sits in their electronic mailbox until they next switch on their computer and see the 'messages awaiting you' signal on their screen.

B. ORAL COMMUNICATIONS

Oral communications are those that are spoken: on the telephone, in meetings, during interviews and assessments, in committee.

The Telephone

Much oral contact within companies is conducted on the **telephone** and many firms have internal telephone systems which allow the employees to have conferences with other staff by phone. Up to five or six members of staff can speak together and have a 'meeting' on the phone, without leaving their own individual offices.

Meetings

Meetings are an important form of internal communication. Some are held by telephone or by video-link (see below) but most are held on a face-to-face basis in a single room.

Interviews and Assessments

Staff can usually communicate with their bosses in an informal oral way at any time, but firms need formal ways of communicating as well. If a member of staff is seriously concerned about something, they can request a formal interview with their superior to try to resolve the matter. In a similar way, the boss might request a formal interview with the employee to bring a serious matter to their attention.

Many companies these days also use formal staff assessment interviews to make sure that staff are happy with their work (and that their boss is happy with *them*), to set objectives for the next year and to investigate ways of helping the member of staff to further their career (through further training or education).

Works committees

Some companies have Works committees which are attended by representatives of both management and employees. The objective of these committees is to provide an opportunity for any ideas or problems which might be identified by either management or staff to be discussed.

C. VISUAL AND ELECTRONIC COMMUNICATIONS

Companies use many **visual** forms of communications internally, including posters – for safety information or to inform employees about special offers – and television. An increasing number of companies have a communications network. Micro-computers which staff have on their desks are linked together so that letters, reports, memos, and other messages can be sent electronically between them without the need for expensive typing and distribution of paper.

D. NON-VERBAL COMMUNICATIONS

We all communicate in **non-verbal** ways but we are so used to reading the signals that we hardly notice it. Most people know what it means when someone winks at them. Without a word being said, we can distinguish between a wink which means 'Don't say a word, I am kidding your colleague here', and one which means 'I like you and I want to be friends but I don't know where to begin'.

Similarly, it does not normally take an expert to tell you how your father, mother, boss, or teacher is feeling, without a single word being necessary. You read their body language: the frown, scowl, smile, raised eyebrow, or slant of the head. These will tell you almost all you need to know but there are many other, more subtle, signs which we also read, such as the way they stand, or hold their hands or the gestures they make.

Non-verbal communication is being studied in many parts of the world and it has become a serious study for many managers. Careful use of an expert knowledge of non-verbal communication can help managers to understand more about how their staff are feeling.

A. WRITTEN COMMUNICATIONS

Written external communications are usually in the form of letters, Annual Reports or newsletters.

Letters

Firms make use of **letters**, brochures and reports as their main forms of external communications. The example of a letter on p. 178 is one to a person outside the company. A memo would *never* be sent to someone outside the firm unless it is a copy of an internal memo in order to help them in some way. However, most memos are considered confidential to the firm and should not be copied to people outside without the permission of senior managers.

Annual Reports

Annual Reports and Accounts are required by law to be sent to all of the shareholders of a limited company. They contain details of the financial performance of the company during the year and details of the directors who will have to be re-elected at the next Annual General Meeting.

Newsletters

Many companies prepare and distribute **newsletters** for their customers. They keep the customers in touch with what the business is doing and inform them about the latest new products and how customers can buy them.

B. ORAL COMMUNICATIONS

Oral external communications are mostly by telephone, or face-to-face conversation.

Telephone

The **telephone** is the most common way in which people outside a company communicate with it. Most companies now recognise the need for special training for staff who have to deal with the public on the telephone. Receptionists and telephone switchboard operators usually have quite long courses on how to deal with people on the telephone.

Face-to-face

The telephone may be very important but **face-to-face** contact is still a vital aspect of many businesses. Shops, banks, building societies, hotels, etc., all have to train their staff to be able to deal with the public directly.

C. VISUAL COMMUNICATIONS

Today's companies are highly skilled in **visual** communications with the outside world. We live in a very visual world in which people are subjected to a large amount of visual communication and the most successful companies are those which make best use of this fact with advertising.

In newspapers and magazines, on the television and on posters, the object is to make people take notice of your product or service by presenting them with attractive and interesting visuals. The advertising can be for your product or service, or for jobs which you would like to attract people into, but it will not be successful unless it draws people to look at it and to read the copy, i.e. the written words which form the main part of the advertisement.

D. ELECTRONIC COMMUNICATIONS

There is a wide range of **electronic communications** and it is growing all the time:

▶ computer links
▶ fax
▶ video

The simplest form of all is the telephone which has been mentioned above. Most of the newer forms of electronic communications rely on computers to send and receive the information.

Computers

Computer communications depend upon a business having:

► a **computer** (usually a micro computer but quite possibly a larger mini computer or mainframe)
► a **modem** (which plugs into the telephone network and enables you to dial into it)
► communications **software** (a computer program which tells the computer how to send and receive messages).

With this equipment – common these days even among private home-computer users – the computer can act as a receiver for all kinds of information and services:

► **databases** – for a fixed fee your computer can be linked to a network of computers and let you access the immense amounts of information contained on those larger machines. **Prestel** is just one of the more common databases but there are many more.
► **telex and e-mail** – again, for a separate fee, you can be linked to an electronic telex service and to electronic mail-boxes into which you can put messages for other people and they can do the same for you. The messages are kept in the memory of a large computer and can be 'read' by your computer whenever you wish.

Facsimile Transmission (Fax)

Fax is a way of transmitting the contents of written or printed pages through the telephone system. If your office has a fax machine and you wish to send a document through to another office in a different city the normal way to do it is by post.

Postal services can be quite slow, though, especially if the other office is in a different country. You might be able to use the telex but this is more expensive and means that someone has to type the whole document out again onto the telex machine. As long as the other office has a fax machine, however, you need simply to feed your letter into the machine, dial the number of the other office and the machine will send the letter through almost instantly. What really happens is that the other office receives a type of photocopy of the letter (the original stays with you).

Fax is a very fast form of communication and is much cheaper than telex. It is also very useful for sending graphics (something which telex cannot do and which, up to now, had to be done through the post or by an expensive special messenger). Designs, engineering drawings, even photographs, can be faxed almost instantly. It is known as 'Intelpost'. Today, some newspapers use a special form of fax system to send whole pages of a newspaper to other printing works around the world.

Like letters and memos, faxes have to contain certain standard information so that the recipient knows where it has come from. It is also important to tell the recipient how many pages to expect. If you send 5 pages and the recipient only receives 4, they have no way of knowing that one has gone missing unless the total number of pages is written on the first page.

The first page of the fax – called the **fax header** – must always, therefore, carry details as follows:

► Name of sender
► Sender's company/organisation
► Sender's fax number
► Date and time fax sent
► Name of recipient
► Recipient's organisation
► Recipient's fax number
► Number of pages in the fax (often stated as 'This one plus ...')

Video-conferencing

Face-to-face meetings are still the most usual way that firms conduct their business. The telephone is immensely valuable but business people still like to see the face of the other person when they are trying to do important business. A person's face can tell you a lot about what he or she really means. Consequently, many people still drive hundreds of miles or fly thousands of miles to have meetings with other people. A great deal of time and money would be saved if all this travel could be avoided.

Video-conferencing attempts to solve the problem. A person who wants to have a meeting sits in front of a bank of screens and a television camera. The camera takes his or her picture and transmits it to the other people and the screens display all of the other people involved in the conference. At present video-conferencing is very expensive. The telephone connections for the TV pictures are slow and not very high quality, and the cost of these lines is very high. Companies which want to take advantage of video-conferencing have to install expensive suites of TV screens and cameras.

However, some large, multinational companies with factories all over the world, have installed video-conference suites, because it is cheaper than sending their executives all over the world for meetings.

Before video-conferencing becomes widely available to everybody, however, a cheaper way of transmitting the pictures and the voices will be necessary. **Fibre-optic** links will be able to do this. In a few years, it will begin to be more common for business-people to hold video-meetings than for them to spend large amounts of time travelling to the face-to-face variety.

E. INFORMATION TECHNOLOGY

In the past, it was not realised that communications like the postal service, were part of the storage and retrieval of information for business. In Victorian times, however, firms which needed to know something had to send letters and then wait for the answer to be returned in the same way – whether it was to ask the price of a piece of equipment which they wanted to buy, or whether one of their customers wanted to re-order some goods. The answers were then acted upon (we hope) and the letters were stored away for future reference. The price list would be stored so that the firm would be able to find out other prices fairly quickly, and the letter from the customer would be stored just in case, at some later time, they claimed that they had not ordered the goods or that they had ordered a different amount.

► Typist types a letter asking for the price list.

► Letter is posted to the supplier.

► One or two days later, letter arrives and is sent to the correct department.

► Sales department receives letter and posts a full price list back after, say, two days.

► Price list arrives through post one or two days later.

► Price list is examined, used and then filed in a filing cabinet.

► If the list is needed a week later, someone must walk down to the filing room, find the correct file, remove the price list and return it to the executive who requires the information.

Figure 16.5 Elementary Information Technology – getting, storing and retrieving a price list

Consider what might happen to the same information flow with today's technology: the microcomputer on the executive's desk would be used as a link to the supplier's computer and, within seconds, the price list would flash up onto the screen. If a record of the list was required, it could be printed out on the printer next to the microcomputer and, if needed for future reference, it could be saved onto a floppy disk. If the executive wanted another price from the list in a week's time, the floppy disk could be selected and inserted, and the information retrieved a few seconds later.

Information technology is not just about speed, however. Modern technology also allows us to store very large amounts of information in a very small space – hence saving money on the cost of floor space and on the labour required to file and retrieve information. Rather than rooms full of layers of shelving, or rows and rows of filing cabinets, the modern company simply has a computer. Most of the book you are now reading was written and stored on a computer. Its twenty chapters, introduction and indexes are actually kept on just one floppy disk. A similar book written several years ago took up three full drawers of files of a filing cabinet (i.e. almost 70 files).

> ▶ Microcomputer used to request information on prices direct from the supplier's computer.
>
> ▶ Within seconds, information appears on screen.
>
> ▶ A written copy can be obtained almost immediately from the printer.
>
> ▶ The price list can be electronically filed within seconds on disk.
>
> ▶ If required, a week later, the information can be retrieved within seconds from the disk.

Figure 16.6 Information Technology in an Electronic Age

Today the availability of **CD-ROM** (compact disk – read only memory) enables vast amounts of information to be stored on just one silver disk. A few years ago, an encyclopaedia could have been stored on about 460 3.5-inch floppy disks; today, that encyclopaedia (together with moving pictures) can be contained on a single CD-ROM.

	Rooms	Cabinets	Drawers	5.25" floppies	3.5" floppies	CD-ROM
One text book	0.1	1	3	3	1	0.002
12-volume encyclopaedia	2.5	28	85	1000	460	1.000

Table 16.1 The impact of modern storage systems

The power of computing systems is also increasing very rapidly. In 1980, the most powerful desktop machines had about 128K RAM, 360K floppies and no hard disks. By the late 1980s, the average desktop had 640K RAM, 720K floppies and 20 MB hard disks. In 1995, office-standard computers had a basic 8MB RAM, 1.4MB floppies, over 500MB of hard drive storage and the capability to read CD-ROMs each of which contains over 600MB of data.

3 ▷ EFFECTIVE COMMUNICATIONS

No matter how fast or efficient a communications system is, it is totally useless if the people who are at the receiving end do not understand what the person at the other end is trying to tell them. Within a company, communications have to be in *two* directions – from the senior people to those who make the goods or provide the service, and the other way round.

EMPLOYEES:	make suggestions
	react to communications from above
	have attitudes
	have problems
	have ideas and views.
MANAGERS:	make decisions
	have reasons for those decisions
	make policy for the future
	make proposals for discussion
	want to change ideas and attitudes

Fig. 16.7 Two-way communications in business.

The most successful companies are those which enable this two-way process to work. Managers cannot run things properly if they do not know what the problems of the workforce are or if they do not listen to suggestions from below; employees cannot work effectively if the decisions of management are not communicated clearly and quickly or if they do not understand where the company is trying to go in the future.

There is no secret to **effective communications** except that everyone must understand that the process has to be **two-way**. To be effective, communication must also be:

▶ **accurate** – you must tell people exactly what you want
▶ **confirmed** – you must make sure that your message has been received and understood.

Neither of these is as easy as it sounds. Your memo to your staff may seem perfectly clear to you but may leave them puzzled as to exactly what you want or when you want it. 'Please make sure that the papers are delivered well before the Board Meeting' could mean many things: Which papers? Delivered to where or to whom? Which board meeting (our company's, someone else's, the next Board Meeting or the one after that, etc.)?

EXAMINATION QUESTIONS

QUESTION 1

A _____ is an informal means of communication between departments of the same organisation.

(ULEAC)

QUESTION 2

In the following questions there is one group of responses A, B, C and D. Each letter in the group may be used once, more than once, or not at all. For each question select the best response and mark its letter in the space provided:

A Telephone
B Postal Service
C Confravision
D Intelpost

From the above forms of communication, A to D, select the one which –

(a) is a means of holding face-to-face meetings between people working in different areas of the country.
Answer_____

(b) is used to acknowledge receipt of a routine order from another firm.
Answer_____

(c) is a means of transmitting facsimiles of documents and drawings at high speed.
Answer_____

(d) is used to discuss a business problem with a colleague at a branch in another town.
Answer_____

(e) is used to link individuals or groups of people in different cities by sound and vision
Answer_____

(ULEAC)

TUTOR'S ANSWERS TO Q.1 AND 2

1. Memo
2. a) C b) B c) D d) A e) C

COURSEWORK

Compile a report, with diagrams, which describes the way in which an organisation, with which you are familiar, communicates.

1. Start by asking the administrators how they communicate with the staff, with the employees or students, and with the outside world.
2. What types of communications media do they use? Identify electronic types, non-electronic types, etc. and do not forget human contact as well.
3. Draw a diagram which shows all these communications routes. Describe how they are used and for what reasons.
4. Try, also, to find out how the communications for your chosen organisation could be improved.

A Review Sheet for this chapter will be found on p. 251.

CHAPTER **17**

INDUSTRIAL RELATIONS

GETTING STARTED

In December 1992, there were 268 **trade unions** in the UK with a total membership of nine million. Some of the trade unions were small with less than 2,500 members whereas others were large, with 20 unions having over 100,000 members and nine unions each had more than 250,000 members each. Over the period 1980–92, the number of trade unions declined from 438 to 268. This was partly the result of smaller unions joining with larger ones. In fact, 20 trade unions with over 100,000 members accounted for 79% of the total trade union membership in 1992 (see Tables 17.1 and 17.2).

Therefore 9 million workers are members of trade unions, out of an employed workforce of approximately $24\frac{1}{2}$ million. What are the main aims of trade unions? What are the reasons for joining a trade union? Are there different types of trade union? What sort of action might a union ask you to take if you are a trade union member? If there is a conflict between the employer you work for and your trade union, then how will that conflict be resolved? These are the main questions you will need to ask yourself while reading this chapter. One point to note is that, although this chapter concentrates on the **conflict** side of industrial relations, trade unions do have other roles to play. For example, they are involved in discussions on the economy with representatives from business and government, and in providing education and training, legal advice and social facilities for their members.

TRADE UNIONS

COLLECTIVE BARGAINING

INDUSTRIAL ACTION

RESOLVING DEADLOCK

ESSENTIAL PRINCIPLES

1 〉 TRADE UNIONS

What are trade unions? They can be traced back as far as the Middle Ages but it is only since the nineteenth century that modern trade unions have developed. They are made up of groups of workers who have a common interest, which may be a common skill, a similar job or the same industry. By joining together as a union the workers can act like a pressure group (see ch. 18). The members of the union will pay a subscription, part of which will go towards employing union officials. These officials will present the views of the union to the employers in a bid to achieve their aims.

Year	Number of unions at end of year	Total membership at end of year (thousands)	Percentage change in membership since previous year
1980	438	12,947	−2.6
1981	414	12,106	−6.5
1982	408	11,593	−4.2
1983	394	11,236	−3.1
1984	375	10,994	−3.2
1985	370	10,821	−1.6
1986	335	10,539	−2.6
1987	330	10,475	−0.6
1988	315	10,376	−0.9
1989	309	10,158	−2.1
1990	287	9,947	−2.1
1991	275	9,585	−3.6
1992	268	9,048	−5.6

Table 17.1   Trade unions: numbers and membership 1980–92

Source: *Employment Gazette* June 1994

Number of members	Number of unions	Membership (thousands)	Number of unions (per cent)	Membership of all unions (per cent)
Under 100	34	2	12.7	0.02
100–499	58	14	21.6	0.2
500–999	25	18	9.3	0.2
1,000–2,499	46	79	17.2	0.9
2,500–4,999	25	94	9.3	1
5,000–9,999	17	120	6.3	1.3
10,000–14,999	5	58	1.9	0.6
15,000–24,999	10	178	3.7	2.0
25,000–49,999	19	699	7.1	7.7
50,000–99,999	9	627	3.4	6.9
100,000–249,999	11	1,710	4.1	18.9
over 250,000	9	5,449	3.4	60.2
Total	268	9,048	100	100

Table 17.2   Trade unions: numbers and membership December 1992

Source: *Employment Gazette* June 1994

✗ A. THE AIMS OF TRADE UNIONS

A trade union will usually seek to be involved in anything which will affect the situation of its members. The main aims of a trade union are:

▶ to improve the conditions of employment, such as wages, holidays and hours of work;

▶ to improve the working environment, such as lighting, heating, safety, noise and ventilation;

▶ to improve the benefits of the members who are sick, retired or who have been made redundant;

❝❝ Note that the reasons for joining a Trade Union are not just to improve the level of pay. ❞❞

► to take up the cases of those whom the union sees as being unfairly dismissed;
► to improve job satisfaction, which may mean promoting education and training;
► to share in the planning and controlling of the company;
► to aid job security;
► to influence government decisions – with this in mind, a number of trade unions sponsor MPs, the aim being to give the union a voice in Parliament.

B. REASONS FOR JOINING A TRADE UNION

When you start your first job, you will normally be contacted by the trade union representative (normally the shop steward) who will ask you if you want to join the trade union. If you do join a union, you will have to pay a yearly union subscription. This could be paid at once, or as a certain amount per week out of your wages.

Your reasons for joining a trade union may include some of the following:

► to improve your level of pay (basic rate) and working conditions;
► to provide support if you think you have been unfairly treated, unfairly dismissed or made redundant – this may be in terms of advice and/or financial help;
► to take advantage of sporting and other social facilities;
► to benefit from training courses run by the union;
► to obtain discounts in certain shops and for certain services such as holidays;
► to identify with colleagues at work who are members of the trade union and who might pressure you to join;
► to gain employment where a 'closed shop' may be in operation.

Closed Shop

In a **closed shop**, only a member of a particular union can be employed by the firm. The trade union may see two benefits of a closed shop:

1. Non-members of the trade union also benefit when a union obtains for its members such things as wage increases, and so they too should pay union subscriptions.
2. The union may feel that a closed shop improves its 'bargaining power' because *all* employees are members of the union.

The main arguments against closed shops are:

1. employees should have the freedom to decide whether or not they wish to join a trade union;
2. it is seen as unfair that a person is not allowed to work in a particular job unless he is a member of a particular trade union.

C. TYPES OF TRADE UNION

There are four main types of trade union, as shown in Fig. 17.1:

1. craft unions
2. industrial unions
3. general unions
4. white-collar unions.

Craft unions

Craft unions consist mainly of skilled workers who often undertake long apprenticeships, and are the earliest type of union. There may be several craft unions within a single workplace, and this can make it difficult for the management, who often prefer to deal with a single union when negotiating. There can also be disagreements between the craft unions about how the work between the various crafts is allocated (i.e. **demarcation** disputes) and the relative pay levels (i.e. **differentials**).

Industrial unions

Industrial unions include all the workers in a particular industry regardless of what job they do in that industry. They tend to be more common in Europe, particularly in Germany, than they are in the UK. The nearest examples in the UK are the National Union of Mineworkers (NUM) and the National Union of Railwaymen (NUR). Even these cannot be viewed as 'true' industrial unions. Within the coal industry, there is also the Union of Democratic Mineworkers (UDM) and within the railway industry there is also the Associated Society of Locomotive Engineers and Firemen (ASLEF). The benefit of this type of union to the management is that they only have to deal with one trade union, in areas such as pay and working conditions. The benefit to the members is that being larger, they are in a stronger position when negotiating with management.

> It is easy to confuse the different types of trade union, particularly the industrial and general unions.

General unions

General unions cut across industrial boundaries and will include members regardless of skill, type or place of work. They do, however, represent a high proportion of semi- and unskilled workers and are large unions. The Transport and General Workers Union (TGWU) and the Union of Shop, Distributive and Allied Workers (USDAW) are examples of general unions. They can be at a disadvantage because of their size, in that the union leaders may find themselves remote from their members. The union may also be very fragmented with their members spread over a large number of industries nationwide.

White-collar unions

White-collar unions include non-manual workers in areas such as clerical, professional, management and supervisory occupations. The white-collar unions have been the fastest growing unions in recent times as individuals see the benefits which can be obtained from belonging to a trade union. The Manufacturing Science and Finance Union (MSF), the National Union of Teachers (NUT) and the Public Service Union (UNISON) are examples of white-collar unions.

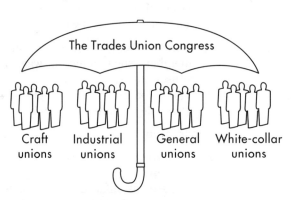

Figure 17.1 The types of trade union

D. THE TRADES UNION CONGRESS (TUC)

Figure 17.1 depicts the **TUC** as an 'umbrella' over the trade unions. The TUC was formed in 1868 and acts as a pressure group, representing the views of trade unions in trying to influence the employers' associations, such as the Confederation of British Industry (CBI) (see below), and the Government itself. The policy of the TUC is decided at the Annual Congress (Conference) which usually lasts for one week in September. Representatives (or **delegates**) are sent from the various unions. The number of delegates each union sends to the Annual Congress depends on the size of its union membership. Delegates have the right to vote on such things as the election of the General Council which is responsible for promoting TUC policies. These will tend to be policies which seek an improvement in the economic and social conditions of the working population.

E. TRADE UNION REPRESENTATIVES

Trade union representatives may be shop stewards or official trade union representatives.

Shop stewards

At the place of work, the trade union **shop steward** will be the union representative you come into contact with the most. The shop steward is elected by the trade union members in the firm, shop or section in which he or she works, although they will still work full-time for the company. They are called shop stewards because they represent the workforce on the 'shopfloor'. (This word originated in the engineering industry which uses the term 'shops' for the various sections of the factory.) The shop steward will form the link between the shopfloor and the union officials. In large companies, a worker representative is required because full-time trade union officials are unable to spend sufficient time in all the companies in which they have members. The shop steward therefore has an important role to play, particularly as national wage agreements have declined in importance and plant bargaining has increased. The shop steward will undertake a number of tasks, including collecting the subscriptions, acting as a voice for the workforce, recruiting new members and distributing information from the union.

Official trade union representatives

Most trade unions will have full-time union officials, who work at the national, regional and district level and have contacts with shop stewards and union members. The top official of the union is often called the General Secretary.

F. EMPLOYERS' ASSOCIATIONS

In its simplest form, an **employers' association** is to employers what a trade union is to employees. Most industries have employers' associations which include employers from that particular industry. These associations may be given the power by their members to negotiate with trade unions on matters, such as the wages and working conditions in that industry. They can also provide advice to members, on such things as Employment Law. Examples of employers' associations include the National Farmers Union and the Federation of Master Builders.

As individual firms grow in size through mergers and takeovers, then the need for them to be in an employers' association declines. Some larger firms, for example Ford, have never felt the need to belong to such an association.

G. THE CONFEDERATION OF BRITISH INDUSTRY (CBI)

Just as trade unions are affiliated to the TUC, so employers' associations are members of the CBI. It was formed in 1965 and represents 3,000 companies, from the smallest to the largest, covering primary, secondary and tertiary production. As well as representing the employers' point of view in talks with the Government and trade unions, it aims at promoting prosperity in British industry. It effectively acts as the spokesperson for industry and management.

As an individual you may be able to go to your employer (who may be a large organisation) and ask for a wage increase or for better working conditions. However, on your own, you may not be successful in your claim; if you were a member of a trade union and they negotiated on your behalf, then the result might be different. The negotiations which take place between trade unions and employers or employers' associations are called **collective bargaining**.

This bargaining can take place at a local or national level. With collective bargaining the relevant trade unions and employers meet to negotiate an agreement, perhaps about pay or working conditions, which could cover the whole industry. In pay negotiations, a national agreement will normally refer to basic rates. These can then be improved at local level where aspects such as bonuses may be negotiated. For example, in collective bargaining over wages (see Fig. 17.2) the union will normally ask for a wage increase (say a claim of 8%) which may be far higher than the employer would be willing to accept. On the other hand, the employer may offer a wage increase (say 2%) which it may later improve upon. The two sides then negotiate to find a wage increase which is acceptable by both sides. This may be an agreement for a 4% wage increase.

Suppose, however, there is no agreement; the trade union is not willing to accept a 4% wage increase and the employers are not willing to offer any more. There may be a number of reasons for this. The company profits may be low, or it may feel that it will have to increase the price of its products (and lose custom!) to pay the higher wage increase. In this case, a **deadlock** is said to occur. To make the employer think again and perhaps offer more than 4%, the workforce may take **industrial action**. The industrial action may have the backing of the trade union. If it has the backing of the union, then the union will have to ballot all the union members, asking them to vote for or against industrial action before the action – which can take a number of forms – can take place.

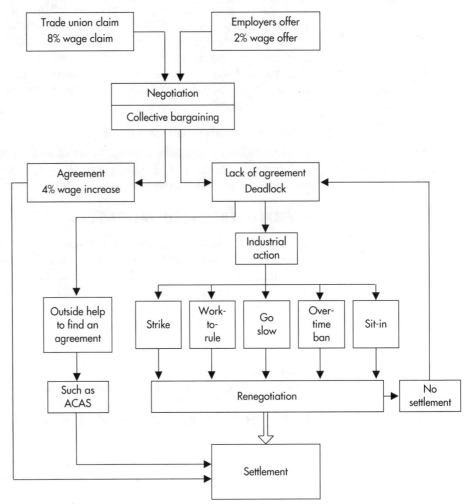

Figure 17.2 The process of collective bargaining

The ultimate weapon which is open to many trade unions is to strike, but as shown in Fig. 17.2 there are other types of industrial action.

▶ strikes
▶ work-to-rule
▶ go slow
▶ overtime ban
▶ sit in.

A. STRIKES

If workers go on **strike**, it means that they withdraw their labour and refuse to work. The strike can take a number of different forms.

Token strike

This is when the workers stage a one-day, half-day or even an hour's stoppage of work in support of their claim.

Selective strike

Here only a certain number of workers, perhaps chosen by areas, are called to strike action by their trade union. Those who carry on working will often pay into a fund to help those who are on strike. This can often be a very disruptive form of action.

All-out strike

With an all-out strike, normally all members of the union withdraw their labour until the dispute is settled. This sort of strike will usually have trade union support which means that the strike is **official**. Here the union will make available a certain amount of strike pay provided there are sufficient resources to support a 'strike fund'. Part of the trade union subscription made on a monthly basis by members will go towards this fund. An **unofficial** strike on the other hand does not have the union's support or backing and can be called a **'wildcat' strike**.

Certain workers may continue to work while the strike is in progress. It may be that they disagree with the strike, or cannot afford to strike because of financial commitments such as mortgages and goods bought on credit. These workers may be called '**blacklegs**' by those who are taking strike action.

When calling for strike action, the trade union in question has, under the Trade Union Act (1984), to hold a **secret ballot** of all its members for the strike to be lawful. The action must be approved by the majority of the union members. If the trade union fails to hold a secret ballot before calling a strike then it loses its legal immunity; the employer could require the strike to be called off and could sue the union for damages.

Picketing

To support their strike action, workers will stand close to the factory gates and try to dissuade other workers and suppliers of goods from entering the factory. You may be aware of picketing in disputes from reports on television or in the newspaper.

Secondary Picketing

This is picketing which takes place *away* from the company or industry involved in the dispute. Those involved in secondary picketing can have injunctions issued against them as introduced under the Employment Act (1980).

Sympathetic Strike

In certain instances, a group of workers may take sympathetic strike action in support of another group of workers.

Blacking

A trade union's support of another group of workers may not go as far as strike action but could include 'blacking'. Here they may refuse to handle equipment, goods, etc. of the industry or firm of the workers on strike.

B. WORK-TO-RULE

Here, workers stick closely to the rules and regulations which govern their work. These rules can be very detailed and are usually viewed only as guidelines. If, however, the workforce follow them strictly they can bring the company to a standstill.

> Make sure you are aware of the different stages an industrial dispute can go through.

C. GO-SLOW

Here, the workforce do their jobs more slowly, deliberately taking longer to complete their normal working operations.

D. OVERTIME BAN

This can be very damaging to a company. With this kind of industrial action, members of the union only work normal hours and refuse to undertake any overtime.

E. SIT-IN

The workforce may refuse to leave the factory, making sure that no goods enter or leave it. A sit-in might occur if the factory is threatened with closure and is, therefore, a strike against the threat of redundancies. The outcome of this might be that workers take over the business, e.g. as a workers' co-operative.

4 ▷ RESOLVING DEADLOCK

The trade union and employers may be in **deadlock**, with neither side being willing to move its position. To help to resolve the dispute, both sides can call on the **Advisory, Conciliation and Arbitration Service (ACAS)**; see Fig. 17.2. ACAS is an independent body set up by the Employment Protection Act (1975) with the role of trying to improve industrial relations. Its main functions, given by the Trade Union Reform and Employment Rights Act (1993), are to:

▶ seek to conciliate on complaints made by individuals under legislation on employee rights;
▶ conciliate in industrial disputes;
▶ arrange independent arbitration and mediation;
▶ advise employers, unions and employees on industrial relations matters.

ACAS provides its services free and is impartial. It is run by a council made up of a chairperson and 11 members representing employers, trade unions and independent organisations.

▶ ACAS provides **Advice and information** on all areas of employment.
▶ ACAS provides **Conciliation**. Here ACAS will be in touch with both sides and will try to find areas which both sides can agree on so that they can come together to start negotiating again.
▶ ACAS provides **Arbitration**. ACAS will, if the two parties agree, refer the dispute to arbitration. An independent group will then listen to the case of both sides and put forward what they view to be a fair settlement. Both sides have to agree in advance to accept the arbitrators' findings.

EXAMINATION QUESTIONS

QUESTION 1

Strikes by workers without trade union support are known as _____.

(ULEAC)

QUESTION 2

An official who acts as a link between trade union members at work and the union's regional office is a _____.

(ULEAC)

QUESTION 3

Collective bargaining is a way of settling wage rates between employers and _____.

(ULEAC)

QUESTION 4

The following article appeared in the 'Daily News'.

Possible Layoffs at XYZ

"We are facing increasing competition from home and abroad". Bob Smith, managing director of XYZ Engineering told our reporter yesterday.

"We must get more up to date machinery and reduce our labour costs. Productivity must improve and we need to become more competitive".

Immediately after the article appeared, Arthur Jones the senior shop steward said: 'This is the first the Union has heard of any changes. I will be calling a meeting of my members tomorrow, and we shall be seeking a meeting with the management as soon as possible. We will resist plans for redundancies.' Bob Smith, when he read the article said: 'They have blown this up out of all proportion. I should have spoken to the unions before letting the press interview me.'

(a) Even before the meeting called by Arthur Jones, many of the members were pressing for immediate strike action. Why might they be suggesting this?

(b) Some members thought that other methods of solving the problem should be tried before taking strike action. What might these methods be and why should the union consider them?

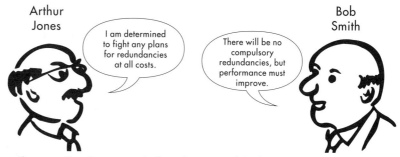

After the meeting between Arthur Jones and Bob Smith, the management put out the following statement.

'The management at XYZ is thinking of buying new machinery for the factory. This may lead to some reduction in manning levels. There will be full consultation with the union at all stages. There will be no compulsory redundancies.'

(c) Why do changes at work usually worry the people who will be affected by them?

(d) What does the management mean by 'There will be full consultation with the union at all stages'? What do you think will be the main points in their discussion?

(NEAB)

TUTOR'S ANSWER TO Q.4

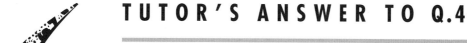

In answering this question it could be easy to write about the other forms of industrial action and fail to mention negotiation. Be careful that you consider all the possible alternatives, including negotiation.

(a) The members of the union may be pressing for strike action for a number of reasons. They will be suspicious that 'up-to-date machinery' will mean less workers, especially since the management want to 'reduce labour costs'. Pressing for strike action will indicate their disapproval of the management proposals for XYZ Engineering and serve as a reminder of what might happen if lay-offs do occur. The members will hope to put pressure on the management at an early stage, by demonstrating their willingness to disrupt the firm's activities if jobs are lost or unacceptable work practices imposed. The union members will probably be unhappy about the fact that the *Daily News* heard of the possible lay-offs before they did.

(b) There are a number of other methods which could be considered in solving the problem. The union members could operate an **overtime ban**, refusing to work more than the normal number of hours per week. This could be very damaging for the company as could a **work-to-rule**, with the workers keeping closely to the rules and regulations laid down by the engineering company. The members may also consider a **go-slow**, undertaking their work as slowly as possible. All of these actions, however, may fail to achieve the desired result for the members of the union. The management may be adamant that lay-offs will have to occur and that productivity will have to improve if the company is to compete with companies at home and abroad. The alternative to industrial action, therefore, could be **negotiation**. Discussions with the management could lead to a satisfactory outcome. The union leaders could agree to **voluntary retirement** or non-replacement of those who leave. They could also agree to **increase productivity** (output per person) as a means of becoming more competitive. Increased productivity and a more efficient company could mean that redundancies are avoided or kept to a minimum.

(c) Changes at work usually worry those who will be affected by them because any change involves **uncertainty**. The workers will have had their security threatened and will be concerned about **redundancy** and having to find another job. There may be high unemployment in the area and they may have to consider moving to another town. This can create all sorts of problems over their children's education, leaving family and friends and having to move house. The change at work could involve the introduction of new machinery. Here, too, there will be the fear of the unknown with new ways of working and, possibly, **training** to be undertaken.

(d) Full consultation means that the management will talk to the union when arriving at their decisions. There will usually be established procedures for management raising issues with the unions *before* a final decision is made. Consultation can involve questions such as: How many workers will be made redundant? What new machinery will be introduced? How will the introduction of the new machinery affect the working conditions of the union members? The final outcome could be redundancies; if so how are these to take place? Are they going to be on the basis of natural wastage, with those over 65 not being replaced, or will there be a need for compulsory redundancies?

S T U D E N T ' S   A N S W E R   T O   Q . 4

(a) Many members were pressing for immediate strike action because they feared that they could lose their jobs if more up to date machinery was brought in. Also, because management communication has been poor, and the article in the paper had appeared unexpectedly, the workers probably feared that they would lose their jobs the same way – with no prior warning. Their strike action would stall any redundancies which might occur.

A good start.

An excellent answer. Uncertainty about the future is an important aspect of this part of the question.

(b) Other methods of solving the problem could be to have better communication between the management and the union. If they have a meeting, they may be able to sort out their differences, before anything drastic happened. If they had problems with communication, they could call in an unassociated body, e.g. an Industrial Tribunal, or ACAS, who may be able to investigate the matter and help to solve the problem.

Good. Better communication might have stopped the problem happening in the first place. Negotiation might help stop the problem becoming more serious. However, alternatives to strike action could have been mentioned, such as an overtime ban, work to rule, go slow, etc.

(c) Changes at work, both large or small, usually worry the people who will be affected by them, as they can cause unrest, disputes or even job losses. For example, when a company wants to bring in more up-to-date machinery, it's usual to replace a worker who is inefficient or uneconomical to the company, therefore the worker will lose his job, as the machinery may be more cost-effective.

Some good points. You might also mention that workers may be 'redeployed' to other parts of the company. Perhaps they will have to move areas, uprooting family, etc. This could happen if they had to look for another job after being made redundant.

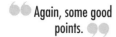 Again, some good points.

Overall, a very good answer to this question.

(d) When the management says 'there will be full consultation with the union at all stages', it means that from now on, there will be a high level of communication between the two bodies. Whatever the management decides, the Union will be informed of it, to try to reduce conflict. They will mainly discuss where the new machinery will be, which workers will be affected, and who will have to reduce their hours or be laid off.

COURSEWORK

**ASSIGNMENT –
INDUSTRIAL
DISPUTES**

INDUSTRIAL DISPUTES

Are you aware of any industrial disputes which have just started? You may have noticed such disputes on the television news. More information is likely to be available on these disputes from the national newspapers. Keep an account of the dispute(s), perhaps in the form of newspaper cuttings. Address some of the following questions:

1. Why did the dispute start?
2. Did collective bargaining take place?
3. What sort of industrial action has the workforce undertaken?
4. Is the dispute official or unofficial?
5. Is the factory/workplace being picketed?
6. How is the dispute being resolved?
7. Has an outside body such as ACAS been involved?

You can write up your findings as a case study. Is the final result of the dispute the one you expected? If not, why not?

A Review Sheet for this chapter will be found on p. 252.

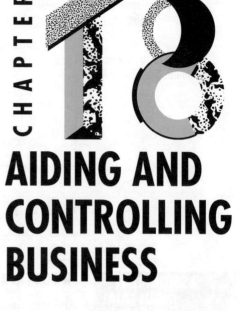

AIDING AND CONTROLLING BUSINESS

LOCAL GOVERNMENT

CENTRAL GOVERNMENT

GOVERNMENT AND BUSINESS

THE EUROPEAN UNION

AID FOR BUSINESS

REGULATING AND CONTROLLING BUSINESS

GETTING STARTED

Business in the UK is surrounded by a very large number of influences which try to either help it or control it:

- local Government
- central Government **plus**
- international organisations
- European Union (EU)
- educational bodies
- pressure groups
- the press and television

- trade associations
- professional bodies
- Industry Training Organisations
- Training and Enterprise Councils (Local Enterprise Companies in Scotland)

Each of these organisations has a rôle in helping businesses or in trying to control them for the sake of the public and other businesses. They operate in a wide variety of ways:

They **aid** businesses:

- by providing information
- by providing money or insurance
- by helping directly in training
- by helping with exporting.

They **control** business:

- by setting up laws which businesses have to abide by
- by exerting pressure in different ways.

This chapter will examine the ways in which business is helped or controlled, but it is necessary, first, to set the scene by considering the structure and role of the various systems of government and institutions which can affect businesses – local, national and international.

ESSENTIAL PRINCIPLES

The system of **local government** which exists in the UK today has only been in operation since 1974. The system prior to 1974 (which had been started in 1888) had many more units of local government. There were, for example, 1,750 authorities at the second tier ('districts') compared to just 422 today.

The most important change since 1974 has been the abolition of the Metropolitan and Greater London Councils (both of which occurred in 1986).

In 1995, the Government created a number of 'unitary authorities' (the city of York is an example) which combine the roles of 'district' and 'county'. We now have, therefore, a fairly complicated system of local government in which most of the functions of local administration are carried out by 'district councils' while, in the country certain other roles are performed by 'county councils' which – in cities – are shared between the districts and new 'single-purpose authorities' for such things as the fire and police services. Since 1995, the new unitary authorities have combined all of these roles under one single local authority.

Table 18.1 illustrates the current situation:

ROLES & RESPONSIBILITIES	METROPOLITAN AREAS (CITIES)	NON-METROPOLITAN AREAS	UNITARY AUTHORITIES (SPECIAL CASES)
Rates (and rebates) Rent rebates Slum clearance Refuse (collection) Public health Housing and home improvement Local planning	Districts (usually called Boroughs	Districts	New Authorities set up in some places in 1995/96
Libraries Personal social services Education		County Councils	
Police Fire Waste-disposal Structure planning	Single-purpose authorities		

Table 18.1 The system of local government in England and Wales

Table 18.1 shows the responsibilities of the various local government types. The main areas of business interest are:

▶ rates
▶ planning
▶ education
▶ roads

> ❝ Councils are composed of *elected* councillors who receive expenses but do not receive a salary for their work. The 'County level' authorities for fire, police, waste disposal, etc., are not elected but are appointed. ❞

Both Districts and Counties have responsibility for planning how their areas are going to develop in the future. This usually means setting aside areas for industrial and business growth, making sure that there will be enough houses to house any new workers, ensuring that there will be enough schools, and making sure that the roads will be able to cope with any new industry or housing. All of this is obviously of great concern to the businesses which are either in the area or considering moving to it.

The way in which these plans are presented to the public and approved by the Councils and the Government is in the form of **Structure Plans**, which state how the authority's area is going to grow, what areas are going to be set aside for house-building and which for business and industry.

Education is provided by the Counties in rural areas but by Districts in the larger cities. Business is always concerned to know that education, especially at the higher levels, is being directed towards the needs of industry and commerce, and that suitable courses are available to train their staff once they have left school or college and joined the firm.

Many services cannot be provided at local level and it is for these that we have **central** or **national** government. **Parliament** is responsible for governing the country and the party or parties with the largest number of seats in Parliament form the Government; see Fig. 18.1.

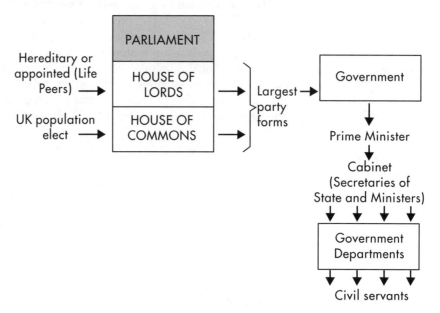

Figure 18.1 The national Parliament and Government

Parliament supervises the work of the Government and is responsible for passing laws which the Government wants to put into effect. By tradition, the Prime Minister cannot come from the House of Lords but several Cabinet Ministers (the most senior Ministers) can be drawn from the Lords. The Prime Minister selects the senior Ministers who form the Cabinet (the Committee which runs the UK on a day-to-day basis). The Prime Minister also selects all the other Ministers who make up the rest of the Government but these Junior Ministers do not sit in the Cabinet. Each Minister of Cabinet rank has responsibility for one of the large Departments and has other Ministers and a great many civil servants to help.

The Government in London – at Westminster – and the large number of local governments, influence business in a great many ways:

The **producer** is affected by government rules on planning and location of industry, by laws on conditions of work and on safety of products, and by taxation.

The **consumer** is affected by the Government's efforts to protect them from unscrupulous producers – by laws on consumer protection and safety, by standards, and by the work of weights and measures inspectors employed by local governments.

The **workforce** is affected by government provision of education and training, by laws on the conditions of employment, by safety regulations, by laws on pay, and by laws affecting trade unions.

Perhaps one of the most significant influences on business in the UK is outside the *direct* control of central and local government, namely the **European Union** – the **EU**.

The **EU** was founded in 1957 by the Treaty of Rome – it included West Germany, France, Italy, the Netherlands, Belgium and Luxembourg. Its objective is to promote unity among the countries of Europe, at least partly by making trade easier. By 1960, Britain had decided to join the EU but it took three attempts and twelve years before the other EU countries agreed to its admission. Along with the UK in 1972, Denmark and the Republic of Ireland also joined. Since then, six other members have joined:

▶ Greece in 1980
▶ Spain and Portugal in 1986
▶ Finland, Austria and Sweden in 1995.

All fifteen members of the EU have agreed to be bound by decisions taken centrally. They have created a 'single market' with no barriers to trade between them. They have also established a *single* set of customs duties between themselves and the rest of the world (called the **Common External Tariff**).

A. MEMBERSHIP OF THE EU

The EU is almost 40 years old. Since its formation in 1957 it has grown as more and more countries have seen the benefits of joining. The UK was invited to join in 1957 but decided not to. Instead the UK formed another organisation called EFTA (see p. 120). By 1960, the UK had decided to join (it did not take long for the Government to see that it had made a mistake in not joining earlier) – however, by that time the European countries (particularly France) felt that it would 'destabilise' the EEC if Britain joined – so they 'vetoed' our application. During the 1960s, the UK made two more attempts to join the EEC and both were vetoed by France. In 1969, however, following a change of government in France, our application to join was accepted and, along with Ireland and Denmark, we became members.

The policy of the European 'community' has always been that it would like to encompass most European countries and would like the EU to be seen as a force for progress and prosperity in trade and international affairs.

For this reason, the EU is a much more influential group than its members would imply. There are numerous 'associated countries' which receive special trade privileges and the recently formed 'European Economic Area' consists of countries which might be seen as 'the next members of the EU'.

OFFICIAL TITLE	DATE	MEMBER COUNTRIES
European Economic Community	1957	West Germany France Italy Netherlands Belgium Luxembourg
	1972	United Kingdom Denmark Republic of Ireland
	1980	Greece
European Community (EC)	1986	Spain Portugal
European Union (EU)	1995	Austria Finland Sweden

Table 18.2 Growth of the European Union

Note: In 1991, the former East Germany 'joined' by being reunited with West Germany.

The EU is now the largest 'single market' (i.e. without internal tariff barriers) in the Western world – around 370 million consumers. If there are disputes between member countries or if the European Commission feels that individual governments or companies are not abiding by the rules, the **European Court** will be the place in which the case is heard.

The Council of Ministers

The **Council of Ministers** actually comprises a number of different 'councils' which consist of political representatives of the member states and *which governs the EU.* Usually we only hear about the Council of Heads of State which meets to take the big decisions but there are other Councils meeting regularly which might consist of the member's Agriculture Ministers, Foreign Ministers, Industry Ministers, etc. depending on what subject is being discussed.

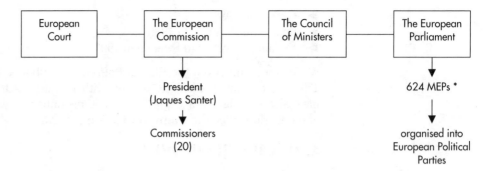

Figure 18.2 EU structure   * UK has 87 of these

The European Commission

The **European Commission** is the body which runs the EU on a day-to-day basis. It consists of 20 people nominated by the member states. The larger members such as the UK, Germany, France and Italy nominate two Commissioners each while the smaller member states nominate one Commissioner each.

The President of the Commission appoints each Commissioner to look after a specific subject area – External Relations, Industry, Agriculture, etc. – just like our own Government's Ministers look after their own departments.

The European Parliament

Every five years, there are elections for **Members of the European Parliament (MEPs)**. Every member state elects MEPs at the same time and their representatives usually work, in the European Parliament, in one of the European Political Parties.

After the 1994 elections, the UK Labour Party returned 63 of the UK's 87 MEPs. Those 63 MEPs took their places in what is the largest party in the European Parliament – the Party of European Socialists (PES). Table 18.3 shows to which parties the UK's MEPs belong, here and in the European Parliament.

UK PARTY	NO OF MEPS	EUROPEAN POLITICAL PARTY
Conservatives	18	European People's Party
Labour	63	Party of European Socialists
Liberal Democrats	2	Liberal, Democratic and Reformist
Ulster Unionist	1	European People's Party
Scottish Nationalist	2	European Radical Alliance
Independent	1	Non-attached

Table 18.3 European Parties and UK MEPs

B. THE EU AND BUSINESS

> The CAP now commands about half of the EU's annual budget.

The way in which the EU structures its budget and its policies has changed in recent years. The Common Agricultural Policy (CAP) has reduced in importance – although still by far the largest element in the EU budget. The most important change has been the rise in importance of what have become known as the 'Structural Funds' – the old Regional and Social Funds plus other elements.

Although we only occasionally hear about the EU in the popular press or on television and radio, the effect that this organisation has on British business is now extremely important.

▶ **Agricultural** business is affected by EU decisions on food prices, on grants for small farmers, and on future agricultural policy.

▶ Business in **areas of high unemployment** can receive significant grants through the EU's Regional Fund to cover buildings and equipment.

▶ The **EU Social Fund** spends a great deal on retraining of young people, women and certain other types of employee; this is especially true in industries such as shipbuilding, textiles, coal and steel.

▶ The **transport policy** helps business by encouraging faster and more energy efficient forms of transport and by helping to build motorways, tunnels, railways and canals.

▶ The **European Investment Bank** gives loans at attractive rates of interest to large and small businesses.
▶ **Competition Policy** makes sure that business does not conspire too much against the interests of the consumer.

The EU today affects almost every aspect of business life and is also involved in trying to improve education on a European-wide basis. One proposal, in 1986, was for funds to be provided to ensure that, by around 1990, 10% of all European students would spend at least part of their course in another EU country.

One of the most important factors for UK business is the increasing importance of the EU's policies on money.

The European Monetary System (EMS)

This policy is based on developments which took place in the late 1970s to try to establish a 'European Monetary System'. The objective of the system was to try to make currency exchange rates less 'volatile'. The worst situation for a business which is trying to trade across frontiers (and the UK has *always* relied very much on trade for its prosperity) is for exchange rates to be constantly changing up and down. This leaves sales people not knowing what price to charge a foreign customer in order to obtain the right amount in pounds sterling.

If you are trying to sell some machinery to a German firm (our most important European trading partner) how do you set the price? The company needs to receive (say) £20,000 for the machine but you have to quote the German company in their own currency (because that is how they will have to pay you). On the day you set your price the Deutschemark is at 3 to the pound (i.e. £1 = DM3). So you quote the Germans DM60,000 for the machine, they agree to buy it and sign a contract for delivery once the machine has been made – in three months' time. In the intervening period, however, the Deutschemark slips to £1 = DM3.5. The machine is delivered and the German company, very happy with their new machine, hand over a cheque for the DM60,000. When your company banks that cheque in the UK, however, their bank account is only credited with just over £17,000! (DM60,000 divided by 3.5) What might have been a profitable sale has been turned into a potentially unprofitable one by changes in currency rates.

The EMS tried to solve this problem by setting limits to the amount that a currency could 'move' against another currency. However, for a variety of reasons, it has not worked as well as the originators intended.

European Monetary Union (EMU)

Today, most businesses in the UK would like to see, instead of the EMS, a more simple solution – the introduction of a single European currency in which everyone could trade. The idea is often called 'EMU' because it would require that all currencies were unified into a single European money. The idea is not at all a new one. Over the centuries, it has always been the way in which larger countries have created better trading conditions for their companies. In the case of the UK, we – effectively – unified our currency when Scotland joined England in the eighteenth century. By using money which means the same thing on both sides of the border, business is able to exchange goods and services without worrying about the effects of exchange rate changes. The name of the European currency has not yet been decided but, if it were introduced, it would probably be called a 'Euro'.

In a 'single currency' Union, the British company trying to sell machines to Germany would simply quote a price in Euros and would receive exactly that price on delivery. The company's staff would be paid in Euros and you would pay for your holidays in the EU in Euros.

The arguments surrounding the possible introduction of a single currency are extremely complex and detailed but one thing is sure – such a currency would certainly help UK firms to trade more effectively in the EU.

5 ▷ **AID FOR BUSINESS**

There are a bewildering variety of sources of **aid for businesses**, which for ease of understanding are broken down into two broad areas of help and assistance:

▶ Government aid for business
▶ aid from private organisations.

A. GOVERNMENT AID FOR BUSINESS

This form of aid falls under five different headings:

1. information for business
2. finance for business
3. help in training staff
4. aid for exporters
5. advice for business.

Information for Business

Most Government **information** is available to businesses to help them plan their products or campaigns. The Central Office of Information (COI) in London has information on almost all aspects of business and most of it is available at the COI Library for researchers to use. In addition, much information is published each year in the form of government statistical booklets, which can be of immense help to business:

▶ *Social Trends* contains information on such things as population trends, wage levels and growth in wages around the country, and how people use their leisure time.
▶ *Annual Abstract of Statistics* has a wealth of economic statistics on such topics as employment, health, education, national income, exports.
▶ *Balance of Payments* (Pink Book) contains details of how much the UK has exported and imported, to and from which countries, and for how much.
▶ *Employment Gazette* contains information on industrial disputes, employment vacancies, growth in earnings, training and other employment-related areas.
▶ *Regional Trends* has a lot of very detailed information and statistics on the economic, social and population changes which have taken place in the UK's regions during the previous year.

Finance for Business

The Government provides **finance for business** in several ways. The most important ones are 'regional' grants and subsidies (see ch.6 on Industrial Location), the grants and assistance provided for small businesses which are just starting out, and the special grants for firms which are in 'high-tech' businesses like micro electronics and automated manufacturing. Grants to help with **research costs** are also available.

One of the most recent ways in which the Government helps small business is through grants for people to start up their own businesses. These **Enterprise Allowances** pay the person a weekly amount for about one year to help them start their business.

There is also a **Small Firms Loan Guarantee Scheme** which was introduced in 1981. Under this scheme the Government will 'guarantee' up to 70% of bank loans for small businesses in return for strict supervision and the payment of an insurance premium.

Help in Training Staff

In these days of very high unemployment, the Government has constructed a number of schemes to help people in finding a job. The main groups these schemes are aimed at are the young and the long-term unemployed.

More detail of these schemes is given in Chapter 14, Section 5.

Aid for Exporters

The UK relies on trade for almost a third of its annual income and trade is, therefore, taken very seriously by the Government. The Department of Trade and Industry offers a great deal of help to British exporters – from statistical information on overseas markets to help with filling in Customs forms.

UK exporters can sometimes obtain grants to help them to begin exporting to certain markets, and there are regular trade visits – organised by the British Overseas Trade Board (BOTB), a subsidiary of the Department of Trade and Industry – to introduce exporters to certain markets. The BOTB provides a variety of services to exporters and these are added to by an organisation known as SITPRO. This is responsible for helping to simplify the extremely complex task of filling in export forms.

The list of government aids to exporters would include:

► publicity for British products through British magazines published by the Government, and through British Embassies abroad;

► free advice on market research;

► financial aid to businesses in employing marketing consultants;

► a well-developed library of books and research findings on export markets which is called the 'Statistics and Market Intelligence Library' (the use of which is free);

► an Export Representative service in which an overseas member of an Embassy's staff will make enquiries and business contacts on your behalf;

► the chance to travel with British trade missions to markets you are interested in.

Many of these services are not free of charge but they are considerably subsidised by the UK Government.

Advice for Business

Through a network of local offices, Government departments provide advice for businesses on industrial location, on regional grants for the assisted areas, on enterprise zones and development areas.

Central Government also offers help and advice on a wide range of business problems including production engineering, industrial design, advanced technologies, and research.

Many local councils have also set up offices offering advice to small businesses.

B. PRIVATE AID FOR BUSINESS

Over the years, business has developed a number of ways in which it is able to help itself. In most areas of the country, there are **Chambers of Commerce** which allow business people to meet and to discuss their problems and successes.

Most types of business have their own **trade association**, such as the Furniture Industry Association. These associations have been established to try to protect their members from laws which they believe will harm them, and to promote the industry with the general public. Examples include the Society of Motor Manufacturers and the Engineering Employers Federation.

At a national level, industry has set up the **Confederation of British Industry (CBI)** to look after its interests. The CBI also gives advice to its members and runs regular courses and conferences. (See ch. 17.)

Education, too, provides aid for business in the form of research and development, as well as consultancy. Many universities have contracts with specific firms to research special areas of science and to provide the firm with the results. A number of such institutions, together with management departments and business schools, also provide consultancy for businesses which need advice. The lecturers are 'hired out' as consultants to the firms to try to solve specific problems which the firms themselves might not be able to solve. The firm receives valuable advice and the university or college receives valuable direct experience for its staff.

6 ▷ REGULATING AND CONTROLLING BUSINESS

Business is heavily surrounded by controls and constraints, most of which have developed over the years to protect workers, consumers and other businesses. They can best be understood by dealing with them under three headings:

1. The Law
2. Government control
3. Non-governmental control

A. THE LAW

There is now a tremendous amount of law relating to business and it is impossible to deal with it all in the space available. There are, however, a number of very important areas of law which need to be noted:

The Companies Acts (1985, 1989)

These Acts of Parliament regulate the formation and running of limited companies. The two main types of company – private limited (Ltd) and public limited (PLC) are governed by the Companies Acts in terms of almost every aspect of their operations. The way they are set up, their Boards and directors, what they are allowed to do as individual companies, how and how often they must publish or file accounts, how they must be checked by auditors and many other things are all covered by the Acts.

The Law of Contract

A **contract** is an agreement between two parties to do something. It does not have to be written down but, in order to be recognised by the Courts, it does have to have certain features: an agreement, some consideration (i.e. a transfer of value), the intent and capacity to enter into a legal relationality.

There has to be an **agreement**, which can be seen by the fact that one party has offered something and the other party has accepted it. In many cases, the 'offer' and the 'acceptance' are not the way you would normally expect them to be. For example, in a shop it is not the shop which is making the offer to you. In law, the shop is merely opening its doors so that you can examine the goods. The customer then makes an offer for the goods and – if it is acceptable – the shop accepts the offer.

Something has to change hands in both directions. A contract does not exist if you receive anything for free. The law of contract demands that, in return for the goods or service there must be **some consideration**, i.e. something must be given in return, either in money or goods.

There must be an **intention to create a legal relationship** – a bargain between yourself and your father would not normally be called a contract unless it was written down that both of you intended to establish a legal relationship. The parties to a contract must be legally able to enter into it. The law calls this **capacity** and all adults who are sane have the capacity to enter into a contract.

There are many other aspects to the law of contract but it is important to understand that a contract does not have to be in writing. You are entering into a legal contract every time you buy something from a shop or pay for your ticket on the bus.

Even where large sums of money are concerned, the law still recognises and enforces unwritten contracts. If you want to buy or sell shares through a stockbroker you may do this on the telephone. The act of telling the stockbroker to buy or sell a certain number of shares in a specified company is a legal and binding contract. You cannot telephone the broker five minutes later and expect to cancel your order.

Protecting the Consumer

The law of contract, if applied literally, allows no way for a consumer to take goods back or to complain about their quality. For hundreds of years, the law said that the buyer of goods was responsible for making sure that they were fit for the use to which they were to be put. This was summed up in the Latin phrase: **caveat emptor** (let the buyer beware). Today, however, the law of contract has been amended in certain ways to give the consumer additional protection (except for sales of goods between private individuals, e.g. for second-hand cars, where the *caveat emptor* rule still applies).

The Sale of Goods Act (1979) gives the customer extra protection when buying certain types of goods. The act effectively says that goods must be the same as they are described on a label or by the shop assistant. The best known provision of the Act is that it now is to be assumed that goods are of '**merchantable quality**' and 'fit for the purpose for which they were sold'. This means that customers can buy goods on the firm assumption that the quality will be appropriate to the use to which they will be put. This does not mean that the goods will never break down, merely, that they will last for an amount of time which a court would regard as 'reasonable'.

Trading Law

The laws by which companies may trade are complex and are divided into those which are established at local level (by-laws governing such things as the size of shop signs) and the national laws.

Weights and Measures Act (1979)

Local councils have departments of weights and measures whose duty it is to ensure that local tradespeople are treating their customers fairly. In years gone by, it was not unusual for traders to add chalk to their flour or to add water to beer or spirits.

Sawdust was often used to give bulk to bread and meat was often sold when it was going rotten. Local shops would often have a wide difference in the weights which they used to weigh out the customer's food. In this way, the customer would believe that they were getting a full pound of flour, butter, bread, or potatoes, whereas, in fact the weight had been filed down so that — although it was marked 1 pound — it weighed less, say, 13 ounces. The shopkeeper's profit would be increased by the saving of 3 ounces on every pound sold. It was common in public houses well into this century for customers to receive 'short measure' in both beer and spirits. The local Weights and Measures Inspectors are still kept busy making sure that scales and drink measures are accurate.

The Trade Descriptions Act (1968)
This act makes it an offence to give a false description of something which you are selling — whether in writing or orally.

Food and Drugs Act (1955)
This Act helps to protect consumers from unscrupulous shopkeepers. The Act makes it a criminal offence to sell food which is unfit for consumption. It also sets standards for hygiene in food premises and sets up a number of regulations on what must appear on the labels of food products.

Consumer Credit Act (1974)
This Act requires the Office of Fair Trading — set up under the Fair Trading Act (1973) — to license any firm which lends money to the public (usually in the form of credit on purchases). The companies must explain to people the *true* cost of borrowing. This is usually given in the form of the APR — or **annual percentage rate** (of interest).

Fair Trading Act (1973)
The Office of Fair Trading was established by this Act with the objective of controlling the way firms do business with the public. It seeks to regulate what are known as **'restrictive practices'** — attempts by firms to 'fix' prices or to 'share' markets. (By agreeing to share a market and not to compete against each other two firms will be able to charge higher prices than they would otherwise.)

Consumer Safety Act (1978)
This Act regulates the construction of most items which can be dangerous in the home, such as fires, cookers, electric irons, microwave ovens and toys.

Consumer Protection Act (1987)
This **Act** also sets out — in great detail — the ways in which companies have to take consumer rights and safety into account.

Competition Law
If businesses are allowed to grow they may form what are known as **monopolies**. A monopoly is a company which is effectively the only company supplying a particular market. In Britain, the electricity and gas companies have a monopoly of the supply of electricity and gas into our homes. Monopolies have the disadvantage that, in view of the fact that they are the only supplier in the market, they can charge almost whatever they like. Economists call this the ability to make super-profits and it is usually seen as being against the interests of the consumer. Not only are prices higher than they might otherwise be but the monopoly has no incentive to improve the service of the product.

It is felt, therefore, that wherever possible, the authorities ought to encourage competition and to try to make sure that large companies which control large shares of particular markets are closely watched.

The Monopolies and Mergers Act (1965)
This Act attempts to control large companies and to encourage competition by making sure that a firm cannot have too much control over a market. A *monopoly* is defined as existing whenever a firm controls more than a third of any market and the Act set up a **Monopolies and Mergers Commission** with the power to investigate and report on any situation which gives cause for concern. Under the Act, the Secretary of State has the power to refer any proposed merger to the Commission and, if the Commission decides that the merger would create a firm which was too large and that it was 'against the public interest', the Secretary of State can forbid the merger.

Since the UK joined the EU, our firms have also been subject to **EU Competition Policy** which tries to do the same thing for the whole of Europe. On a number of occasions, several very large firms have been fined millions of pounds for trying to restrict competition by 'price fixing', i.e. coming to secret agreements that they would not undercut each other's prices.

Employment Law

In this area, there is a great deal of government legislation designed to protect the employee. The need for employment law goes back to the nineteenth century when some workers used to be paid in the form of 'truck'. This meant that the worker did not receive money at the end of the week but, instead, received vouchers which could only be exchanged at the company's store where the food, clothes and other stock were extremely expensive. Several 'Truck' Acts, beginning with one in 1831, were needed to deal with this exploitation of working people. During the nineteenth century, the government also began to regulate the hours which women and children could work. Today, there is a very large amount of law concerning the treatment of people at work and every business-person needs to know most of it in some detail.

Factories Act (1961)

This Act is the most recent of a long series of Factories Acts which govern conditions of work inside manufacturing plants. Most of the original rules contained in the Act come from the nineteenth century and govern such things as:

- ▶ no machine can be cleaned while it is still moving
- ▶ women cannot work in a factory within 4 weeks of childbirth
- ▶ women are not allowed to work down a mine
- ▶ women and young people (under 18) cannot work more than 9 hours per day or more than 48 hours per week.

Health & Safety at Work Act (1974)

This is an extremely important law which makes it a criminal offence to expose either employees or non-employees to risk. It covers all industrial and commercial premises and the products which a firm manufactures. The Act also makes it a duty of every employee to take care of the health and safety of themselves and their work colleagues.

Race Relations Acts (1968, 1976)

These laws make it an offence for an employer to discriminate in any aspects of business on the ground of race, ethnic origin or nationality. These aspects are:

- ▶ recruitment
- ▶ promotion
- ▶ conditions of service
- ▶ training
- ▶ dismissal.

Equal Pay Act (1970)

This legislation came into force in December 1975 and requires that women are paid and given the same benefits as men if they are doing the same work.

Sex Discrimination Act (1975)

Although this Act overlaps to a certain extent with the Equal Pay Act, it requires that women are treated equally in other ways too: that they are not discriminated against in recruitment, promotion or training. It should be noted that this Act also applies to men. The law makes it illegal to advertise jobs in such a way that it appears that only one of the sexes will be considered. The only way that it is possible to advertise for a 'sales-girl' or for a 'postman' is if the advertisement also states that either sex will be considered.

Employment Protection Act (1978)

Employees receive certain rights under this Act which requires, for example, that an employer should keep a woman's job open for her if she leaves, temporarily, to have a baby. The Act also requires that staff be given a minimum amount of notice if they are to be dismissed; the actual amount depends on how long the employee has worked for the employer. An employee is also entitled to redundancy payments if his or her job is to be abolished, and to compensation if they are unfairly dismissed.

Sex Discrimination Act (1987)

Employers, under this Act, are not allowed to discriminate between men and women as far as retirement dates are concerned.

In 1980, 1982 and 1984 the Government passed two Employment Acts (1980, 1982) and a Trade Union Act (1984) which set out rules by which trade unions are able to conduct their affairs.

B. GOVERNMENT CONTROL

The Government exercises a great deal of *control and influence* over business in other ways, e.g. taxation, NI, credit restrictions, export restrictions, policy on location of industry, and public expenditure.

Taxation

All companies have to pay tax just like individuals. Their profits are taxed under **corporation tax (CT)** and it has to account for **value added tax (VAT)** on the value of everything it sells.

National Insurance (NI)

All employees must pay a contribution to the benefits they are entitled to receive under the National Insurance regulations. These benefits include such things as medical care, unemployment pay, supplementary benefit, and sickness benefit. The employer also pays an additional amount which is added to the money paid by the employee. The employer's National Insurance payment is regarded by many as a form of **tax on employment**.

Credit Restrictions

The Government controls most of the banking system by exercising complicated restrictions on the amount of money that the banks can lend. Although there are no such laws at the moment, it is also possible for the Government to control how much business firms can do by placing limits on the amount of credit they can give. At one time the law stated that, before you could buy a car, you must be able to pay a cash deposit of cash at least 33% of the price.

Export Restrictions

These do not affect many companies these days but there are still rules – mainly for defence reasons – about what can be exported to certain countries.

Location of Industry and Regional Policy

The Government tries, through its system of regional grants and loans, to encourage firms to locate where it wants them to locate (usually in areas of high unemployment) rather than where the firm might have wanted to go.

Public Expenditure

The Government spends a very large amount each year – around £160 billion – and the way in which this money is spent has an effect on UK business. If the Government decides that it has to cut spending and to build fewer roads, schools and houses, then the construction industry will have fewer orders and will be able to employ fewer people. Similarly, Government decisions on spending can create more demand for almost every type of product. If a new hospital is to be built, business will be created not only for the builders but also for the firms who will provide all the office furniture, typewriters, beds, sheets and blankets, carpets, lights, radios and so on.

C. NON-GOVERNMENT CONTROL OF BUSINESS

There are three main ways in which business is subject to control from private sources:

1. from codes of conduct
2. from pressure groups
3. from the media (press, television, radio, etc.).

Codes of Conduct

Industry, today, follows many different **codes of conduct**. These codes are not laws, they have never been passed through Parliament, and they can not be taken to courts. The idea of the codes is that industry is able to set them up and control them themselves rather than having the Government do it for them under an Act of Parliament.

Examples of two codes illustrate how codes are used:

1. **Garages** have a code of practice which they have drawn up themselves. It states what all member garages must follow when repairing people's cars. The code says what sort of quotation should be given, how much information it should contain, how the garage should set out the bill for the repairs, and many other things.
2. **Advertisers** also have a code of practice, supervised by the Advertising Standards Authority, which states that all advertisements should be legal, decent and honest.

Pressure Groups

Pressure groups are sometimes called interest groups. They are groups of people who link together to try to influence the way things are run or the way decisions are taken. There are many different pressure groups:

▶ Some seek to influence Government, like the Campaign for Nuclear Disarmament or the Campaign for Electoral Reform.
▶ Others try to influence both Government and business, such as the AA and the RAC, the CBI (Confederation of British Industry), trade unions, the Consumers Association, etc.

It is with the second of these two types that we will be concerned here. The best way to understand how pressure groups influence business is to look at the way they operate.

The Automobile Association (AA) and The Royal Automobile Club (RAC)

Both the AA and the RAC were set up to try to protect the interests of motorists against both the Government and the car and motorcycle manufacturers. Like most pressure groups, they have members who pay an annual fee to join. This money is then used by the pressure group to help it to do its job. In the case of the AA and the RAC, they try to make sure that any laws which are passed with respect to motorists are good ones and that the products of the car and motorcycle manufacturers are of the right standard.

The Consumers' Association

The Consumers' Association is best known for its monthly publication: *Which?* The object of this pressure group is to represent the interests of the buyer of goods and to try to make sure that the consumer enjoys the best possible value for money. The Association regularly tests all products to find out whether they are safe, how long they will last, and whether there are any problems about using them. Over the years, *Which?* has had a great deal of success in protecting consumers against businesses.

Trade Unions

Trade unions, too, are pressure groups. They seek to protect the interests of their members – the employees – against the firm. (They are dealt with more fully in ch.17.) Unions have been quite successful in improving the working conditions and wages of workers.

Environmental Groups

As more and more people become aware of the danger which modern industry can represent for the environment, so more environmental pressure groups are established to try to control the activities of both governments and business. Groups such as The Green Alliance, Greenpeace, and Friends of the Earth, spend a great deal of time watching what businesses are doing and opposing them if they feel that their activities will harm the environment or wildlife.

The Media

The 'media' means any of the ways in which people receive information. Nowadays, it is usual to divide it into two:

1. paper
2. electronic.

The **paper media** include newspapers, magazines and journals, while the **electronic media** includes radio and television. Almost all of these media have reporters whose job it is to look out for stories which will be of interest to the readers, listeners or viewers of the medium for which he or she is working. Business topics are not very popular in the tabloid press or on peak-time television (see ch.9 for more information on what makes up these categories) but such topics can be found in the quality press and on radio and television programmes which are designed for 'serious' viewers, and provide very interesting information.

Of course, business is itself influenced by the popular media; various programmes which reveal the sharp practices of businesses are very popular and may lead to firms having to change their policies, to give refunds, or, even, to go out of business altogether.

COURSEWORK

Local government has a significant effect on business, and firms pay a large proportion of the income of local councils in the form of rates. Unlike private householders, who also pay rates, businesses do not vote at elections and, therefore, have no say about how their rate money is used.

Conduct a survey to find out how local businesses feel about the services they receive from local government and how they would like to improve the situation.

You will need to draw up a questionnaire which will give you details of what type of business it is and how big it is (number of employees is the easiest measure).

1. The questionnaire will need to glean the reaction and *comments* of business people on a wide variety of subjects including:
   - ▶ Rates
   - ▶ Refuse collection
   - ▶ Education
   - ▶ Roads and lighting
   - ▶ Public health
   - ▶ Weights and measures
   - ▶ Planning
   - ▶ Housing for employees

2. You will need to survey a good range of business: large and small, including shops, offices and factories.
3. Obtain a copy of the local Structure Plan from the Council offices. It will tell you a lot about where business is growing and what the Council's attitude to the expansion of business is.
4. Write up your results into a final report with illustrations, tables and – if helpful – graphs.

In this project you will have to find out how businesspeople feel about the various laws which affect them.

A questionnaire will be necessary, asking for reactions to a wide variety of laws covering:

- ▶ employment
- ▶ contract and sales of goods
- ▶ consumer protection.

1. Try to find out whether any single person is responsible for the 'legal side' of things and who that person is.
2. Cover as many different types of business as you can.
3. Ask for and compare firms' terms and conditions of business. These are usually to be found on the back of order forms or invoices.
4. Do the firms (e.g. garages) have to comply with a code of practice? If so, what is it and who supervises it?
5. Complete the project with a written report which gives the results in the way you think most sensible, for example, by law, by size of business, or by type of business.

A Review Sheet for this chapter will be found on pp. 253–4.

BUSINESS IN A CHANGING WORLD

GETTING STARTED

In 1885, two German engineers named Benz and Daimler were just beginning to develop the first motor cars and the first petrol engines; by the turn of the twentieth century, these 'horse-less carriages' were beginning to appear on the muddy roads of Britain. A few people are still alive today who were born into that Victorian world at the end of the nineteenth century. Then business was conducted by letter and by telegraph. Telephones only began to be used in offices very gradually after about 1889. Clerks wrote account books, invoices and statements by hand, by the light of gas lamps, and even the typewriter (manufactured by the American company of Remington since 1876) was a rare sight. Documents were methodically filed by hand and cross-referenced with other files using large card indexes. Goods were transported by horse and cart, by steam train, and by steam ships. Factories operated almost entirely on the power provided by steam engines, and the most important energy source was coal.

CHANGES IN THE BUSINESS ENVIRONMENT

CHANGES IN TECHNOLOGY

CHANGES FOR HUMANS

ESSENTIAL PRINCIPLES

1 CHANGES IN THE BUSINESS ENVIRONMENT

A. BUSINESS TRANSPORT

Business transport has developed rapidly from the horse and the steam engine to include motor cars and lorries, aircraft carrying over 100 tonnes of freight, high speed diesel and electric freight trains, and fast cargo ships carrying anything up to 100,000 tonnes. The Channel Tunnel now allows freight to travel by land-based transport from almost any part of Great Britain to any part of Europe and Asia. Although the 20 miles of sea between ourselves and the Continent are not very far they have meant, in the past, that every single freight journey had to be interrupted to a certain extent. In the mid-1990s, a container can be placed onto rail freight and transported without transfer to almost any point in Europe. Over the next ten years, rail-freight terminals will be established all over Britain through which manufacturers will be able to send goods *direct* to Europe and Asia.

In business transport, the carriage of people is almost as important as that of freight. In the modern world, business-people have to travel to meet, discuss, and to negotiate. Fast, efficient transport systems have developed which enable meetings to take place in any part of the world. In Britain, a business person can leave Leeds or Manchester in the early morning by train or plane, have a full day in London and still be back home in time for dinner. Such an itinerary is equally possible between Britain and most of continental Europe and, by Concorde, business-people can have a morning meeting in New York and be back home by dinner time (a round trip of 7,000 miles). It takes four hours to travel the 400 miles between London and Edinburgh by train, and just 3.5 hours to travel from London to New York by Concorde.

B. BUSINESS COMMUNICATIONS

Business communications have improved. Every company uses both telephone and telex as standard forms of communication and many are now using facsimile (fax) machines. The speed and convenience of these methods have been vastly increased by the advent of satellites in orbit around the planet (having partly replaced long-distance telephone cables). In 1994, British Telecom introduced the UK's first 'video-phone' which can use ordinary telephone lines and, in 1995, the first desk-top computers with built-in video-conferencing facilities were being sold.

Communication is the heart of business and efficient electronic communications are now taken for granted. Fax is becoming the standard means of communication between and within companies and **E-mail (Electronic mail)** is fast gaining a foothold.

C. PRODUCTION OF GOODS

Production of goods has changed from being extremely labour intensive – requiring lots of people to operate all the machines or to make the goods – to being very capital intensive – having many more machines, some of which can operate on their own with only minimal human supervision.

D. INFORMATION STORAGE AND HANDLING

Information storage and handling has changed out of all recognition. The clerks, filing cabinets and card indexes of the turn of the century have been almost completely replaced by complex computer systems which store the same information electronically. The draft chapters of a book such as this would take up an entire drawer of a filing cabinet if they were typed out, placed in individual folders and filed away. Instead, all 20 chapters plus index, introduction and contents can be stored on just one floppy disc. Rather than the 90cm by 60cm space of the filing cabinet drawer, the disc takes up just 100mm by 75mm. No less than 70 full books could be stored in this way in the space taken up by just one chapter using the old method.

In one lifetime, society has moved from the steam engine to nuclear power and from filing cabinets to computers. Most of this change has been technical and mechanical. However, behind the technical and mechanical wizardry there has occurred an even more significant change – in the way people work. As late as 30 years ago, it was common for people to expect to stay in the same job – and sometimes with the same employer – for their whole working lives. By the mid-1990s, that situation has become the exception. Most people now know that they will have to change jobs regularly and most understand that they may well have to change careers as well. Into the twenty-first century, change is going to be even more far reaching. The tremendous change that your parents and grandparents have experienced will look very tame beside what is coming! There are different aspects to such changes.

First there are developments in **technology** which are already beginning to affect our lives. These include **bio-technology**, the science of using man-made organisms to create new chemicals or to change existing ones, **factory automation** and the **information revolution** based on the microprocessor – the computer on a chip.

Then, there are the changes which will happen to our lives – the **human** change. Last, but not least, we need to deal with change and at increasing speeds. It is all very well to talk about change but we now have to live with it and adapt to it on every day of our working lives. In by-gone days, a young person would 'learn a trade' at 16 years old and that skill would suffice for an entire working life. In the twenty-first century, things will be changing so quickly that there will be no chance to 'sit back and rest on our laurels'. Instead, at all levels of work, we will need to keep up with changes in technology and working practices throughout our lives.

The speed at which we work, today, is another aspect to which we will have to adjust. In the first half of the twentieth century a business-person had quite a lot of time to consider options and make decisions. For example, if – in the 1920s – a client wrote to you to ask whether you would sell him five machines at £1,000 each you would have had a couple of days to consider the matter and compose your reply before writing back to them. Today they would probably phone (in which case you would only have seconds to decide what to do) or they might fax (in which case you might have a few hours to decide before faxing back). Modern technology means that all business transactions move at high speed and managers have to be extremely quick on their feet in order to stay 'ahead of the game'.

Anyone who has tried to keep up with changes in computers will know what faces us in the future. Continual, rapid change brings the need for regular updating courses and almost continual learning. It may also mean that we have to learn to deal with the stress that change causes. Most doctors agree that rapid change in the working environment can cause severe stress. They also agree that physically fit people cope with that stress a lot better than those who are relatively unfit. It seems that one of the consequences of modern technology is that it is going to force us to keep fit!

2 > CHANGES IN TECHNOLOGY

We first consider technical changes in the **factory** and then in the **office**.

A. IN THE FACTORY

Change in the factory will involve both **automation** and **expert systems**.

Automation

The factories of the near future will certainly have far fewer people working in them. The machines will either be 'intelligent' – i.e. they will have their own computers which tell them what to do – or they will be linked up to large central computers which will control the whole manufacturing process.

There are many computer aided machines in operation today. The difference in the future is that **computer integrated manufacturing (CIM)** will control *all* of the machines, together with the input of raw materials from stores, the warehousing of finished goods and the despatch of goods which have been sold. Human operators, at least in the early stages, will be required to program the computers, to repair the machines and to repair the electronic components.

Robots are simply computer controlled machines. They are important because, unlike the machines which they replace, they can be reprogrammed at very short notice to do a different job.

For example, machines have been welding motor-car bodies for a very long time. In the past, however, each new design of car had to have a special welding line built for it. The welding machines would have to be positioned exactly and would then weld the right spots on the car bodies as they were taken past on the conveyor. If the firm decides to change the shape of the car body the whole line of welding machines has to be moved and re-arranged – an extremely expensive and lengthy job.

Robot welding lines are much more flexible. The robots, once installed, can be 'taught' to weld the correct spots on a new car. Each robot usually has a working 'arm' which it uses to reach over and weld exactly the right bits. If the company decides to redesign the car body, none of the robots needs to be moved. An operator simply reprograms them ('teaches' them a new set of movements) and the line can start work on the new shape of the car. Weeks or months of expensive dismantling and moving of machines is avoided. With robots, the new car can be going through the production process in a matter of days.

Expert Systems

Computers are going to affect factories in a wide variety of ways. Not only is CIM going to increase the number of firms which are almost completely automated, but new **expert systems** are going to be helping, and possibly replacing, human beings in the areas of the firm where, up to now, humans have felt secure in their jobs.

Up to now computers have been essentially just automatic machines. They have had to be told absolutely everything. They could weld a car body, but they could not *design* it and they could spot a flaw in a piece of metal but they were incapable of *deciding* whether the flaw was dangerous or not.

It seems likely that this will begin to change in the not too distant future. Some computers are already being programmed, not with instructions but with **rules**. The computers then use these rules to design machines and to make their own decisions.

> **True expert systems are still a long way off. They require immense computing power and speed, improved computer languages, and better ways of acquiring and coding information.**

In effect, these expert systems work just like an expert human being. When you go to the doctor to find out why you have a pain in your back, he will use his expert knowledge to narrow down the cause. He will ask you what you think caused the pain: Were you lifting anything? Have you fallen over? Were you playing sport? In most cases, the doctor will be able to tell you how you did it and what to do about the pain without even examining you. In making this diagnosis, the doctor is simply applying a large number of complex areas of knowledge, which he learned at medical school and through years of experience, to the problem of your back.

It is, of course, much more complex than this and the doctor would also have to examine you to make a final decision but the essence of an expert system is there. Already, in the US, expert computers are being used to save doctors' time in giving basic diagnoses of many ailments.

In a similar way, expert systems are now being developed which can design buildings, machines and other computers. The automated factory of the future will probably not require human beings even to analyse faults in the system. The factory and its computers will work out the solutions to problems themselves and then instruct less intelligent robots to put them right.

B. IN THE OFFICE

Change in the factory is going to be very great over the next few decades but change **in the office** is already looking as though it will be even more significant. It will involve:

▶ Information technology
▶ Expert systems
▶ Voice input
▶ Telecommunications

Information Technology – The Information Revolution

Computers have already made the storage and retrieval of information much easier but they have also made all sorts of office work completely different to the way it was only a few years ago.

Hardware

Hardware is the physical equipment needed for information technology. In computer terms it means the parts which make the computer do what it does, and then all the extra bits which enable the computer to be so useful.

Tables 19.1–19.4 describe some of the major terms used in today's computer-world.

CPU	CPU stands for 'central processing unit'. It is the main 'brain' of the computer which does almost all of the calculations and work. In 1980, a computer would have a CPU operating at about 8 MHz (a megahertz is a measure of the power and speed of the chip). Today many CPUs in ordinary office computers operate at between 75 and 100 MHz. In the 1970s an average radio would contain 8–12 transistors to help it work. One of the fastest CPUs in a modern computer – the Intel Pentium chip – has over six million transistors on it.
Floppy disk	Disks are used, these days, to store information. They consist of a circle of magnetic material similar to that used in an ordinary cassette tape. Nowadays, most disks used in business are 3.5" with a storage capacity of 1.4Mb.
Hard disk	The hard disk is so-called because it is made of aluminium coated with other materials. Hard disks can store a very great deal of information. In 1988 an average desktop computer would have 20–50Mb of hard disk. In 1995, a business desktop would need a minimum of around 300Mb and – ideally – would have 500Mb.
CD-ROM	CD stands for 'compact disk' - the same technology that is used for music CDs. ROM stands for 'read-only memory', i.e. memory which can only be read from but not written to (like a book – you can only read a book, you cannot write any more of it or add to it in any way). In the same way, you can read data *from* a CD-ROM but you cannot write anything *to* most of them. What are called 're-writeable CDs' are now becoming more common but it is still an expensive technology.
Modem	Modem stands for 'modulator-demodulator' and is a communications device which can sit inside or be attached to a computer. It allows computers to 'talk' to each other and to exchange information down a phone line. The modem is probably one of the most important developments of IT for the early twenty-first century. A business connected by modem can be linked to any other business and can exchange information almost instantaneously.
Video-card	Computers can use television screens (called monitors) to show information. To show pictures (or graphics) it needs a video card which helps the CPU to process all of the information needed to show colour detail. Most video-cards have their own memory and processors. Note that a video-card is *not* the same as the card which a computer needs to be able to show *moving* pictures from the television or from satellite broadcasts – these are usually called 'TV cards'.
Tape streamer	The most dreaded event for anyone who uses a computer regularly is a major 'crash'. If the computer suffers a fault (normally just called a crash) it can lose *all* of the information contained on its main storage medium – the hard disk. This could, potentially, lose a company *all* of its accounts, its customer records, its reports and work, its designs, etc. Some studies have shown that a very high proportion of companies that suffer a major crash and loss of data go out of business as a result. To avoid disaster, always keep a 'back-up' copy of everything on the hard-disk. Ten years ago, this could be easily done on two or three floppy disks. Today, with very large hard disks, back-up needs a tape streamer, a special tape recorder which can back-up lots of computer information at high speed. Ordinary tape streamers can usually store up to 250Mb on a single small tape. Newer 'digital' tape streamers using DAT tapes can store up to 2–3Gb.

Table 19.1 Computer hardware

Table 19.2 Computer memory and storage		
Bit	One unit of charge – either positive or negative – which stores either a '1' or a '0' in the computer.	
Byte	Eight bits – each bit being '1' or '0'. It takes eight bits to store any particular piece of information in the 'hexadecimal' system.	
Kilobyte (Kb or just k)	One thousand bytes. Computer memory used to be measured in 'k' and certain types of computer memory still are. In 1981, the first commonly available home computer, the Sinclair ZX81 had just 1k of memory	
Megabyte (Mb)	One million bytes (or 1,000 Kb). With the advance in memory systems many types of memory are now measured in this way.	
Gigabyte (Gb)	One billion bytes (one thousand million or 1,000,000,000). New hard disks are commonly available which can store up to about 5 Gb and new storage media such as CD-ROMs can also store up to this amount.	
	A gigabyte is an immense amount of information – an entire encyclopaedia can be stored in around 650Mb.	

Table 19.2 Computer memory and storage

Random Access Memory (RAM)	This is 'temporary' memory which only exists while the computer is switched on. It forms a stack of programs and program detail which can be accessed very easily. When started up, modern computers transfer many of the programs and instructions they need immediately to RAM. In this way, it can be accessed faster than having to go back to the hard disk every time
	Modern desktop computers need a minimum of about 4Mb of RAM and, with Windows-based systems, ideally need 8–16Mb.
Fixed memory	Almost all fixed memory in computers is on hard disks. However, some, more advanced systems, use 'solid state' chips to store information. Some of the newer 'palm-top' computers use 2Mb solid state cards to store their data.

Table 19.3 Types of computer memory

Mainframe	The very first electronic computers, used in Britain and the USA during World War II, took up entire floors of buildings and had the power of one of today's average desktops.
	Those computers – and their descendants – were called mainframes because they were built using large aluminium framing. Mainframes are still used but the term now refers to the very biggest and most powerful computers. 'Supercomputers' are a very special type of mainframe which can operate at extremely high speed. They are used to do millions of calculations every second for such tasks as weather prediction or the design of buildings, cars, missiles and aircraft.
Mini-computer	These are smaller versions of mainframes. Today's minis take up a small room and can contain vast amounts of information.
Desktops	Although quite small, desktop computers are used for almost every type of modern computing. At the smallest end of the market, they are used for home computing while, at the other end, companies use very powerful desktops as design tools and as 'servers' for many other desktops.
Portables	Smaller than desktops these are commonly called 'luggables'. They are powerful but portable and usually weigh 8–10kg.
Laptops	True portables, these weigh 1.5–4kg. They range in size but can almost always be fitted into a standard briefcase. The smallest laptops are sometimes called 'Notebooks'.
Palmtops	These are the latest types of portable computers. True 'palmtops' are real computers with around 1Mb of memory and lots of different types of software. The most successful one to date has been the Psion '3 series' palmtop.

Table 19.4 Types of computer

Software

Software is the set of instructions which a computer needs to follow to do its work. It is the modern term for computer 'programs'. Computers may change – every year we see smaller computers able to do more and more – but the real developments over the next few years are going to be in the field of the software which the computers use. Without software, a computer is just a mass of electronics. The first computers had all these instructions built into them but, today, even the simplest of home computers can 'run' a wide variety of software. In this way, a home computer can be playing a game at one minute and helping you to organise your home finances the next.

To 'run' any form of program, a computer needs one very important type of software: the **operating system**. This computer program tells the computer how to deal with all the other types of program. Different types of computer use different operating systems but – today – they fall into two clear types: 'heavy duty' operating systems are mostly used on commercial systems (whether mainframe or desktop) such as UNIX and many others; and 'general purpose' operating systems used on business and home computers. These began with what were called Disc Operating Systems (DOS) in the 1980s. The best known forms are MS-DOS (produced by Microsoft) and PC-DOS (developed by IBM).

A newer form of operating system is the 'Windows-type' which gives the user a picture or series of pictures, to help them to find their way around the computer. These systems are available from Apple (for the Mackintosh series), from Microsoft (as 'Windows' itself) and from IBM (as the 'OS2' system). These systems have the advantage that they are much more user 'friendly' but they have the disadvantage that they use a great deal of memory.

Most business computers are now almost totally flexible. With the correct software they can help the business to write its letters, design its invoices, keep track of debts, plan future investments, compile the end-of-year accounts, keep long lists of customers or staff, and communicate with other firms or with other computers. There are five important areas of modern 'software'.

1. wordprocessing
2. databases
3. spreadsheets
4. accounts
5. communications

Word-processing packages

A word-processor can do everything that a typewriter can do but it also enables the user to change what has been written very easily. You can now write a whole report and then swap bits of writing from one place to another and change the style of typeface being used. Modern word-processors have spelling checkers added to them and most can be used with what are called 'mail merge' programs to produce personalised letters to many people from one, single standard letter.

Databases

These are the computer equivalent of a card index. Any information which has to be stored in some sort of order – lists of customers, of staff, of stock, etc. – can be kept on a database. The programs enable the operator to find information quickly and, if they are good enough, to list or print the material in virtually any way they want.

For example, a database of customers could be printed out as:

▶ a list of names in alphabetical order
▶ a list of customers according to which area of the country they live in
▶ a list of customers by sex
▶ a list of telephone numbers of STD-code order.

Spreadsheets

These offer ways of dealing with lots of figures. Where databases keep lists of **words** and can manipulate them, so spreadsheets keep details of **numbers** and can manipulate them in almost any way you wish. Spreadsheets are like a grid of boxes drawn inside the computer. Each box can have a number in it and the computer can handle the number in many ways.

Spreadsheets are normally used for financial information. They can keep details of sales over a period of months and then add them up, divide them by twelve to calculate an annual average, show them as a graph or take them away from figures of costs to get a profit figure.

ANNUAL SALES REPORT	
Jan-95	12,500.00
Feb-95	14,750.00
Mar-95	17,500.00
Apr-95	26,800.00
May-95	12,800.00
Jun-95	15,700.00
Jul-95	13,850.00
Aug-95	15,000.00
Sep-95	16,550.00
Oct-95	28,900.00
Nov-95	10,500.00
Dec-95	7,500.00
Total	192,350.00
Average	16,029.17

Table 19.5 A spreadsheet-created analysis of annual sales

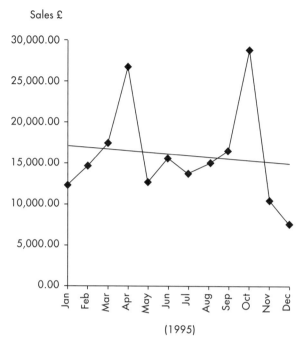

Table 19.5 shows the sales for a company during 1995. The actual figures do not tell us very much but, when placed into a spreadsheet and transferred to a graph (Fig. 19.1) they begin to tell a story about the company's performance. The graph shows that the company had two distinct peaks for its sales – in April and October. A lot might be learned by the company asking itself why this is the case. Even the graph itself does not help much more – the points seem to be pretty haphazard. Once the spreadsheet is asked to do some analysis of the figures a piece of very useful information becomes clear. We ask the spreadsheet to show us what the 'trend' of sales has been during the year and, after working it out mathematically, the spreadsheet shows that the overall trend in sales is *downwards*. In fact, having started the year averaging over £17,000 per month, the company ended it with a trend line at just £15,000 per month. This would be a worrying piece of information for the Managing Director who would now be trying very hard to find out the reason or reasons for this state of affairs.

Accounts packages

Almost every business uses some form of computer accounts system these days. It should be noted, however, that they are not the answer to every business's problem. They can be complex to use and, for small businesses, they may be more trouble than they are worth. For most medium to large firms, however, computer accounts systems keep their complex financial records and are able to compile everything from a trial balance to a set of final accounts.

Communications software

Computers tend to use different languages and they find it difficult to 'talk' to each other. Software engineers have, therefore, developed special programs which allow computers to communicate – often over long distances. In the office, separate computers can be linked together to form networks which allow staff to send information to each other without using paper. By linking a computer to the telephone system and by using the correct software, it is possible for even the humblest of home computers to be linked in to a worldwide communications network.

Even at the relatively low level of small businesses and home banking this revolution has meant that it is now possible to pay bills, keep up with your finances and transfer money from account to account without leaving your office or home.

Expert systems

Just as expert systems are set to change the way in which computers help to design products and diagnose problems in industry, so similar systems will begin to enter the office of the future. They will be able to analyse marketing problems, suggest solutions to insurance problems, perhaps, even, to run businesses by themselves.

Voice input

Before this comes about, however, the office will almost certainly go through yet another revolution. At present office skills involve typing – in fact, as computers become more important so the need for typing skills has increased. However, typing is really a very awkward and time-consuming way of putting information into a computer. It would be more convenient if the material could be simply spoken into the computer. This is more difficult than it might appear – how, for example, does a computer tell the difference between the words 'pare', 'pear', and 'pair' when spoken to it? Most major computer companies already have voice-computers in the prototype phase and it will not be many years before these machines begin to enter service.

Telecommunications

Many business people are already finding that improved communications means that they need to travel less. Until recently it has been difficult to do the obvious thing – to link several business-people together by phone and television to replace a single meeting. The television and telephone lines needed made this technically difficult and very expensive.

Today, however, optical-fibre communications lines can carry a great deal more information than the old copper electric telephone lines and video-conferences are beginning to be economic and convenient. Instead of four or five people having to travel hundreds of miles to a meeting, they all stay in their own office and pictures and sound from all of the others are transmitted onto screens in front of them. They can see everyone and hold the same meeting without leaving their own offices.

3   CHANGES FOR HUMANS

Changes for humans are inevitable, and many aspects need thought:

- ▶ higher skills
- ▶ education
- ▶ job mobility
- ▶ earlier retirement
- ▶ more leisure time
- ▶ handicrafts and human skills.

All around us the machines and what they can do are changing rapidly. It appears that human beings are rapidly being replaced by extremely intelligent robots and that there will soon be nothing for humans to do. This view of the future is not likely to come about quickly even if it happens at all; but there is no doubt that human workers are now less necessary to modern commerce and industry than they have ever been.

There are two alternative ways of looking at this situation:

1. Human beings are being 'robbed' of the work which up to now has given their lives meaning and dignity. There are many people who take this view and who resist the mechanisation of factories and offices.
2. Computers and robots are now going to release human beings from the back-breaking and boring jobs which they have been tied to in factories and offices. Humans will be released to do jobs or to follow hobbies which will give them far more pleasure in the long run.

The chances are, of course, that neither of these views will turn out to be correct; but it is clear that humans are going to have to adjust to a very different world over the next 20 years or so. We look now at a few changes about which we can be fairly certain:

A. HIGHER SKILLS

The first jobs to be taken over by machines are always the easiest and the most repetitive. For example, people used to have to stand all day long just feeding bits of flat metal into machines which stamped them out into pots and pans. Very early in this century, those jobs were taken over by an automatic 'arm' which fed the sheets in steadily. Today, it is not just the mechanical jobs which are being replaced by machines. As computers become more skilled they are replacing more and more workers.

Case Study – Banking

This is not only the case in manufacturing industry. One of the industries most affected by automation and computing has been the banking industry. In the past, the banks employed thousands of administrators and clerks to keep track of all the cheques and payments going through the system. Today almost all of that work is performed by computers. One example is the way in which cheques are dealt with: people in Britain write millions of cheques every day; even in the recent past, these had to be dealt with by hand with skilled people examining each cheque to make sure it was correctly filled out and to add up all the money on them. Nowadays this task is done at massive speed by computers which 'read' the cheques as they stream by on a conveyor. The computers have 'optical character reading' (OCR) software which enables them to read the information on the cheques. Further reading is done by magnetic strips and 'bar-code' readers.

Case Study – The Printing Industry

During the nineteenth century newspapers required lots of workers – between the journalist and the printed page stood dozens of people who worked the 'hot-metal' machines which set the journalist's words into metal plates; man-handled the metal impressions of any photographs or drawings down to the presses and placed them on the printing drums; the ink and paper also had to be applied manually and the presses needed constant watching to repair any breakdown.

In the computerised world of today's newspapers, there are very few people between a journalist and the printed word. The journalist can type his story directly into the computer which will then allow another person, the sub-editor, to amend it if necessary; the story is then electronically set and photographically printed. Apart from a few highly trained engineers who ensure that the system works smoothly, the paper does not require anything like the staff it had for the old-fashioned process.

New technology does not necessarily only cause human beings to lose their jobs. Technology can also *create* jobs in a number of ways. It can create totally new jobs which did not exist prior to the invention of the technology and it can create the capacity for jobs where there was simply no possibility of work.

Technology creating new jobs

New information technology, for example, has created a number of new types of jobs which simply did not exist before: computer programmer, computer analyst, computer operator, etc. In companies which used outside printers, some work can now be done 'in house' by computer operators doing their own desktop-publishing. In motor car servicing, there used to be a relatively simple job of 'electrician'. That person looked after the electrical system of the car from the battery and wiring to the headlights and the distributor. It was all relatively straightforward electrics. Today, however, motor car maintenance requires technicians who understand the computers that govern the way that the car works and the new electronics which manage the way the engine runs.

Technology creating totally new possibilities for work

Modern technology has created the possibility for employment where it would have been impossible in the past. Even 20 years ago, the concept of 'homeworking' would have been almost unheard-of. By the turn of the century, the Government expects almost 5% of the working population (i.e. around 1.3 million people) to be working from home using computers to link into offices and to other homeworkers. Exam questions are beginning to be set on this area, such as: 'Explain how new technology can create jobs' (Midland Examining Group – May 1994).

The lesson behind all this is that the human beings who are required by modern industry are those with skills. Most of the unskilled work can now be done by machines. It is the engineers – electronic, production and software – who are needed and will be needed well into the next century. Commerce needs those who have developed skills in a wide variety of areas – such as accounting, marketing, purchasing, sales, communications, and secretarial.

B. EDUCATION

The need for these skills means that the modern worker must be well-educated and – what is more important – prepared to carry on being educated throughout their working life. There are very few areas of business and commerce left in which a worker can leave school, find a job and stay there for the rest of their life without developing their skills or their knowledge. The modern world is one in which education does not end with leaving school or college. To keep up with change, it is necessary to retrain while at work. This is called **lifetime learning**. Almost every job now requires that people take part in learning across their whole working life. This will make jobs much more interesting over the long term.

C. JOB MOBILITY (CHANGING JOBS)

As technical change speeds up, people will find that the firms they work for may go out of business or change. Even now many people need to have more than one type of job during their working lives and this will almost certainly increase in the future. Having a career has already become an almost old-fashioned idea. It is becoming more and more common for people to change their careers once or twice during their working lives.

In the 1980s a large number of coal miners were put out of work by changing technology. Faster and cheaper transport has meant that ships can carry coal from many other places in the world and sell it profitably in Britain.

Many of those put out of work did not believe that they would ever be able to work again. However, with retraining, many have completely changed their careers and are now employed in areas as diverse as plumbing and social work, and education and electronics.

D. EARLIER RETIREMENT

With relatively high unemployment likely to be with us for some time to come, firms can let employees retire earlier.

From a business point of view there are two important results from this trend:

1. There will be an increase in the demand for all the goods and services which these retired people will need – everything from education in subjects they never had the time to study while at work, to holidays.
2. People will have to be taught how to make best use of their leisure time. A person who retires at 55, these days, has many years of life to fill with interesting things to do.

E. MORE LEISURE TIME

More leisure time is going to be a problem for almost all of us, not simply for those who retire earlier. As the working week becomes shorter, the amount of free time we have becomes much greater. Up to now, very few people have had the chance to learn how to use this leisure or to try out different hobbies. For many people 'leisure' simply means watching television or visiting the local pub for a drink. With more time at our disposal, we will need more to occupy us and will need to consider many different ways to fill our leisure hours with interesting hobbies and activities.

F. HANDICRAFTS AND HUMAN SKILLS

Luckily, there appears to be a tremendous variety of things to do. If you look around your own area today you will see that there are many types of business which did not exist 20 years ago. Many of these firms are providing high quality handicrafts which are now in demand again.

Case Study – Hand-Knitted Woollens

In the 1960s, the increase in the supply of machine-knitted woollens seemed to mean that there would never again be a demand for hand-knitted clothes. The machine-made clothes were much cheaper, of reasonable quality, and could be made quickly in immense quantities. Today, people are buying hand-knitted clothes again as a type of status symbol and many small businesses are making a good living out of this return to the old crafts.

Craft industries are sprouting up in all sorts of areas and in most trades. At one time it seemed, for example, that the old-fashioned craft of thatching was going to die out altogether. In the late 1960s, there were probably only a few people in the entire country who knew the old skills. It was thought that, because tiles were cheaper and easier to maintain, they would replace thatched roofs completely. It has not turned out that way. In areas of the country like Suffolk and Oxfordshire, thatched cottages have been renovated and repaired and this has provided work for an increasing number of thatching companies.

COURSEWORK

ASSIGNMENT – TECHNOLOGY

Technology is changing our lives all the time. Advanced technology may not interfere with our everyday lives but lots of technological change is occurring in our homes, schools, colleges and workplaces.

Put together a file which describes how technology is changing your life and that of your parents and friends. You should divide it into sections such as:

▶ work (in shops, offices and factories)
▶ school or college
▶ home
▶ leisure.

You might begin by listing the various ways in which technology is changing your life and then find photographs or advertisements to go with the description you have written.

Alternatively you might look at specific types of technology and find out how they are affecting our lives:

▶ the computer
▶ new forms of transport
▶ new types of telecommunications
▶ new household gadgets or electronic equipment.

One way of approaching such an assignment might be to ask yourself how modern technology has made ordinary household tasks easier or improved our entertainment.

ASSIGNMENT – THE HUMAN EFFECT

How does change affect humans? Build up a list of the ways you think that change in the modern world affects people. Think not only about machines and technology but also about changing jobs, pressure within jobs, the need to learn new knowledge and skills, etc.

Now choose three different types of jobs – one skilled job, one in administration, and one in management – and repeat the list for each job. What differences can you see in the pressures of change which affect the different type of jobs?

Finally – for each job – write a short account of the ways you would suggest that people reduce the pressure on themselves or help themselves to deal with change.

A Review Sheet for this chapter will be found on pp. 255–6.

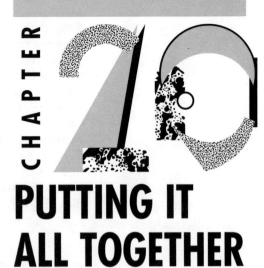

CHAPTER 20

PUTTING IT ALL TOGETHER

INTEGRATED EXAMINATION QUESTIONS

At the end of each chapter, this book has included specimen examination questions to give you an idea of the types of questions you can expect when you undertake the GCSE Business Studies Examination. You will find that the examination papers set by a number of the Examination Groups, will include what are known as integrated questions. This means that the questions asked may each cover more than one area of the syllabus. As you will see from the questions below, they may take the form of a short passage followed by a series of questions drawn from various areas of the syllabus. Note that although these questions include a short passage they could include a piece of visual information or a table instead.

This chapter could, perhaps, be used at the end of your course and before your examinations as a source of revision and examination practice. You could tackle these questions under mock examination conditions. This would mean sitting down in quiet surroundings, maybe in your bedroom or, if this is too noisy then in the local or school library, and trying to answer the questions. The marks allocated for each question are important because they give you a rough guide as to how detailed your answer should be.

A tutor's answer has been given to questions 1 and 2.

INTEGRATED QUESTIONS

QUESTION 1

Read the following passage carefully and answer the questions below.

J Morgan, a private **limited** company producing a cheaper chocolate, is facing considerable **cash flow problems** because of cut price selling from the brand leaders. At an emergency meeting of the Board of Directors it is decided to ask for permission to increase their **overdraft** at the firm's bank, and also discuss with the trade unions the possibility of redundancies for some of the 200 employees.

There has also been a meeting of the local branch of the Trade Union who are aware that the firm is considering some redundancies. The Union are discussing what their attitudes should be towards the problem. The workers are worried about their job security and wish to know what their rights are if they lose their jobs and how the firm is likely to decide who should be sacked.

(a) State what you understand by the following terms as used above:
    (i) limited;   (2 marks)
    (ii) cash flow problems;   (2 marks)
    (iii) overdraft.   (2 marks)
(b) (i) What is an agenda? What function does it perform for a meeting of the board?
                                                                                         (2 marks)
    (ii) Using the information in the passage, state three items that may appear on the agenda.   (3 marks)
(c) Who would be members of the Board of Directors in this firm?   (2 marks)
(d) If the firm made a loss in the financial year, what would be the effect of payments to
    (i) shareholders;   (2 marks)
    (ii) debenture holders.   (2 marks)
(e) As a result of the directors' meeting the Trade Union are informed that 150 employees are to be made redundant.
    (i) On what basis do you think the firm should decide which employees should be made redundant?   (4 marks)
    (ii) What information and advice do you think the unions would offer to those employees being made redundant?   (4 marks)
                                                                                                       (WJEC)

QUESTION 2

ADC plc is a firm involved in the extraction of sand and gravel. It wishes to increase the size of its business. The Board of Directors have decided to try and take over firms involved in the secondary and tertiary stages of production.

(a) (i) Give ONE example of secondary production and ONE example of tertiary production   (2 marks)
    (ii) What is the purpose of the Board of Directors?   (4 marks)
    (iii) What is a 'take over'?   (2 marks)
    (iv) Explain why ADC plc would wish to become involved in the secondary and tertiary sectors of production   (10 marks)
(b) The Board of Directors have decided to move their Head Office to another town which is 100 miles away. This would mean that all office staff would also need to move.
    In order to try and stop this, the office workers have decided to hold a union meeting to discuss the problem.
    (i) Why might the office workers not wish to move to another town?   (8 marks)
    (ii) What action might the union members decide to take?   (6 marks)
    (iii) How would ADC plc overcome the problem of the move for the workers?   (8 marks)
                                                                                                               (SEG)

QUESTION 3

Read the following passage carefully, and answer the questions below.

Walestran, a successful public limited company specialises in overnight delivery of parcels throughout the United Kingdom. It hopes to expand by taking over a firm that carries bulk goods so that the range of transport services can be diversified. Increasing the size of the business might require a new site for the main transport depot. The Board of Directors are prepared to consider any suitable site within Wales.

Moving to a new site will give the firm a chance to modernise the office and make use of computers. However, several members of the Board think much of the firm's business depends on local customers, who may be lost if the firm moves, and want to expand on the present site.

(a) Give two advantages to the firm of expanding their range of transport services. (4 marks)

(b) Explain why each of the following factors might be important in deciding whether a new location is suitable:
   (i) being close to main roads; (2 marks)
   (ii) being close to towns and villages; (2 marks)
   (iii) the cost of land; (2 marks)
   (iv) government aid. (2 marks)

(c) If the company computerises its main office several jobs will be created.
   (i) What skills and abilities will the firm be looking for? (2 marks)
   (ii) Draft an advertisement which might attract someone with these skills and abilities. (7 marks)
   (iii) State two different places where would you expect the firm to advertise the vacancies. (2 marks)

(d) You wish to object to the firm expanding the existing depot because of the very large number of lorries which will be using the local roads. State and explain three reasons you would give for your objection. (6 marks)

(e) Why would the people who work in the company's office at the moment be worried about the possibility of the introduction of computers? (6 marks)

(WJEC)

QUESTION 4

Read the following extract from the *Middlebridge Evening Post* and answer the questions below.

EXPANSION PLANS FOR UNITED

United Foods PLC have reported a large increase in profits for the year ending June 1985. The Company has grown rapidly. It manufactures a wide range of canned foods sold under its own brand name as well as supplying several supermarkets who sell under their own labels. The directors have decided to invest part of their profits and diversify into the soft drinks market.

At their last meeting, one of the main decisions concerned the new factory in which the soft drinks would be produced. Most of the workers will be employed on an assembly line and the discussion was about job satisfaction and whether workers should be paid on an hourly rate or on a piece-work system.

(a) What does the abbreviation PLC stand for? (1 line for answer) (1 mark)

(b) (i) Explain what you understand by the term 'brand name' and provide an example to illustrate your answer. (2 lines for answer) (2 marks)
   (ii) What is 'job satisfaction'? (2 lines for answer) (3 marks)

(c) United have decided to 'diversify'. Give TWO advantages of diversification to them.
   1. _____

   2. _____
   _____
   (2 marks)

(d) Suggest how the company might have found that the soft drinks market had room for another competitor. (6 lines for answer) (5 marks)

(e) At present United sells its food products only to supermarkets. What new and different outlets might be appropriate for the sale of canned drinks? (4 lines for answer) (4 marks)

(f) Say, with reasons, whether you think the assembly line workers should be paid on time rate or piece rates. (6 lines for answer) (4 marks)

(MEG)

QUESTION 5

John Cooke has just been made redundant from his job as a car worker. He has decided to set up a taxi and courier service to provide a service for the public and deliver letters and packages for business.

He still has to decide whether to work from home or to rent a small office in the town centre.

(a) Where would John obtain the capital to start up his business? (4 marks)

(b) (i) What would be the disadvantages if John worked from home? (6 marks)

(ii) What would be the advantages if John decided to rent a small office in the town centre? (6 marks)

(c) Which place of work would you advise John to choose? Give reasons for your choice. (10 marks)

(d) John has received a number of applications for jobs as drivers with his business.

(i) What qualities would be important for this type of work? (4 marks)

(ii) Draw up a contract of employment which could be used for one of John's employees. (10 marks)

(SEG)

QUESTION 6 CASE STUDY

Superpanes Ltd is a double glazing firm making and selling replacement windows and doors, and conservatories.

Features of its marketing mix include the following:

BUY NOW! and pay nothing until October 1993

Special Low Rate credit from only 23% APR

All UPVC frames fully aluminium reinforced to British Standards

For limited period only up to 35% discount for volume purchases

Multi Point Locking for all windows and doors offering maximum security

Comprehensive 10 year transferable insurance-backed guarantee on all materials and labour

Extensive showroom open 7 days a week Special late nights to 8.00 pm Thursday/Friday

FREE ESTIMATES with no obligation to buy

Free champagne and picnic hamper on all orders this June

1 What is a marketing mix? (6)

2 How will this marketing mix help Superpanes sell its double glazing products? Select four of the features to explain your answer. (12)

3 How might market research help Superpanes improve its marketing mix? (8)

Superpanes is organised in three departments: Production & Assembly, Fitting & Maintenance, Sales & Administration.

Like many double glazing companies, it has a high labour turnover.

The figures for the past year are shown below.

Department	Total Number Employed	Left and Replaced
Production & Assembly	42	7
Fitting & Maintenance	50	10
Sales & Administration	16	4

4 Using the information given above, explain the term high labour turnover. (6)
5 What problems might high labour turnover cause Superpanes? (9)
6 How might Superpanes try to reduce labour turnover?

One new competitor, Econoglass, is set up by three friends made redundant by a national double glazing company. They use their redundancy money and a bank loan as starting capital. At first, they plan to form a partnership because it is quite easy to set up.

A business counsellor asks whether they have considered forming a private limited company. The counsellor also warns them, 'Setting up a new small business is quite risky. For example, many businesses experience marketing and financial problems in their early years.'

7 Do you think the three friends would be better advised to set up a private limited company? (12)
8 Explain some of the problems Econoglass might experience in its early years of business. (8)

After 15 years of operation, Superpanes has the largest market share in its region. It has built up an annual sales turnover of £17 million through a reputation for high quality products and service. Superpanes aims to maintain steady sales and strong profits by using a wide product mix targeted at middle to high income earners.

The new competitor, Econoglass, has been operating for 18 months. It has decided to aim at one market segment by offering a cheaper product. It is planning to build up sales by concentrating on a narrow product mix. Econoglass expects low profits while it tries to establish itself in a highly competitive market.

9 Using examples, explain the term wide product mix. (8)
10 How might a wide product mix help Superpanes maintain annual turnover? (8)
11 Using examples, explain how a market may be divided up into segments. (6)
12 Compare the business objectives of Superpanes with those of Econoglass. (9)

At the end of its second year in business, Econoglass reviews its financial position. This includes the following figures for the past year.

Sales Revenue	£280 000	Current Assets	£60 000
Cost of Sales	£130 000	Current Liabilities	£40 000
Expenses	£134 000	Total Capital Employed	£200 000
Net Profit	£16 000		

The average rate of return on capital employed for this type of business is 15%.

13 Calculate, clearly showing your workings:
   (a) Gross Profit; (4)
   (b) the ratio of Net Profit to Sales Revenue; (5)
   (c) the current (or working capital) ratio; (5)
   (d) the return on capital employed (ROCE). (8)

14 (a) How successful has Econoglass been in its second year of operation? Use your calculations and any other figures from the data to help explain your answer. (12)
   (b) What other information would Econoglass find useful in measuring its success? (5)

The price of most goods and services bought by consumers includes Value Added Tax (VAT).
VAT has to be charged on double glazing products.

15 How might Econoglass be affected by an increase in the rate of VAT? (8)
(NEAB)

TUTOR'S ANSWER TO Q.1

(a)   (i) **limited**: a 'limited' company is one which is registered under the Companies Act. There are two types of limited company, the public limited company (PLC) and, as here in the case with J Morgan, a private limited company. The basis of limited companies is 'limited liability' where the owners/shareholders are only responsible for the debt of the company up to the amount they have put into the company. A private limited company is not able to sell its shares to the general public.

   (ii) **cash flow problems**: these happen when a company's cash outgoings exceed (temporarily or permanently) its cash incomings. In the case of J Morgan, the chocolate manufacturer, the cash flow problem stems from a possible reduction in its cash incomings. While it will still have to make regular payments, such as wages, rent, rates and bank interest on loans, it may now be receiving less revenue from the sale of its product. This is because the major producers of chocolate are cutting their price, which will probably make J Morgan's cheaper chocolates less attractive, reducing demand for it. Selling less chocolate at the same price will reduce the revenue of J Morgan.

   (iii) **overdraft**: an 'overdraft' is the amount which the bank agrees to let the company take out of its account *over and above* what is in it. *Note:* be careful not to confuse an overdraft with a loan (see Ch. 7).

(b) (i) An **agenda** is a list of items to be discussed at a meeting. At a Board Meeting it lists the matters which will be dealt with by the Directors. A typical agenda will include: (1) **Apologies** from those who are able to attend the meeting. (2) **Minutes** or notes from the last meeting which have to be approved. (3) **Matters arising**, so that those present at the meeting can discuss/comment on the last meeting. (4) **Reports** which individuals, such as the Chairman may want to present as important information to the meeting. (5) **Special Matters**, which may have arisen. (6) **Date of the next meeting** (7) **Any other business** (AOB), so that any matters not included in the agenda can be discussed.

(ii) The three items that may appear on the agenda for J Morgan under **Reports** or **Special Matters** are: (1) The need for an overdraft (2) The possibility of redundancies (3) How those who might be made redundant should be selected.

(c) The members of the Board of Directors in this firm are likely to be the members of the Morgan family together with any other major shareholders. This is because it is a 'Private' Limited Company.

(d) If the firm made a loss in the financial year then the effect on the **shareholders** who are the owners of the company, might be (1) That a dividend would not be paid. At best the firm's reserves might be used to pay a **small** dividend. (2) On the other hand **debenture** holders would be in a different position. These are the creditors of the company, and must be paid or they can force the company into liquidation. Interest payments must still be forwarded to debenture holders.

(e) (i) The basis on which the firm should decide which employees to make redundant include (1) The skills still required in the 50 remaining employees. The firm will not want to make employees redundant whose skills are still vital to its operation. (2) The levels of seniority. The firm may want to keep more experienced, senior staff. (3) The nearness to retirement age. Those near to retirement age may be less concerned about redundancy. On the other hand, long-standing employees will qualify for more redundancy pay, and will therefore prove more expensive to dismiss. (4) The nearness to appointment. Those 'last in' may be 'first out'. (5) Those who volunteer for redundancy. Those near to retirement may volunteer for redundancy. Taking volunteers may create less bitterness with the remaining staff and with those leaving.

(ii) The information and advice the unions would offer to those employees being made redundant include (1) Information on the rights to redundancy pay. (2) Help in finding a new job. (3) Advice on whether **industrial action** would be likely to stop the redundancies. If so, advice on the type of industrial action to take. (4) Advice on the possibilities for **retraining**, the government grants available, the types of retraining suitable to each person.

TUTOR'S ANSWER TO Q.2

(a) (i) A secondary producer would be a company involved in the manufacture of goods, for example, a cement producer. A tertiary producer would be a company involved in the provision of services, for example, consultancy service to the building industry.

(ii) The Board of Directors are a group of individuals who are elected by the shareholders to whom they are accountable. The purpose of the Board of Directors is to run the company. This involves deciding what the company policy is to be and making sure that the policy is carried out. All the major decisions within the company, such as the purchase of expensive machinery, the takeover of another company or the redundancy of employees will also be the responsibility of the Board of Directors. A Managing Director is likely to be on the Board and be the director most actively involved in running the company.

(iii) **With this question you need to make sure you do not confuse a takeover with a merger.** A takeover is where a company (ADC plc), wants to take control of another company which might otherwise resist its approach. The control of the other company will usually take the form of obtaining sufficient shares in that company. A merger, on the other hand, is where both companies are willing to join together.

(iv) The extraction of sand and gravel is a **primary** stage of production. If ADC plc becomes involved with the secondary (manufacturing) and tertiary (service) stages of production, this would be **forward vertical integration**. There could be a number of benefits to the firm from this.

1. **Less risks.** Being involved in other activities may be helpful if the demand for sand and gravel should decline.

2. **More secure outlet for its products.** By owning a manufacturing plant which uses sand and gravel, ADC plc can be sure that someone will take its product. **This reason is similar to 1**.

3. **Lower costs for the firm.** By adding extra activities, the size of ADC plc will grow. Being a larger firm will help it reduce the average costs of production, i.e. benefit from economies of scale.

4. **Control over the outlet for the product.** ADC plc might take over retail or wholesale outlets (tertiary stage) as well as manufacturing. It may therefore be able to control the price of products (such as cement) which uses its sand and gravel. By keeping the price low, ADC plc can help encourage demand for cement and with it the demand for sand and gravel.

5. **Extra Profit.** There may be profit that can be made at the secondary and tertiary stages of production. This profit can be added to the profit it is already making at the primary stage.

(b) (i) The office workers may not wish to move to another town 100 miles away for social and economic reasons. In social terms the office workers will have to leave their family and friends. Leaving their 'roots' may prove to be very difficult. Many of the office workers may have children at school and be reluctant to move them, particularly if they are soon to take their examinations. In economic terms moving 100 miles would prove to be very costly. There are removal and legal expenses associated with buying a new house in a new location. If the town is closer to London then the house prices are likely to be much higher. If the office workers live in rented accommodation then they will face a problem if the new town has a shortage of rented accommodation.

(ii) Before any action takes place the unions will want to negotiate with the company. In their negotiations they will want to explore all the possibilities. Is the move the only option open to the company? If so, then they will want to know whether they will be given any financial help with the move. If the union members believe other options are available to the company they may decide to oppose the move. If negotiations break down they may operate an overtime ban or a work-to-rule. As a last resort they may go on strike.

(iii) ADC plc could overcome the problem of the move for the workers by giving them financial assistance with the move. If the house prices are more expensive in the new town then the company may give housing subsidies. Rented accommodation might be provided free of charge, for, say, the first six months. Higher salaries could be given to office workers in the new location. Information may also be made available on the new town such as the types of facilities which are available, the schools, shops, and hospitals.

STUDENT'S ANSWER TO Q.5

❝❝You could also mention that he may have received redundancy pay.❞❞

❝❝Good points, but more could be made! There would probably be complaints from his neighbours about noise, etc. He would need planning permission to carry on the business at home, which might not be granted, etc.❞❞

❝❝A good answer.❞❞

❝❝Good points, which show that you are thinking about John's situation. Perhaps near to the railway station would also help.❞❞

❝❝Honesty will also be important as drivers will handle money. Being on time is also important.❞❞

5) a)   John could obtain his capital in the form of a bank loan or from the government.

   b) i) If he worked from home, his business would not be so noticeable or seen by many potential customers. He probably has to travel a costly distance before he'd reach the pick-up destination, normally in the town centre.

      ii) to rent a small office in the town centre would be a benefit because it would be more easily recognisable as a business in operation, it is already in (the) a busy town. Therefore, as well as being on the door-step of his customers, more people are likely to see his office and therefore use his services.

   (c) John would be wise to have his office near to the town centre where organisations wanting taxi or courier services are near-by, and where there is easy access for his vehicles. He needs to be established near potential customers but away from competitors so that he obtains a maximum custom. He needs plenty of parking space so that his service can run efficiently without causing any congestion in the road.

   (d) i) A clean driving licence is essential. Good driving experience. Good knowledge of the area, streets as well as places (businesses.)

       ii) —

❝❝A great pity. You will lose all the marks for this part of the question, spoiling what has so far been a very good answer. Always try to make an attempt at every part of the question. Make sure you revise the Contract of Employment.❞❞

REVIEW SHEET (CHAPTER 3)

1 What are meant by the terms 'unlimited wants' and 'limited resources'?

_____
_____
_____

2 Using examples, explain what is meant by the term 'opportunity cost'.

_____
_____
_____
_____

3 Distinguish between the various factors of production.

_____
_____
_____
_____

4 What is the difference between fixed capital and circulating capital?

_____
_____
_____

5 What is meant by the chain of production?

_____
_____
_____

6 Define the primary, secondary and tertiary types of production.

_____
_____
_____
_____

7 Which of the following are consumer durable goods: a bar of chocolate, a tin of soup, a bottle of shampoo, a refrigerator, a daily newspaper, a dining room suite, a carton of orange juice?

_____
_____
_____

8 Give two examples of primary, secondary and tertiary industries.

_____
_____

9 Why has there been a decline in the primary and secondary types of production in the last 30 years?

_____
_____
_____

10 What are the advantages and disadvantages of a market economy?

_____
_____
_____
_____

11 Outline the difference between a market economy and a planned economy.

_____

_____

_____

_____

12 Define a mixed economy.

_____

_____

_____

13 Distinguish between the maximisation of profits and the maximisation of sales, as different business objectives.

_____

_____

_____

_____

14 What is meant by the Business Plan?

_____

_____

_____

15 Explain what is meant by a satisficing management objective.

_____

_____

_____

_____

16 What is meant by a 'mission statement'?

_____

_____

_____

_____

17 Explain what the term 'competitive advantage' means.

_____

_____

_____

_____

18 List four sub-headings which you would expect to find in a typical 'Business Plan'.

_____

_____

_____

_____

REVIEW SHEET (CHAPTER 4)

1   A friend of yours is currently a company employee but is considering starting a business, as a sole trader. What advice would you give to your friend?

2   Smith's Plumbing Engineers was initially set up as a sole trader before becoming a partnership. Briefly outline the advantages and disadvantages to the business now that it is operating as a partnership.

3   What advantages does a partnership have over a private limited company?

4   What advantages does a private limited company have over a partnership?

5   Outline the difference between a private and a public limited company.

6   What are the advantages of a business becoming a public limited company?

7   Explain the difference between limited and unlimited liability.

8   Which company would find it easier to raise finance – a private or a public limited company? Give reasons for your answer.

9 Briefly outline the process a company must go through to become a limited company.

_____
_____
_____
_____

10 Distinguish between the Memorandum and Articles of Association.

_____
_____
_____
_____

11 What reasons have been put forward, in the past, for the nationalisation of industry?

_____
_____
_____
_____

12 Name four privatised companies.

_____
_____
_____
_____

13 Outline the reasons put forward for privatisation.

_____
_____
_____
_____

14 What is meant by contracting out?

_____
_____
_____
_____

15 What are the advantages and disadvantages of contracting out?

_____
_____
_____
_____
_____
_____

16 Distinguish between retail and producer co-operatives.

_____
_____
_____
_____
_____
_____
_____

17 Explain what is meant by franchising and give two examples.

_____
_____
_____
_____
_____
_____

REVIEW SHEET (CHAPTERS 5 and 6)

Chapter 5

1 Outline what you view to be the main functions of management.

2 What is meant by an organisation chart?

3 Outline two factors which may influence the shape of a company's organisation chart.

4 Explain the difference between a pyramidal and horizontal management structure.

5 In what situations would Chocolate Delight plc make use of a matrix style of management structure?

6 Give two advantages derived from organising a company in terms of departments.

7 Distinguish between formal and informal organisation.

8 How do autocratic and democratic types of leadership differ?

9 Define 'the span of control'.

10 As a company grows in size it may suffer increasing problems with its chain of command. Briefly outline two problems it may experience.

11 Outline two reasons why a manager may be afraid to delegate.

Chapter 6

12 List three factors which would be important to a hairdresser when considering the location of his or her salon.

_____
_____
_____

13 What is meant by the 'economies of concentration'?

_____
_____

14 Distinguish between natural and acquired advantages of location.

_____
_____
_____

15 Outline the advantages a firm may derive from relocating to a Development Area.

_____
_____
_____

16 Give two reasons why (a) profit and (b) number of employees may have drawbacks as measures of the size of a particular company.

_____
_____
_____
_____

17 Name two economies of scale.

_____
_____

18 Distinguish between internal and external economies of scale.

_____
_____
_____

19 Why may a company suffer from diseconomies of scale?

_____
_____
_____

20 Outline two ways in which a firm may grow in size.

_____
_____
_____

21 Give three examples each of backward and forward vertical integration.

_____
_____
_____

22 What advantages may a company obtain from undertaking a horizontal merger?

_____
_____
_____

23 Give two examples of conglomerate integration.

_____
_____
_____

REVIEW SHEET (CHAPTERS 7 and 8)

Chapter 7

1 Name and explain three of the main reasons that companies are likely to need finance.

2 List four sources of external finance for a company.

3 Why are some profits called 'retained profits'?

4 If you were the Chairman of a public company, why might you prefer to raise finance through an issue of debentures rather than an issue of shares?

5 What is the riskiest type of share from an individual investor's point of view?

6 What, exactly, is being placed in a 'placing'?

7 Why would pebbles not be a particularly useful form of money?

8 Name and explain three of the uses of money.

9 What is 'intrinsic value' where money is concerned?

10 Explain the main differences between credit cards and debit cards.

11 What is the difference between 'key man' assurance and 'public liability' insurance?

12 If you were selling someone your car, why would you ask them for a banker's draft instead of an ordinary cheque?

13 What sort of services does Lloyds of London deal with?

14 What sort of companies would have their shares traded on the unlisted securities market (USM) and why?

Chapter 8

15 Explain why the initials PPQQTT are important.

_____

_____

_____

16 In some circumstances, a buyer has to ensure that the quality of a component is not too high. Why is this?

_____

_____

17 List and explain the three main types of production.

_____

_____

_____

18 What is the difference between 'continuous flow' and 'mass' production?

_____

_____

19 What type of production would you opt for, if you were setting up a factory to make grand pianos, and why?

_____

_____

_____

20 Modern aircraft are complex pieces of machinery. What sort of production do you think is used to build them?

_____

_____

21 Explain the crucial difference between 'process' and 'product' layout on the production floor.

_____

_____

22 Draw a flow diagram similar to that in Fig. 8.1 which shows how you would produce either a refrigerator or a suite of furniture.

23 Why do you think that 'group' working often reduces absenteeism?

_____

_____

_____

24 What is a 'progress chaser' and what would one do to help the production of a product?

_____

_____

25 Explain the difference between an 'automated' machine and a 'robot'.

_____

_____

26 Explain the differences between CAD, CAM and CIM.

_____

_____

REVIEW SHEET (CHAPTER 9)

1 Why is market research so important to a company?

_____
_____
_____

2 List and explain the differences between three types of markets.

_____
_____
_____

3 What is the 'marketing mix'?

_____
_____
_____
_____

4 Draw up a list of five questions you might ask if you were researching a proposed new bus service. Why would you ask those particular questions and how would they help the bus company?

_____
_____
_____
_____
_____
_____
_____
_____
_____
_____
_____
_____
_____

5 What is the difference between a 'product-oriented' company and a 'market-oriented' company?

_____
_____
_____
_____

6 On a separate piece of graph paper draw a 'product life cycle'. What are the main stages in that cycle?

_____
_____
_____
_____

7 Where in the product life cycle would you place 'mens' hats' and 'disk-based computer games'? Explain why you have placed them in those particular places on the cycle.

_____
_____
_____

8 Complete the equation: total costs (TC) = ? + total variable costs (TVC)

_____

9 Why is 'break-even analysis' so called?

_____
_____
_____

10 What things would you need to know about a product before you could begin to calculate its demand curve?

_____

_____

_____

11 What is 'loss-leading'?

_____

_____

12 A car manufacturer has to decide what type of car it will design and produce for the year 2005. Design must start now and the machines and tools for the production floor must be ordered soon. The company has the choice between producing a very basic small car with very few 'extras' and gadgets or the same size car with a slightly bigger engine (smoother and quieter) plus a luxury interior and lots of gadgets. The latter car will, obviously, have to be more expensive than the 'basic' model. What sort of demographic information will the manufacturer ask of its market research company? Given what you know about demographic change in the UK over the next decade or so (see also Chapter 13) how would you advise the company to proceed?

_____

_____

_____

_____

13 What does an advertising agency do?

_____

_____

14 What is a 'medium'? List and describe five different media.

_____

_____

_____

_____

_____

_____

15 Name a product which would be most effectively advertised in or on each of the following:

(a) _The Times_

_____

(b) Cinema advertising

_____

(c) _The Sun_

_____

(d) Channel 4 television

_____

16 Explain why in Question 15, you chose those particular products to be advertised on those particular media.

_____

_____

_____

17 What is the difference between 'desk research' and 'field research'?

_____

_____

REVIEW SHEET (CHAPTER 10)

1. What proportion of UK exports of goods and services go to the countries of the EU?

   _____
   _____
   _____
   _____
   _____
   _____

2. Excluding Europe, which is the UK's next most important trading partner?

   _____
   _____
   _____
   _____
   _____

3. What is 'invisible trade'?

   _____
   _____
   _____
   _____
   _____
   _____
   _____

4. What two figures would you need to enable you to calculate the 'balance of trade'?

   _____ + _____ = balance of trade

5. What further figures would you need to be able to calculate the UK's 'balance of payments in current account'?

   _____
   _____
   _____
   _____
   _____
   _____

6. What is a 'tariff' and why is it a barrier to trade?

   _____
   _____
   _____
   _____
   _____
   _____

7. On March 1st, you agree to sell an Australian friend your computer for A$1,000. On that day, the pound is trading at A$2 = £1. You send the computer to Australia and, on March 30th, you receive back your friend's cheque for A$1,000 as agreed. When you take it to the bank you find that the rate has now changed to A$3 = 1. Is this good or bad and why?

   _____
   _____
   _____
   _____
   _____
   _____

8. How does a 'sight draft' differ from a 'term draft'?

    _____
    _____
    _____
    _____
    _____

9. What is the 'Single Market' and how does it affect UK business people who are trying to trade with other EU countries?

    _____
    _____
    _____
    _____
    _____
    _____
    _____
    _____
    _____

10. Name four 'barriers to trade' and explain how they operate to restrict trade?

    _____
    _____
    _____
    _____
    _____
    _____
    _____
    _____
    _____

11. What do the letters IMF, WTO and EU stand for?

    _____
    _____
    _____
    _____
    _____

12. Why do exports need to be 'guaranteed' by organisations such as the ECGD?

    _____
    _____
    _____
    _____
    _____
    _____
    _____
    _____

REVIEW SHEET (CHAPTER 11)

1. A new manufacturing company wants to predict its cash flow for the next six months. It will be starting business with no money of its own and hopes to survive on an overdraft from its bank. It has regular salary payments of £3,000 per month to make plus 'overheads' (rent, rates, electricity, etc.) of £500 per month. To produce its goods – micro-computers – it needs to buy in £4,000 worth of components every other month beginning in Month 1. It also estimates that other costs – general costs and packing and shipping the computers – will be £500 in Month 1 but will increase by £50 per month after that. It expects to sell one computer – at £750 – in the first month, 3 in the second month, 5 in the third month, 10 in the fourth month and 12 in each of Months 5 and 6.

    (a) Draw up a cash flow forecast for this company showing what its bank position will be at the end of each month.

	MONTH 1	MONTH 2	MONTH 3	MONTH 4	MONTH 5	MONTH 6
Costs:						
Salaries						
Overheads						
Components						
Other						
Total Costs						
Total Sales						
Net Revenue						
Bank Balance (month-start)						
Bank Balance (month-end)						

Table 11.12

    (b) What will be its maximum need for an overdraft and in what month will it reach its peak?

    _____
    _____
    _____
    _____
    _____

    (c) When does it begin to make a 'trading profit', i.e. a profit in just that month?

    _____
    _____
    _____
    _____
    _____

    (d) How many computers must be sold to meet its monthly costs in Month 5?

    _____
    _____
    _____
    _____
    _____

    (e) How much is the overdraft going to be in Month 6?

    _____
    _____
    _____
    _____

2.   Why is a 'trial balance' important?

_____
_____
_____
_____
_____
_____
_____

3.   Explain what 'depreciation' is and why it is important for a company to allow for it in its accounts.

_____
_____
_____
_____
_____
_____
_____

4.   Why might a company be profitable and yet still go out of business?

_____
_____
_____
_____
_____
_____
_____

5.   Explain the difference between a 'debtor' and a 'creditor'.

_____
_____
_____
_____
_____
_____
_____

6.   Why is a measure of 'stock turnover' useful information for the Directors of a company?

_____
_____
_____
_____
_____
_____

7.   Is a rise in the 'current ratio' from 3:1 to 5:1 good or bad for a company? Explain your answer.

_____
_____
_____
_____
_____
_____

8.   What formula would you use to work out the 'net profit margin' for a company?

_____
_____
_____
_____
_____

REVIEW SHEET (CHAPTERS 12 and 13)

Chapter 12

1 Give two reasons why it is necessary to produce and keep business documentation.

_____

_____

2 Name two 'non-financial' documents that a company produces.

_____

_____

_____

_____

3 Name four 'transaction documents' produced and kept by companies.

_____

_____

_____

_____

4 What information would you expect to see on a company's letterhead?

_____

_____

_____

_____

5 How might the letterhead of a partnership differ from that of a limited company?

_____

_____

_____

_____

6 Explain how and why a company might use the following:

(a) a quotation

_____

_____

(b) an invoice

_____

_____

(c) a credit note

_____

_____

7 What does 'E & OE' mean when seen on a business document?

_____

_____

_____

_____

8 What are the 'terms' of an invoice?

_____

_____

_____

_____

9 What information needs to be stated at the top of a 'fax' before it is sent?

_____

_____

_____

_____

Chapter 13

10 What is the 'fertility rate'? Explain why knowing it might be important for certain business-people.

_____

_____

_____

_____

11 List the four ways in which population can change.

_____

_____

_____

_____

12 What has been happening to the 'death rate' since 1900?

_____

_____

_____

_____

13 Can you think of any reasons why the average age at which women are having their first child is rising?

_____

_____

_____

_____

14 What two things make up 'migration'?

_____

_____

_____

_____

15 What do we mean when we talk about the 'sector of employment'? List the three main sectors.

_____

_____

_____

_____

16 What does 'self-employed' mean and how does it differ from being 'employed'?

_____

_____

_____

_____

17 Name and explain three types of unemployment.

_____

_____

_____

_____

18 Give two reasons why the employment of women has been rising in recent years compared with the employment of men.

_____

_____

_____

_____

REVIEW SHEET (CHAPTERS 14 and 15)

Chapter 14

1 Read the advertisement below and then answer the questions that follow.

GREENLINE INSURANCE

An opportunity has arisen at our Cambridge office for a member of the sales team.

Aged between 25 and 35, the successful applicant will ideally have had 5 years experience in the financial sector, be highly motivated, capable of working under pressure and be a good communicator.

This position offers excellent prospects, a company car, a salary of up to £30,000, a bonus related scheme and membership of BUPA.

If you feel you have the right skills then forward your CV to the Personnel Officer, Greenline Insurance, Jones Street, Cambridge CB2 8JP

(a) How is Greenline Insurance aiming to attract employees?

_____

_____

(b) What other information would a prospective applicant like to know before applying for the post?

_____

_____

(c) This advertisement appeared in a local newspaper with a small circulation. Give two reasons why this may not have been the best place for the advert.

_____

_____

(d) Briefly describe three ways (other than the local newspaper) that Greenline Insurance could have advertised the post.

_____

_____

(e) List four pieces of information you would include in a CV if you were to apply for the post advertised.

_____

_____

(f) Give two advantages Greenline Insurance would have obtained by asking applicants to fill in an application form rather than sending in a CV.

_____

_____

(g) Before the applicant is appointed, the company may insist on a medical examination. Explain the reason for this.

_____

(h) The person who is appointed to the sales team by Greenline Insurance will probably take part in an induction programme. What are the advantages to the company and the new employee of such a programme?

_____

_____

Chapter 15

2 What is meant by a contract of employment?

_____

_____

_____

3 List four factors which might influence the motivation of a worker.

_____

_____

_____

4 Distinguish between wages and salaries.

_____

_____

_____

5 What are meant by wage differentials?

_____

_____

_____

6 Distinguish between time rate and piece rate.

_____

_____

_____

7 Define gross and net pay.

_____

_____

_____

8 Outline the compulsory deductions from an employee's pay.

_____

_____

_____

9 What allowances is an individual able to claim before paying tax?

_____

_____

_____

10 How is the tax code calculated?

_____

_____

_____

11 List five fringe benefits.

_____

_____

_____

12 What factors influence a worker's job satisfaction?

_____

_____

_____

13 Distinguish between job enlargement, job enrichment and job rotation.

_____

_____

_____

REVIEW SHEET (CHAPTERS 16 and 17)

Chapter 16

1 Name **five** groups of people that companies have to communicate with.

2 What is 'body language'? Why is it important for business-people to be aware of it?

3 List and explain the five main types of communication.

4 What three main sections should appear in a 'report'?

5 What is an 'agenda' for a meeting? What should it contain?

6 How does a set of 'minutes' differ from a 'transcript'?

7 Name three types of oral communication.

8 Is there such a thing as 'visual communication'? If there is, how might a company make use of it?

9 What is a 'database'?

Chapter 17

10 Explain the main differences between 'telex' and 'fax' communications.

_____

_____

_____

_____

11 List three reasons for joining a trade union.

_____

_____

_____

_____

12 Give two reasons for the fall in the total membership of trade unions over the period 1980–92.

_____

_____

_____

_____

13 Distinguish between an industrial union and a general union.

_____

_____

_____

_____

14 What is the role of the Trades Union Congress (TUC)?

_____

_____

_____

_____

15 Give two functions of a shop steward.

_____

_____

_____

_____

16 What is meant by collective bargaining?

_____

_____

_____

_____

17 List three forms that industrial action might take.

_____

_____

_____

_____

18 What role might ACAS play in resolving a dispute?

_____

_____

_____

_____

REVIEW SHEET (CHAPTER 18)

1. What is a 'unitary authority' in local government and how does it differ from a 'district' authority?

   _____
   _____
   _____
   _____
   _____
   _____

2. Name three things that local government is responsible for.

   _____
   _____
   _____
   _____

3. How does local government obtain the money to pay for the services it provides?

   _____
   _____
   _____
   _____
   _____
   _____

4. What is the name of the place where our MPs discuss and decide on national policy?

   _____
   _____
   _____
   _____

5. What are the three main institutions of the EU?

   _____
   _____
   _____
   _____

6. In what year was the European Economic Community (EEC) – the forerunner of the modern EU – first formed and which countries formed it?

   _____
   _____
   _____
   _____

7. How many countries are now members of the EU and list member countries?

   _____
   _____
   _____
   _____

8. How does the UK government help business?

   _____
   _____
   _____
   _____
   _____

9. What is the main training scheme used today to help young people receive job-related training and experience?

    _____

    _____

    _____

    _____

10. List **four** important Acts of Parliament which directly affect business.

    _____

    _____

    _____

    _____

11. What is a 'pressure group'?

    _____

    _____

    _____

    _____

12. Name three pressure groups and explain how they might affect business.

    _____

    _____

    _____

    _____

    _____

    _____

REVIEW SHEET (CHAPTER 19)

1. Describe **three** ways in which the business environment has changed in recent years.

   _____
   _____
   _____
   _____
   _____
   _____

2. What is 'bio-technology'?

   _____
   _____
   _____
   _____

3. Give a brief account of how an 'automatic' machine differs from a 'robot' machine.

   _____
   _____
   _____
   _____
   _____
   _____

4. What is the main advantage of a robot over an automatic machine?

   _____
   _____
   _____
   _____

5. What are the main effects of change for businesses?

   _____
   _____
   _____
   _____

6. The skill and knowledge of a doctor might be put into an 'expert system'. What other types of occupation might be put into such systems? Describe **two** and say why you think that they could be replaced by expert systems.

   _____
   _____
   _____
   _____
   _____
   _____
   _____
   _____

7. How many megabytes are represented by 2,300,000,000 bytes? How many kilobytes are in the same number of bytes?

   _____
   _____
   _____
   _____

8. Describe the main differences between a floppy disk and a hard disk.

   _____
   _____
   _____
   _____

9. What type of computer software would you use to do the following?

a) Create a set of business accounts

_____

_____

b) Keep records of all your customers' names and addresses

_____

_____

c) Write a report for the Board of Directors.

_____

_____

10. Why is a modem an important piece of equipment for a modern computer?

_____

_____

_____

_____

_____

_____

11. List three ways in which changing technology will affect human beings in the future.

_____

_____

_____

12. What type of jobs will be the first to be affected by new technology?

_____

_____

_____

_____

_____

_____

13. What is 'lifetime learning'?

_____

_____

_____

_____

_____

_____

INDEX